Advertising Fictions

Literature, Advertisement, and Social Reading

The Social Foundations of Aesthetic Forms series
Edward W. Said, Editor

Advertising Fictions

LITERATURE, ADVERTISEMENT, & SOCIAL READING

JENNIFER WICKE

COLUMBIA UNIVERSITY PRESS
NEW YORK 1988

Columbia University Press
New York   Guildford, Surrey
Copyright © 1988 Columbia University Press
All rights reserved

LIBRARY OF CONGRESS
Library of Congress Cataloging-in-Publication Data

Wicke, Jennifer
   Advertising fictions : literature, advertisement & social reading
Jennifer Wicke.
      p.   cm.—(The Social foundations of aesthetic forms series)
   Bibliography: p.
   Includes index.
   ISBN 0-231-06604-X
   1. English literature—History and criticism.   2. American
literature—History and criticism.   3. Advertising in literature.
4. Advertising—Books—History.   5. Dickens, Charles, 1812–1870—
Knowledge—Commerce.   6. James, Henry, 1843–1916—Knowledge—
Commerce.   7. Joyce, James, 1882–1941. Ulysses.   8. Advertising—
Great Britain—History.   9. Advertising—United States—History.
I. Title.   II. Series.
PR409.A38W53   1988
820′.9′355—dc 19   88-5015
                                                                         CIP

Printed in the United States of America

Hardback editions of Columbia University Press books are
Smyth-sewn and printed on permanent and durable acid-free paper

Contents

• Acknowledgments

COLLEAGUES AND FRIENDS AT YALE UNIVER-
sity have provided the critical and the emotional climate to make
the work one does possible, and I thank them. I am grateful also for
the Morse Fellowship from Yale, and for a Whitney Humanities Center
grant that allowed me to inspect the advertising collection of the British
Museum Library. The New-York Historical Society was a rich and
gracious resource. From an earlier life, warmest thanks are due to the
Pickwick Club (Mark Schenker, Annie Schenker, Peter Antelyes, and
Greg Myers), to J. Ellen Evans and to Harry Cornelius. My greatest
debt is to Edward W. Said, teacher, friend, and inspiration, for his
intellectual generosity and his unfailing solidarity.

Advertising Fictions

Literature, Advertisement, and Social Reading

Introduction:
Advertising & Criticism

A coronation is the picture of pomp and dignity. Cut one minute
of this proceeding out of its surroundings: the crown is being placed
on the head of the king in his coronation robes. —But in different
surroundings gold is the cheapest of metals, its gleam is thought
vulgar. There the fabric of the robe is cheap to produce. A crown
is a parody of a respectable hat. And so on.
            —Ludwig Wittgenstein, *Philosophical Investigations.*

What, in the end, makes advertisements so superior to criticism?
Not what the moving neon sign says—but the fiery pool reflecting
it in the asphalt.
            —Walter Benjamin, *One Way Street*

ADVERTISING ARISES AS A RADICALLY NEW
discursive practice over the course of the nineteenth century.
Despite the long and rich history of advertising incunabula, the institutional formation of modern advertisement did not begin to be discernible until the mid-1800s. Within that period, advertising can retrospectively be seen to have become an institution—a center of
knowledge production, a determining economic site, as well as a representational system comprising a vastly heterogenous set of individual
artifacts. In this book I want to examine advertising as a language and
a literature in its own right—as a preeminent discourse of modern
culture. The advertising institution did not arise in isolation, but was
concurrent with the establishment of the novel as the literary form
achieving its predominance in the nineteenth century, and the dialectic
between advertising and the novel reveals both how advertising was
able to take on the status of a mass literature, enforcing its own codes
of social reading, and how the novel relies on the conditions of advertising to permit it to become the major literary form. In what follows,
I will be tracing the filaments of this dialectic, as well as proposing
new theoretical ways of engaging advertisement as a discourse. On a
methodological level, this is to suggest the intimate relationship between "high art" and its conditions of production, and its shadow
partner, the mass communication form that constitutes its matrix. The
intertwining of literature and advertising enmeshes two interdepen-

dent discourses, neither of which can be fully read without reference to the other. Additionally my project hopes to recast the history of the novel by placing works of Dickens, James, and Joyce, a formidable triumvirate in the tradition of the novel, within the new social lexicon of advertising, arguing that modern "reading" can only arise in the dialectical space opened up between novel and advertisement.

Why award advertising this signal importance, moving it center stage and giving it star billing in the cultural theater? Advertising has been so thoroughly stigmatized as a subject even in ordinary conversation, that to invade its purview for more than rapid ideological critique may seem to be a retrograde or even perverse critical enterprise. Advertising's fruits, after all, range from desert highway billboards to the global calligraphy of the Coke logo: even in terms of sheer mass, the task for analysis appears unwieldy. To place all the disparate spawn and spoor of advertisement over the last hundred years or so under one analytic rubric is to conjoin the homemade tailor's sign with the first ultrasophisticated neon signs of 1907, the circus poster with the discreet ladies' magazine advertisement, the street-corner handbill with the full-color advertising insert. Yet the centrality of advertisement to modern culture, and its radical reshaping of both literature and ideological production in general, demands complete critical investment: advertising has to be seriously accepted as a formative cultural discourse.

To take on the loose, baggy monster of advertisement as a discourse, I have adopted a method that derives from Wittgenstein's famous argument about family resemblance and its relation to proof. Considering advertising as a discursive practice makes it possible to connect advertising styles and practices that have only resemblance, not complete homology, in common. The diachronic and synchronic axes can also be rotated at will, as the kindred artifacts of advertisement, widely separated by historical time, location, and use, enter into "a complicated network of similarities overlapping and criss-crossing: sometimes overall similarities, sometimes similarities of detail."[1] Advertising will be defined and discerned along these fuzzier boundaries, so that physical activities, performances, written artifacts, lights, mechanical reproductions, and all occurrences that exhibit the advertising impulse can be included as instances of the material discourse of advertising.

Literature is as problematic a field to define as advertising; the theory of family resemblance comes into play there as well. "Literature" takes refuge behind a somewhat suspect monolithic facade; the "canon," another ever-shifting boundary, embraces medieval drama, the realist novel, the satyr play, and the phillipic, to note only a few antipodes. Criticism makes itself comfortable with this artificial designation, and the ambivalence that results is usually accommodated by keeping periods and fields very disjunct. Consequently, the argument that follows will be fought in a very specific trench, the great novelistic tradition, but with its strategies directed toward a larger contested battleground, i.e., the changing place of literature per se in contemporary culture. This segmentation is partly necessary for evidentiary purposes, as these claims need minute investigation that generality cannot give. If the catalytic relations between advertisement and the works of Dickens, James, and Joyce can be carefully reproduced, the reader can follow through with connections to Balzac, Hardy, Baudelaire, Gissing, T. S. Eliot, Twain, Melville, Valéry, the Futurists, Flaubert, Pynchon, etc. An inherent assumption of my argument is that just such revision of literature is possible and pressing. Advertisement takes its place as an equal object of interest, however. Literature *qua* literature illuminates the outlines of advertisement in an irreplaceable way; there is no sense in which a purely sociological, historical, or economic theory of advertisement can approach unveiling its cultural dynamic. Advertising only leaves its vital trace with the litmus test of literature—it is incomprehensible without this parentage. And to state this is to admit that literature and advertisement are cultural kindred.

One way of situating the relationship of literature and advertisement is to look at their association over time.[2] Post-Gutenberg literature has always had advertisement as a shadow partner, but what is more remarkable is that advertisement was a concomitant of the early printing industry, and needed literature for *its* first appearances. The technology of print opened a space for the creation of advertisement, and although advertising was to develop as an independent form within two hundred years, initially it sprang from the emergence of printed literature, and was at home within the book.

The development of advertising can be traced by the use of the term *avertissement*. Once the word had signified a note placed in the colophon (back) page of a scribal manuscript to indicate that copying had been done during the holy days, meaning that it should not be sold. The *avertissement* was the antitype of advertisement, because it put a manuscript off limits for commercial purposes. Eventually, this scribal disavowal became the term for the page printers placed *first,* announcing their work, describing it, and giving their emblem and shop address. The self-effacement and anonymity of scribal production gave way to the technology of print, whose side effect was the discovery of advertising. These printed books and pamphlets had dual roles: they were new entities on the social scene, from whatever discipline or commercial activity they emerged (Vulgate Bibles, mercantile handbooks, accountancy manuals, scientific treatises), *and* they were *prima facie* exhibits for the new art of printing. Printing was the first invention in Western culture to be involved in a priority struggle, with rival national claims to the invention and attempts to monopolize it. Fierce contests over the ownership of the printing mechanism also produced a climate in which printers needed to establish and announce themselves, argue for the virtues of printing and their own methods, and articulate a new mode of social production not yet controlled by church or state. These necessary exhortations translate into the early codes of advertisement.[3]

Early printers had a unique pride and an unusual class position. There was great militancy among them, with many strikes occurring over the problem of full employment. Such emergent class agitation required polemical self-presentation, and maximum public visibility; the combination sufficed to turn the meek *avertissement* into the bold advertisement page set at the front.

> Early printers in their prefaces did all they could to reinforce the impression that theirs was an unusual calling. They cultivated all the arts of self-advertisement and pioneered as press agents on their own behalf. At the same time they catered to the needs of other merchants by issuing handbooks and manuals that were dignified by the addition of practical prefaces and an abundance of classical allusion.[4]

Far from being a pathetic or degraded stepchild of print, then, advertisement bolstered a solidarity among printers as a new type of self-sufficient and nonfeudal worker; it produced a network of connection between a rising new merchant class and a new world of literature; it participated in the secularizing trends and classical revivals by announcing and arguing for the importance of these texts. So ingeniously did this work that the Catholic *Index Librorum*, the list of proscribed books, provided Protestant printers with a free advertising list, also alerting interested Catholics. Early printers were in the extraordinary position of controlling the new publicity apparatus, and thus had an unprecedented relationship to all other enterprises, in that they actively sought out new markets, trades, and products, and profited from their expansion. Printing and advertisement, not really separable at this juncture, brought notice of and furthered an intense process of social reorganization.

The impact on literature was equally great. By the sixteenth century the advertising methods invented by printers to inaugurate their reproductive process had begun to realign the literary scene. "In the course of exploiting new publicity techniques, few authors failed to give high priority to publicizing themselves. The art of puffery, the writing of blurbs and other familiar promotional devices were also exploited by early printers who worked aggressively to obtain public recognition for the authors and artists whose products they hoped to sell."[5] Gradually the advertising material at the front of the printed text became a complex site for the celebration of individual authors, the prefatory remarks that could set a literary work in a compelling context, paeans to cultural classics, and portraits and poems setting up cults of authorship. Almost no books appeared without the obligatory advertisement, a tremendously complicated orchestration that "explained" the merits of the (usually) secular work, created a role for the author, and addressed the various classes and groups who might be audiences for the book. Printing itself had been a test case for the new legal category of intellectual property, when it was undergoing patent struggles. The advertising exordiums at the front of printed material were focal in allowing books to be seen as intellectual property also, with authors as celebrity figures (and here we can think of Erasmus, Paracelsus, Galileo), so these two aspects of early advertisement converged in the formation of "authorship" as a new property category.[6] In this sense, then, it is impossible to place modern literature, conceived as a set of great works by individual authors, outside the advertising context which supplied these boundaries.

If advertisement was present at the creation of "modern" literature, what ambivalences kept this intimacy from being acknowledged later, when literature flourished as a self-sufficient genre? Advertisement was absolutely central to the formation of "the author" and to promulgating a reading public outside the religious sphere, but the establishment of authorial practices and reading protocols cut two ways. Tensions arose when literature, heady in its newfound social place, was also forced to compete in its new market prominence. The early printers, many of whom had been authors themselves, became consolidated in larger, more corporate printing and publishing houses. "Claims to superior historical dignity and spiritual value were uneasily reconciled with turning out best-selling works that sold like drugs on the market—and were similarly advertised in the daily press."[7] The printing realm was growing cluttered, and literary work fought for space with journalistic production, political tracts, nostrums, spells, and scientific pamphlets. Advertising was no longer a charmed nimbus hovering about, and thereby describing, the secular book per se.

Early advertisements were restricted to delineating the contours of "literature," being by definition the prefatory pages that invented and furthered the methods of literary circulation and allowed literature to come into its own. By the late seventeenth century, however, publicity techniques called "advertising" had slipped out from the covers of literary works and had helped to create the newspaper—*The Advertiser* became a generic name for journalistic offerings. The lability of advertising allowed it to shape a separate print medium, newspapers, which sprang directly out of that liminal advertising space. This caused a further petrification in literary advertisement, now needing to differentiate itself from advertising as "news."

Literature had a precarious and variable status in the marketplace of print, and although advertisement had not yet come into association with any products except printed documents, as was to happen in the nineteenth century, it no longer beamed with especial beneficence on literature alone. From this period on begins the excoriation of the "cash-nexus" prison of literature, most famously formulated by Carlyle, a tendency that has had enormous repercussions on the reception and creation of literature. Elizabeth Eisenstein summarizes these perturbations within print culture:

> The more strident the voice of one generation, the more deafening the static interference became for the next. Among the variety of reactions that ensued two might be singled out: on the one hand, a museum culture, preserved in anthologies and taught in the schoolroom, was savagely assaulted; on the other hand, modern cultural "anarchy" and the society that sustained it were nostalgically repudiated. Nihilistic images pertaining to a "dustbin of the past" and a "wasteland of the present" were, in turn, dutifully recorded and expounded. . . . Thus the same process that had, earlier, introduced an eponymous authorship and harnessed the drive for fame to print-made immortality, led to an overpopulation of Parnassus.[8]

Advertising was crucial in making "literary production" possible, but advertising had also proved traitorous. If print culture as a whole was envisioned by literary producers, critics, and educators as a Tower of Babel, advertising had become a new kind of menace: the nineteenth century witnessed the foundation of an independently organized advertising language, and the twentieth century, its triumph in the marketplace.[9]

So powerful and so formidable on the cultural scene, advertising comes into view as an object for theory trailing sundry filaments that link it to the major cultural questions of our period, irrespective of disciplinary categories. The theoretical study of advertising has a dual parentage (normally enough), a critical heritage comprising strange bedfellows indeed. One vigorous progenitor is the field of mass cultural studies, where advertising is subsumed as a cultural technique along with mass-market publishing, film, radio, television, and state propaganda. A second, equally vital parent owes allegiance to an opposite ideological camp and a more recherché cultural pursuit—the simultaneous description and preservation of a traditional "high" literature, while advertising becomes visible as a demonized, twentieth-century rival. Each partner in the critical misalliance is embedded in its own set of complex affiliations, whose histories I will sketch in what follows. Nevertheless, the most powerful sources in advertising theory flow from this schismatic marriage—on the one hand, a tradition of wider cultural critique, and on the other, a literary debate whose stakes are of the highest political importance.

Having marked off those two larger divisions, one can chart the main split *within* the cultural critique that includes advertisement as one of its subjects. Put very broadly, the two primary critical approaches to advertising as a mass cultural system have originated from the writings of the Frankfurt school, in particular the work on commodity culture as exemplified by Horkheimer and Adorno in the *Dialectic of Enlightenment*, and from a Barthes-oriented semiotics best represented in his own work by *Mythologies, Systeme de la Mode*, and the essay "Rhetoric of the Image." Of the handful of key texts on advertising, Stuart Ewen's *Captains of Consciousness* (1976) contains a sociological and historical investigation whose terms are derived from the Frankfurt school, and current theorists of advertising artifacts, such as Judith Williamson in her brilliant *Decoding Advertisements* (1978) takes over a Lacanian-informed semiosis going back to Barthes. Raymond Williams has made his own way in the debate; his seminal article, "The Magic System," provides a sense of the global importance of advertising, while nonetheless shrouding this discovery in the apocalyptic garb often featured by highly conservative commentators on modern culture. Marshall McLuhan broke theoretic ground not only in his inclusion of advertisement within an all-encompassing technological reappraisal of image versus print culture, but in borrowing a writing style whose blocking, collagelike effect can only have been derived from advertisement itself—see *The Mechanical Bride*.[10]

These figures form an eclectic assemblage arrayed on the mass cultural side of the debate about advertising. The bride I have chosen for this Frankenstein is the specifically literary orientation toward advertisement crystallized in the school of F. R. Leavis, which would include I. A. Richards, Queenie D. Leavis, and Denys Thompson. I will briefly explore some of the fundamental arguments this school makes about advertising, because the group, focused chiefly on *Scrutiny* magazine, initiated a stance toward mass culture and especially advertising which is extraordinarily widespread and undeniably influential in schools and university studies, in cultural criticism, and in common parlance as well. Q. D. Leavis' book, *Fiction and the Reading Public* (1932), sets the tone for Leavisite cultural analysis *tout court*. Fiction, according to this view, had once been in harmonious alignment with a reading public: good literature had also, in effect, been popular literature, and there was no discrepancy between popular *taste* and high culture. Fiction lost this intimate bond with its audience only under the pressure of the sudden emergence of mass cultural forms, in the Leavis version; mass culture was an alien wedge interfering with literature, and a chief saboteur was advertising. When Q. D. Leavis looks for a culprit for this historical sundering, she traces it to the spread of a perfervid advertising system that soon was able to turn groups— in actual fact, whole classes, including the middle class—away from high culture to an artificially exciting new alternative: ads, mass market genre fiction, magazines, tabloids, and, ultimately, film.

One can make many inroads in the argument that "high" literature was once all that existed; in particular, this is to neglect the general excoriation of the novel form as a "low" habit, and to forget the tatterdemalion antecedents of fictional forms.[11] But by inverting the history of fiction in its British guise in order to shape a historical narrative to account for the proliferation of mass forms against a backdrop of some early golden age, Q. D. Leavis does foreground the extraordinary power of advertising and demonstrates its vital linkage to the fate of literature in general. The mythology of a cultural organicity, of a time when all classes read the same books, can be cut through to examine how profoundly advertising and mass culture are demystified in the process.

For the *Scrutiny* group the lowering of all cultural standards and the perversion of the social environment by mass production and alienating industrial labor could be traced to advertisement. As Francis Mulherne points out:

> The cultural effects of advertising were not all the result of the economic constraints that it imposed. Distinct both from the mainly informational notices of the first newspaper and from the merely hyperbolic publicity material of the early popular press, modern advertising—the systematic investment of commodities with meanings more or less un-related to their use-values—was itself a genuinely new element in the cultural ensemble. The active cultivation of delusory social values ("optimism," "Progress," the "herd instinct") and the discernible stylistic convergence between popular fiction and advertisements were testimonies of the direct action of the copywriter in the sphere of culture. [12]

I have tried to sketch out why advertisement is inextricable from the modern notion of literature; in the nineteenth century, their two histories begin to diverge and advertising is launched as a new mode of writing in its own right. That it is a new kind of writing, able to lay claim on the English language and to ravage it, provides the basis of F. R. Leavis' critique. "The decisive use of words today is . . . in connection with advertising, journalism, best sellers, motorcars and the cinema," he declares, and asks the public to "consider the probable concomitants of a change from the Bible, the prayer book, Bunyan, Shakespeare and Milton as the main influences upon our emotional vocabulary, to newspapers, advertisements, best sellers and the cinema." [13]

The litany of literature Leavis cites is notable because it is speech-based; either there is a tradition of hearing it read aloud or spoken in dramatic performance. What advertising really kills for Leavis is literature as transfigured speech, the art he places at the root of creative language use. In theories reminiscent of those of nineteenth-century philologist Max Müller, and the poetics of Gerard Manley Hopkins,

Leavis traces the legitimate use of *words* to those words which are linked to organic, craft traditions. One primary example for him is wheelwrighting, a form of village production that for Leavis engenders a vocabulary associated with intimate, holistic rural life. Advertising language can only spring, in this view, from the utterly deficient modes of industrial production, so that the words used by advertising epitomize the industrial transformation of speech communities and the advent of an alienated labor force.[14] An idealism of the word comes into play here, one certainly not restricted to Leavis. The woodland notes are heard in most litanies deploring advertising language. Marshall McLuhan, for example, credited advertising with the demise of the tradition of great folk orators and evangelists of late medieval times, who vanished, taking their organic words with them, under the hailstorm of publicized pamphlets.[15] Advertising came to be seen as the destroyer of an organic spoken language, and thus of the possibility of literature, since literature in this light has a privileged origin at the heart of speech communities. A goodly amount of animus has been directed against advertising on the grounds that it muddies the pool of pure speech from which the well of literature is supposedly drawn up.[16]

Leavis also sets advertising and fiction up against one another as direct rivals. One danger confronting unwary modern readers, particularly the inexperienced, is that advertisement tries to disguise itself as fiction, making it very difficult to differentiate them. Much of *Culture and Environment* emphasizes pedagogical heuristics designed to inculcate the proper ability to penetrate advertising's multiple guises and to sort out ads from literature. Leavis explores some of the tricks of advertising language in its chameleonic role. Style is one avenue (look for literary mannerisms and archaisms in ads), and content is another (ads use fear, snob-appeal, mob passion). He also invites critiques of misguided persons who would assimilate fiction and advertising; Mrs. Naomi Mitchison, notable novelist and critic, writes:

> Reviewers and people like that—I am sometimes one myself, so I know—have a horrid habit of talking about the decline in fiction. This is so silly of them. They keep their eyes firmly turned back onto Walter Scott and Dickens and Hardy, and they neglect the new and admirable branch of fiction which has sprung and blossomed like a daisy round the feet of the great oaks: they do not read advertisements. For what after all is the main difference between

Pamela and *Clarissa Harlowe* and one of the charming set pieces which adorn the pages of this book? Surely the difference is merely one of length. . . . Best of all it is written not for the soothing of a heart-throb, but—like Shakespeare's plays—for money.[17]

Stronger hearts than Leavis' might blanch at this bland declaration, and especially its final encomium. For Leavis such critical fatuity signified that training in critical awareness, or training for *resistance*, as he puts it, was vitally necessary in modern society, and essential if literature was to be preserved.

The fury against advertising in Leavisian practice is problematic because it is attached to impotent longings for a traditional culture, and to fear and hatred of "herd solidarity." Many left critiques that spring from ideological studies advocate a program technically if not politically indistinguishable from Leavis', however, where the emphasis is on training people to be more critically aware of advertisememts. John Berger, for example, developed a television show, the remarkable "Ways of Seeing," that sought ways to unmask the advertising image of women. A current definition of cultural literacy in some quarters would include the ability to "read through" advertisements, or at least to see them as important ideological constructs whose operation extends far beyond selling products.[18] The latter conviction certainly grounds this project as well, but what I want to complicate is the certainty about the status of advertising as an ideological production, where advertisement is almost always figured as the "other." More salient critiques of advertisement require an analysis of its affinities to a host of cultural practices—among them, literature.

Generally, these critiques resoundingly choose to view advertisement as "the other," as a sinister cultural production with no connection to what seem to be more positive or more transgressive cultural practices—whether evaluated from the left or right end of the spectrum. My study hopes to break down some of this confidence in advertising's divorce from other cultural productions, to set it in motion with the chief modern discourses. Two major investigations that, in different ways, do place advertising within a broadly defined cultural context come from the work of Barthes and Benjamin. In both cases, the contexts chosen ultimately prove somewhat problematic in assessing the confluence of literature and advertisement during the latter's formation.

Roland Barthes may have initiated the post-Leavisian discussion of advertising. In *Mythologies, Systeme de la Mode,* and other works he takes the entire cultural field as a set of signifying practices, and begins to work on "decoding" the sign system of advertising. The classic essay on an Italian pasta ad, "The Rhetoric of the Image," analyzes the tripartite nature of its image: its linguistic denotation and connotation, and the level of pure image or picture.[19] Advertising differs from the other sign systems for Barthes in having an intentional signification. Its affinity to literature lies in its deliberate self-reflexivity, where each statement also contains the message "I am speaking." Barthes' work on this subject undeniably opened and enlarged the cultural field of study, although the semiotics that follows in Barthes' wake has so fetishized the "sign" that there is no historical movement at all on this giant signboard; Barthes' writings on advertising subjects are invaluable, but even within his essays key problems emerge. Ads— like all signs—become hierophantic, emblematic, completely static except insofar as they interact differentially. No historical change in advertisement is discernible; each individual ad can be "entered" to probe its codes, but the larger effect of advertising language is lost. The only explanation for advertisement offered comes in "Mythology Today," where ideology (and thus advertising) is conceived as an unfalsifiable myth, like the Freudian unconscious, incapable of being subjected to the truth-testing that obtains in "reality."[20]

"The Work of Art in an Age of Mechanical Reproduction," Walter Benjamin's seminal essay on the status of art in a period where capitalist technologies alter the ontology of art and its very creation (read production), has been regularly rediscovered by virtually every critical school.[21] Literature does not lend itself to the critique of this particular essay, whose paradigms come from the plastic arts, but even in the case of film and photography Benjamin has missed a fateful context. Far from being aesthetically revolutionary forms supplanting painting, sculpture, and literature, both film and photography originate in commercial, advertised enterprise. To strip a complicated history down to simple elements, photography's first and primary use was to document business sites and commercial development to convince financial speculators of the "reality" of various properties, and the first rudimentary motion picture apparatus was devised to capture complicated machinery in operation, in order to advertise sophisticated equipment to manufacturers. The story of Thomas Edison's corporatist development of film is a cautionary tale for utopian Benjaminians, reiterating as it does Wittgenstein's dictum "meaning is use" with a vengeance.[22] Since Benjamin carefully avoids discussing the penumbra of advertising activity shrouding even these mass media (admittedly in order to better present the powerful aesthetic capacities of still-despised mass art forms), it is not surprising that he does not single out advertising as a truly salient instance of the new work of art. Politically, this would have had devastating implications, although Benjamin comes close to voicing this in several footnotes, and in pieces in *One Way Street*.[23] Though Benjamin perceived brilliantly the changed field of art in capitalist society, his visionary prediction of the liberating potential of new mass art technologies would be shattered by acknowledging that advertising had already installed itself in the forefront of those techniques. The theoretical categories of Benjamin's essay are irreplaceable, yet the Brechtian optimism that cloaks its treatment of mass cultural forms fails to confront the specificity and intransigence of the advertising form.

I will borrow Benjamin's most diffuse point—that modern art forms, in this case literature, are put under vast pressure by the burgeoning of technologically assisted cultural production. In what follows, the historical affinities of literature and advertisement will be traced, culminating in their intense rivalry over contested space in a changed linguistic economy. Advertising artifacts will be used as an archive, in the Foucauldian sense, treated as a repository of cultural materials not readily ordered under any institutional heading or disciplinary category, but whose presence on the cultural scene is resoundingly evident. The archival approach differs from semiotic or sociological analyses because it sets an entire body of advertising "discourse" up against a formally acknowledged cultural discourse, what is termed literature. Whatever the status of advertising today, and this point will be returned to in the epilogue, its prehistory shows it to be intimately related to literary practice.

Secondly, the archival investigation of advertising does not focus on readings of individual advertisements, whether to unfold the workings of particular artifacts or to make inferences about the ideological purposes of individual ads. Single ads are evanescent, ephemeral structures; of more moment to my argument is the reshaping of cultural discourse as a whole by the massive presence of a huge archive of advertisement. Richard Simon, for example, has written of advertising as literature, but his comparison of advertising and literature is a thematic one; current television commercials form a closed, fantastic and folkloric world, analogous to the presumed inner world of fiction.[24] Argument by analogy is somewhat limited, however—advertising does not merely resemble literature in setting up miniature stories, nor "happen upon" its narrativity and copy it. Both literature and advertising are composite, heterogeneous language practices, which need to be read off each other to gauge their respective outlines.

I have organized my text as a series of such mutually penetrating readings. In each section a major novelistic work or advertising document serves as a prism to refract a particular dialectic. The choice of Dickens, James, and Joyce as the specimen novelists is not accidental or arbitrary. In the first place, while other genres of literature can certainly be scanned for the advertising presence (and one of course thinks of the poetry of Mallarmé, Baudelaire, and others), the novel is without doubt the most important literary form during the nineteenth and twentieth centuries. The palimpsestic nature of the novel, its ability to contain, suppress, stratify, and transform a host of cultural discourses, is a key claim of the theory informing this project. While many aspects of M. M. Bakhtin's dialogic theory of the novel are extremely problematic, his assumption of the "heteroglossic" nature of the novel as a genre is suggestively relevant here. "The stylistic uniqueness of the novel as a genre consists precisely in the combination of these subordinated, yet still relatively autonomous, unities . . . into the higher unity of the work as a whole: the style of a novel is to be found in the combination of its styles; the language of a novel is the system of its 'languages'."[25] We can perhaps reject the idealism of a novel's higher unity but salvage the technique of disentangling languages within narrative works. "Certain features of language (lexicological, semantic, syntactic) will knit together with the intentional aim, and with the overall accentual system inherent in one or another genre: oratorical, publicistic, newspaper and journalistic genres, the genres of low literature (penny dreadfuls, for instance), or, finally, the various genres of high literature."[26] If "the real task of stylistic analysis consists in uncovering all the available orchestrating languages in the composition of the novel," then one can use the archeological strategy to uncover the advertising archive set within the novel, and a similar procedure to search for the stratifications of literature within the procedures of advertising. Bakhtin said that "it is precisely in the most sharply heteroglossic eras, wher. the collision and interaction of languages is especially intense and powerful, when heteroglossia washes over literary language from all sides (that is, in precisely those eras that most conduce to the novel), that aspects of heteroglossia are canonized with great ease and rapidly pass from one language system to another."[27] This notion conforms exactly to the great crisis in literature brought on by the rapid eruption of advertising, both languages ricocheting off one another in the cultural field. The "heteroglossic" pressure on the novel is supplied, in my view, by the active capitalization of narrative language, the establishment of powerful centralized writing factories in the form of advertising agencies, the usurpation of public space for new modes of social reading, and the revolutionary writing techniques advertising was able to engender, with its technological expertise.

Dickens, James, and Joyce are apposite choices for an archeological expedition seeking the record of the cataclysms wrought by advertisement. Dickens' career is concomitant with the institutional formation of advertising, and the economic crisis of overproduction that engendered it. James writes during the transitional phase of advertising (beginning in the 1880s), when it becomes the handmaiden of oligopolistic economic concentration, as the corporate period begins. Joyce's *Ulysses* is published on the cusp of a third great shift in advertising practice and power: by 1925 advertising was a primary industry, capable of setting the cultural agenda of radio, film, and later, television as well.[28]

It is a crucial challenge for criticism to address the material and political forms of our daily life. For left criticism especially, the contours of contemporary culture must certainly be explored to map their political implications. Virtually every text on advertisement, with the exception of the hagiographies issued from Madison Avenue itself, ends with a peroration *against* advertisement, a plea for its extinction, an attempt at an exorcism. A "what is to be done?" plaintiveness sets in, occasioned by the very real specter of global advertisement haunting every surface, mediating every exchange. In writing about advertisement's affiliations with print culture, and its origins within what can loosely be called "textuality" I hope to resituate the discussion of advertising, essentially by *familiarizing* it as a practice. This is not to ignore the extraordinary ideological force of advertisement, nor to efface its profound effects in both communicating and buttressing the political system of industrial and postindustrial capitalism. These effects are powerfully demonstrable and crucial to conditions of modern hegemony. But advertising does not serve as a simple messenger-boy of ideology, if only because ideology does not exist in some place apart before it is channeled through advertisement. The richness of advertisement as a cultural structure—and this is in spite of the advertising industry's own claims to positivist efficiency, psychological control, and logical management—ensures that advertising will not, and cannot, wither away. Its roots in myriad discourses afford it too much cultural nourishment; its plenitude as a lexicon, an idiom, a display, a site for the reading of our culture, guarantees this.

Advertising, in short, is one practice, but is not isolable to any one central function—not even "selling products." Indeed, in the contemporary saturation stage, advertisements are so numerous it is often impossible for agencies and marketers to ascertain whether specific ads have made a profit difference. The most significant feature of advertisement—or at least the one I will highlight—is its *overdetermination*, which advertising shares with all other cultural phenomena. Put in other words, every cultural artifact is produced by individual makers, by institutional settings, by collective aspirations and values, by its historical relation to the forms and genres that surround it, by its adoption and use by a public, and by its place in an overall political economy. When we "read" cultural artifacts all these forces are in play. The force-field of advertising is equally rich, and has its own unique overburdened structure. Add to this advertising's pride of place as a narrative form absolutely central to modern economic production and the corporate system, and its freight is considerable, because advertisement will also have to reenact and recreate a political economy simultaneous with its personal desire structure.

Advertising's cultural tasks are many. In the absence of a personalized market, it must compensate for older forms, like the buying fairs with their carnivalesque elements of exchange. Vanished human relations of exchange and barter are compensated for within advertisement (thus the many "old friends" in advertising where most real purchasing situations are impersonal). Public traditions of decoration and excess—the shop sign, the town gate, and so on—also flow into advertising's cultural space, so that the proliferation of billboards and box signs also serves to produce a public iconography. Where channels of public speech have broken down—the church pulpit, the town meeting—advertisements' illusory surface of collective discourse finds a place. Finally, within advertisements themselves the culture finds a location for staging the contradictions inherent in the myths of general desire. Only advertisements, lodged as they are within the heart of the commodity form, can theatricalize the conditions of politics, gender, class, and race—by neutralizing their conflicts—that impinge on our individual and collective Robinsonnades. Advertisements are cultural messages in a bottle—messages we read to learn just how alone we are.

1 • The Dickens Advertiser

"Promise, large promise, is the soul of advertisement."
Samuel Johnson, *The Idler*, 1750

"Tolstoy has to be read, but Dickens can appear on a cigarette card, and all the world knows him."
George Orwell, *Charles Dickens*

GEORGE ORWELL'S REMARKABLE APPRAISAL of Charles Dickens in his 1936 essay[1] crystallizes the unique quality of Dickens as a writer. One can think of many other authors to stand on Tolstoy's side of the equation, but the link that Dickens has to the "cigarette card" belongs to him as a determining characteristic. Although Orwell makes no explicit reference to it elsewhere in his essay, his remark is evidence of the inextricable intertwining of Dickens' work, and his career, with advertising. The apparently mundane cigarette card, born out of and born into a world saturated with advertising, is in reality a universal token, a representation that offers a familiar mode of knowledge beyond its bare paper and print. While Tolstoy, for example, must be *read* to be known, there is another possible road to apprehending Dickens. Dickens is a phenomenon of mass culture, a writer who is present at the creation of advertising as a system, and whose work and personal career participate in shaping that system.

Orwell's hint in 1936 at the magical power that lies behind Dickens' formidable impact—his relationship to advertising—has not been followed up. The investigation is a key one for comprehending both the phenomenon that is Charles Dickens and the phenomenal way advertising was to install itself as the primary medium of cultural communication during his lifetime and since. Dickens has been called by Steven Marcus the first capitalist of literature; moving beyond this insight, it appears that Dickens was able to exert such force precisely because his literary capitalizing intersected with the aestheticizing of capitalism—a period during which advertising was able to become the virtual literature of capitalism.

There are four main axes of this investigation, although they will necessarily overlap at times, and their mapping can only be done in close readings of texts themselves. The first line of inquiry lays the necessary historical groundwork for an appreciation of how radically new the advertising institution was, and how it was linked from its inception to texts, particularly literary works and newspaper journalism.[2] This involves an excursus into the economic practices of the beginning of the nineteenth century and the coffee-house milieu in which advertising was engendered, with a scrutiny of the very early work of Dickens as it registers the alterations advertising was beginning to impose. Dickens' own personal history is vitally relevant to this juncture, not as simple biographical overlay, but to make concrete his texts' transformations of his own literal encounters with the material conditions of advertisement.

The second phase of my analysis proposes that advertising be defined as a social writing that presupposes a particular form of social reading. The "textuality" of advertising increasingly saturates mid-nineteenth-century culture, and as the public is taught to read it, the text/image nexus of advertising is able, by virtue of its universal dissemination, to shape social narrative and to provide the sense of proferring social reality. Dickens' work takes up this problematic of social visibility vigorously, in one sense because his novels are an attempt to make the society visible to itself,[3] and also in that within his novels visibility and invisibility are often a function of the ability of people or a class to manipulate advertisement on their (its) own behalf. The novels' intense preoccupation with the way advertisement has come to take on this function of social arbitration is responsible for the prophetic quality of the texts: in an extraordinary range of cases they delimit and invent advertising methodologies that were only to be used many years later—when advertising, in a sense, had caught up to Charles Dickens. It will be important to chart the ways that Dickens' texts are both a reading of advertisement and a harbinger of it.

The third thrust of this chapter is to show that advertising is a central subject in Dickens' novels. I will be claiming that Dickens' work is a palimpsest of advertising practices. Beginning with *Sketches by Boz* and continuing through *Pickwick, The Old Curiosity Shop, Martin Chuzzle-wit, Bleak House,* and *Our Mutual Friend,* advertising emerges as a subtext or organizational principle of many of these texts. The Dickens ouevre carefully charts the changes occurring in advertising, from scattered shop signs and impromptu street fairs to its adumbration in the later novels as the totalizing advertising world of text, publicity, and image. The entire panoply of advertising indices is unfolded within his books, not as incidental backdrop, but because these changes are critical for both the writer and the reader. This premise can make better sense of books that are seemingly marginal—like *The Old Curiosity Shop* and *Martin Chuzzlewit*—while providing new readings of other works that open a window on the procedures of advertising as it reshapes the modern cultural and economic spheres.

I have mapped out an exploration of Dickens' texts within an advertising context, seeing the works and advertising in a dialectical relationship to one another. The final area I will be discussing pulls back from the texts to look at them as objects per se: Dickens' novels were directly connected to advertising as products. The characters and incidents of his novels yielded a stream of products the books had already pre-advertised, and they were also used to form the basis of advertisements, as in the respective examples of the Weller cab and the Pickwick cigar. In addition, Dickens cannibalized his own texts in order to excerpt from them, forming the basis of his reading career, for which he also fashioned the advertisements. The "popularity" of Dickens' work and his person was allied to conditions that obtained for Dickens as for no other writer, and reveals the confluence of advertising and literature in the nineteenth-century market.

INCUNABULA OF ADVERTISING

One of the earliest documented advertising jingles appears on the label of Warren's Blacking, England's then-paramount shoe polish. The label, dating from 1787, shows a cat staring at its reflection in a boot, and reads:

> As I one morning shaving sat
> For dinnertime preparing
> a dreadful howling from the cat
> Set all the room a-staring

Suddenly I turned—beheld a scene,
I could not but delight in;
For in my boots so bright and clear,
The cat her face was fighting.
Bright was the boot—its surface fair,
Its lustre nothing lacking;
I never saw one half so clear
Except by *Warren's Blacking*.[4]

The idea of combining individual packaged products with a textual accompaniment was a new one; most goods sold in England at the time were either found in anonymous bins within stores marked only by iconographic shop signs, or they were purchased or exchanged at the large itinerant "buying fairs" held in the larger country towns.[5] The Warren's Blacking firm was a prescient one: within a few decades the need to transform manufactured goods from bulk anonymity to aesthetically announced "product" would be felt throughout the industrial and business worlds, although no straightforward procedure for accomplishing this transformation was at hand. Advertising remained a congeries of loosely allied practices, a crossroads between newspaper, coffee-house, freelance writer, and the firm with the product until the latter half of the nineteenth century. But in the beginning was Warren's, making its solitary attempt to perform the transmogrification on its own.

Although many histories of advertising take the practice back to its supposed avatars in the clay tablets of Pompeii or the signs of the middle ages, it seems more reasonable to agree with Raymond Williams' contention that advertising is more than the simple "announcement" described in Shakespeare; it takes on its recognizably modern contours late in the seventeenth century.[6] The appearance of advertising is concomitant with the appearance of the first newspaper, which has been traced to Nathan Tyler's 1647 *Intelligencer*. The system Nathan Tyler had arrived upon was an elision of news with advertisement, with the two separate strands very difficult to disentwine. The one-page sheet served notice that certain ships had come into port; in a different section, a list of goods that might or might not be carried by a particular ship was set out. No open exhortation to connect the docking of the ships with possible purchases was made, and the circulation of the newspaper seems to have been limited to the ship companies themselves. However, the decision to regard as "news" that which was also a form of commercial announcement sealed the new status of advertising, falling between the rhetorical and the informative.

The subsequent papers that began to proliferate in the eighteenth century commonly had the subtitle "The Advertiser," and within the text of the one- to two-page document the advertisements were printed directly with the "copy," such as it was. Typographical distinction of news from advertisement was a refinement that took until the nineteenth century to be definitively established, and the similar device of sorting out the ads to their own column was also long in coming.[7] This timidity on the part of newspaper editors reflects the problematic status of advertisement as it was gradually being formed—there *was* no practical distinction to be made between the advertisement for a runaway slave or servant, and the "news" that such an escape had taken place. Given this difficulty, a result of property relations, many gazettes simply gave themselves over to compilation of such advertisements, written by the injured party, and generally calling for the redress of wrongs to property or marital happiness. These homemade advertisements have the quality of compressed narratives, as a specimen from the *Gazetteer* of 1789 shows:

> To announce that Mary Jane Tombs has fled my house on January twelve or thereabouts, having taken with her our red shawl and assorted items, can be known for her stoutness. She will head North; advertiser offers a reward for the return.[8]

Advertisement was bifurcated between two relatively distinct provenances on the threshold of the nineteenth century. On the one hand, it defined a species of social communication or narrative that was aligned with news, another highly unstable new social practice; on the other, advertisement began to make inroads at the gathering places where a constant stream of visitors could be expected: the coffeehouses. Not accidentally, the coffeehouses were the site of much of the foregoing newspaper activity; both the *Spectator* and the *Idler* were coffeehouse papers with voluminous advertising.[9]

The informal aspect of advertising in the coffeehouse world involved the posting of casual signs or the message-board system that allowed small tradesmen to put up notices for interested parties. Gradually, the message system became more codified, with the coffeehouse owner taking on, sometimes for a fee, the job of relaying commercial messages, or putting buyers and sellers in touch with one another. This system functioned on a verbal level, but it had a great impact in that the coffeehouse was an urban gathering place that cut across class lines and created a public perhaps more receptive to these unique messages. In order to have invaded the coffeehouse at all, a patron needed a certain susceptibility to the then-exotic practice of coffee-drinking. Among the very earliest advertisements arising out of this matrix are those for coffee and tea—again, delivered in the form of news accounts, because their appearance was news, but with the stirrings of narrative later to become so pronounced:

> Tchai, or Tai, or Tee can be bought from the Morrish Rose teahouse. Discovered by Chinese emperors and the Manchu families. With great difficulty brought in ships to England.[10]

The seminal place of the newspaper in the development of advertising is expressed by Anthony Smith:

> The ways in which the content of a paper is coded for the reader—as news, as comment, or as advertisement—resulted from the canons of editorial policy. There can be no absolute distinction. In one society the announcement that a ship is arriving or departing is news; in another it is read as an advertisement. . . . In the course of history many kinds of news have turned into advertising, and vice versa. For example, the London newspaper of the eighteenth century would pay theaters for the right to print information concerning the performances, the names of the author, actors, and director. For its part, the theater would pay the newspaper for the right to print comments on the quality of the production (these were the "puffs" that came to earn ridicule and eventually contempt). . . . The two sections of the newspaper—information and advertising—came to occupy equally important roles, separated only through tradition and a gradually clarifying ethic.[11]

Advertising, as yet not a sui generis form, was allied to another text besides the newspaper at this point. The documented advertisements in greatest abundance in the eighteenth century are all for literary works. This practice apparently started when a printer, William Caxton, created flyers on scrap sheets for *The Pyes of Salisbury*, a text on church law, which the clergy then distributed after services.[12] Because of printers' proximity to the printing press itself, already used to print the book in question, it was an easier task for booksellers to break through to the notion of printing up an accompaniment to sell that text. Most eighteenth-century books had a leaflet describing the book sewn into the front pages, and titled "Advertisement." This leaflet combined a virtual abstract of the text with praises of its humor, loftiness, or piety.[13] The intimate liaison maintained by book and advertisement was profoundly deepened in the nineteenth century, when a newspaper tax on ads was suddenly levied. The monthly paper-covered editions of books became the natural, and less expensive, location for the placement of ads, given the alliance of text and ad in the past.

While these features connect advertisement to texts, the ads themselves were not written specifically for certain products. Returning to the Warren's Blacking jingle that initiated this historical excursus, one recognizes that this relatively unimpressive piece of writing affixed to the individual bottles of blacking marked more than a revolution in packaging. The act of pasting labels to differentiate one product from another—in fact, the nascent notion of "product" itself—is the primitive phase of the industry that was to become indispensable for economic production as a whole, however unprepossessing the short poem may be.

The period of Charles Dickens' childhood that he kept secret until late in his life, what his unfinished autobiography calls his "secret agony of the soul,"[14] found him employed at the Warren's Blacking warehouse, pasting labels very like the one featuring the cat onto the bottles until "each one looked as smart as a pot of ointment from the apothecary's shop."[15] This labor, while as grueling as the factory work so many other children (and adults) were engaged in, was also different from it in that it had added, in embryonic form, the stage in which product was beginning to be conjoined to text.

The link between a product and its advertising text was still a tenuous and unstable one, and so could often be substituted for by a physical or performative activity. Not only was the young Dickens assigned to paste the advertising labels on the shoe polish, but he was placed in a niche at the exposed street-level window, embedded as an attractive human pendant to the title "Warren's Blacking" above him, to serve for passers-by as a "working advertisement"[16] for the seriousness and assiduity of the warehouse as a whole. The glimpse of his nominally middle-class son exhibited as an advertisement in a public street galvanized John Dickens into finally removing him from the warehouse and sending him back to school.[17] The warehouse experience was a totally transforming one for Dickens, but also more generally reveals a radically new social relationship: the insinuation of text between labor and product. The Warren's Blacking jingle placed itself in a new space opened between the warehouse workplace and the shoe polish labeled on the store shelf, making it almost impossible for the public reader of that label to mentally traverse the route back to the reality of the labor that the young Dickens, for one, saw only too clearly indeed.

The casual and incongruously aligned practices of advertising were also beginning to demand writers. In the early nineteenth century the modeling of advertising on the circuit taken by the book had not yet been achieved, but the need for authors of these ephemeral texts was becoming felt. The handful of firms using "advertising" generated it in a haphazard way on their own, usually seeking out the services of a writer to help them fashion their home-made announcements. Dickens became one of these writers for the firm of Warren's Blacking, during his much better known career as a parliamentary reporter. His uncle, John Barrow, in fact described him as an advertising writer in introducing him to John Payne Collier for a job.[18] The boundaries sharply delineating newspaper writer, advertising writer, and aspiring "author" were still shifting, so that Dickens' foray into advertising is an attempt at realizing himself as a *writer*—his own description of this stage of his career. None of Dickens' proto-ads apparently survive, especially since they were launched into the void of free-lance copywriting ephemera before there was any advertising profession as such. But Dickens, as distinct from any other nineteenth-century novelist, begins his career from within and without the world of advertising, and is one of its original practitioners.

URBAN POETICS: THE WARREN'S BLACKING TRANSFORMED

Sketches by Boz (1836)[19] and *Pickwick* (1837)[20] launched Dickens as a "real" writer, one who carved out the first mass-market reading public in achieving his popularity. The *Sketches* can be read as transitional in this process of integrating advertising, since the text comments continually on signs and ads, and still retains tenuous ties to Dickens' "advertising writer" phase. *Pickwick* looks back to an earlier scene, struggling with the anachronism unavoidable in portraying a pre-advertising society, and in so doing it manifests the tensions within the nascent advertising culture. Simultaneously, *Pickwick* becomes a marketing success and an early advertising instrument as it is in the process of its formation; the book itself begins to fill up an advertising vacuum that Dickens takes eager advantage of.

The *Sketches* delineate a London without the palpable advertising evidence that would pervade it as little as a decade later, when "all London is a circus of poster and trade bill, a receptacle for the writings of Pears and Warren's until we can barely see ourselves underneath. Read this! Read that!"[21] This early book takes its models from the newspaper sketches of London life in vogue at the time, but it is unlike them in its emphasis on "reading" the city like a text (p. 17). Throughout the *Sketches*, and particularly in those sections devoted to shops and neighborhoods, Dickens uses writing, announcement, and text as analogs for all forms of human communication. The signs that determine a neighborhood for an outside visitor are called "a few illegible hieroglyphics" (p. 68). One sketch focuses on a particular house going through a metamorphosis from one dismal business site to another. The sketch makes no reference to human occupants or to their various fates; their presence is inferred from the gradually accumulating crazy-quilt of advertisements painted on the front windows, until the original purposes of the house are hopelessly erased by succeeding signs. Dickens textualizes the entire neighborhood of the Dials, "reading the book from its covers" (p. 18), by using the signs, bills, window lettering and shop-window display as the "book" to be read. While most of the signs are still the older iconic ones, such as the thistle within a gold ring that announced Gillies' bookshop, or else the extremely wordy, hand-lettered signs that give a history of a shop and its problems, the city is "read" by Dickens through these advertisements, and reading and writing are the operative terms of the *Sketches* as they move through the London scene.

Dickens ends his sketch of the Dials with a description of an advertising writer:

The shabby-genteel man is an object of some mystery, but as he leads a life of seclusion, and never was known to buy anything beyond an occasional pen, except half-pints of coffee, penny loaves, and ha'portions of ink, his fellow-lodgers very naturally suppose him to be an author; and rumors are current in the Dials, that he writes poems for Mr. Warren. (p. 157)

The elision here between advertising writer and "author" will continue to be highlighted in Dickens' next few books, until the text is able to maintain the ironic, disdainful tone taken toward "Slum," the advertising poet of *The Old Curiosity Shop*. The shabby-genteel writer is a new denizen of the city, as well as being the exemplar of a writer for the class of people that surrounds him in the neighborhood, who, although semi-illiterate, can be said to "read" his works. The London of the *Sketches* is undergoing an apprenticeship in the social reading that will come to dominate social exchange. In this initial book, Dickens is at once the first pupil of the advertised landscape, and a newly escaped Warren's Blacking "author," capable of doing both the reading and the writing on the social scene.

Pickwick considerably complicates the reading/writing nexus of the beginnings of advertising. Textually, it lies in the flux between its ostensible dating thirty years before, and its accommodation of the current times (1837). The anachronisms become clues to the changes newly wrought by the presence of advertising, as does the nostalgia for a "country" England in a book that keeps veering back to the city. Mr. Pickwick's exposure to the realities of urban life also engages him, and the book, in a confrontation with advertising. Finally, *Pickwick*'s sensational debut ensconces Dickens firmly within the advertising milieu.

Because the book is planned to capture the quixotic ramblings of the Pickwick club, its rural trajectory seems natural enough; in fact, the country scenes and town visits become the only places of retreat from a city that, try as he will, Dickens cannot burnish with a retrospective nostalgic glow. A quintessential feature of the countryside is its *absence* of advertising and of the need to advertise. The only intrusive "sign" in the landscape is the comforting tavern symbol that always greets the weary band. The multitude of taverns and inns still preserve the superannuated iconic symbologies, and the text celebrates these in detail:

Mr. Pickwick gazed with an air of curiosity, not unmixed with interest, on the objects around him. There was an open square for the marketplace; and in the centre of it, a large inn with a signpost in front, displaying an object very common in art, but rarely met with in nature—to wit, a blue lion, with three bow legs in the air, balancing himself on the extreme point of the centre claw of his fourth foot. (p. 161)

Pickwick goes on to note with approval the few labeled shops and stores, in a village square he can still "read" at a glance. The Blue Lion Inn, with the addition of Dingley Dell, remains a base of operations for the rest of their journeyings. Other stopping-places are also marked by iconic signs: "The Great White Horse [is] rendered conspicuous by a stone statue of some rampacious animal with flowing mane and tail, distantly resembling an insane cart horse, which is elevated above the principal door" (p. 384). Mrs. Weller keeps a public house with a flagrantly expressive signboard depicting the Marquis of Branvy as "the head and shoulders of a gentleman of apoplectic countenance, in a red coat with deep blue facings, and a touch of the same blue over his three-cornered hat, for a sky" (p. 449). Sam Weller spots his father's pub, the Blue Boar, by noticing a signboard "on which the painter's art had delineated something remotely resembling a cerulean elephant with an aquiline nose in lieu of a trunk" (p. 537).

These signs are "nostalgic" within *Pickwick* because they are the few remnants of a once-universal graphic vocabulary, relics of a time when each establishment could represent itself pictorially. Shop and tavern signs since the Middle Ages had elaborated on an immense and complex pictorial code, an eloquent representational grid drawn from disassembled coats-of-arms and guild banners. The thistles, unicorns, scissors, headless knights, and animals once blazoned on all shops were identifications, marks on a social and a political map, not solicitations. The signs made no attempt to suggest new needs—there was a magic air to advertisement when few people could read that made the simple announcement culturally sufficient. The inn signs *Pickwick* lingers over were part of "a world of symbols and colors, amplified by corresponding street cries, songs and rhymes,"[22] that was vanishing, with a few exceptions. (Autolycus' song in The *Winter's Tale* is an example of the street-fair song that had once served as a complement to the elaborate artifice of shop signs.) Mr. Pickwick also notes with relish the market-

places and market fairs of the country towns; up until the nineteenth
century, scheduled markets were held for the exchange of locally
produced commodities. *The Book of Fairs* (1775)[23] shows how a trading
network of this scope and complexity was organized, and also demonstrates that the network of fairs was the major outlet for commerce
in all of England. The fairs did not have advertising, obviously; instead,
traveling players, puppet shows, and other acts made the circuit of the
fairs. *The Old Curiosity Shop* investigates the detritus remaining after
the dissolution of this market fair system, while *Pickwick* valorizes each
market square, inn sign, and shop signboard the Pickwickians run
across, with an impassioned political nostalgia.

An ironic result of *Pickwick*'s affection for these tavern signs and old-
fashioned market exchanges, and an emblem of the tensions in a text
at the cusp of changes in economic production, is the outcry occasioned
by one of the original illustrations to *Pickwick*. Depicting Mr. Weller
helping his son Samuel compose the famous valentine, as they linger
within the Blue Boar, the picture clearly shows a placard on the mantel
above Mr. Weller's head, reading distinctly "Guinness Dublin Stout."
The placard was originally the wooden crate side of the box containing
Guinness; by being replicated in the illustration for Pickwick, it became an ad peeping out over Weller's head. Percy Fitzgerald describes
the resulting furor in *History of Pickwick*.[24] The conjunction of the
picture with the huge public *Pickwick* was reaching created a new
reading of the illustration, implying that the excitement readers found
in the episode also extended to the stout, and yielded a host of
manufacturers who wanted the same heady exposure for their products.
By the completion of *Pickwick*'s serial run, the illustrator had begun to
be in demand for advertising pictures, and Dickens' famous collabo-
rators, Hablot K. Brown (Phiz) and George Cruikshank, were later
able to build hugely successful advertising careers.[25] The novel gives
birth to an advertising scenario.

Mr. Pickwick may be innocent of advertising, but the book's urban
dwellers are not. The town of Eatanswill, in whose affairs the Pickwick
Club becomes enmeshed, is dominated by two rival newspapers, the
Eatanswill Gazette and the *Independent*. These presses are clearly shown
to preserve no boundaries between their publicity campaigns and their
reportage. Mrs. Leo Hunter, literary doyenne and aristocratic poetess,
is able to use the paper to promote herself and her garden party, while
the announcement passes for news.

Mrs. Hunter's grounds . . . would present a scene of varied and delicious enchantment—a bewildering coruscation of beauty and talent—a lavish and prodigal display of hospitality—above all, a degree of splendour softened by the most exquisite taste; and adornment refined with perfect harmony and the chastest good keeping—compared with which, the fabled gorgeousness of Eastern fairyland itself, would appear to be clothed in as many dark and murky colors, as must be the mind of the splenetic and unmanly being who could presume to taint with the venom of his envy, the preparations made by this virtuous and highly distinguished lady . . . (p. 257)

Pickwick and his friends are unable to comprehend the promotional nature of the soiree when they attend it, because their perception of the possibilities of textual self-promotion belongs to an earlier time. They accept the self-evaluation of the literary group, and are awed at their celebrity. The darker connotations of this technique of social visibility are limned in *Our Mutual Friend;* in *Pickwick*, the disjunction between the mundane actuality of the literary party (and also of the Blue and Buff political campaigns taken up by the enemy papers) and the inflated publicity and covert advertisement surrounding it is still a comic one.

Social invisibility is a keen problem for the middle class, unable to command the society columns, in *Pickwick* as well, best represented by the struggles of the two unruly medical students Mr. Pickwick meets on their vacation at Dingley Dell. Bob Sawyer and Benjamin Allen try to make a go of their medical practice in London, with only meager results.

Mr. Benjamin Allen and Mr. Bob Sawyer sat together in the little surgery behind the shop, discussing minced veal and future prospects, when the discourse, not unnaturally, turned upon the practice acquired by Bob the aforesaid, and his present chances of deriving a competent independence from the honourable profession to which he had devoted himself "which, I think, Ben, are rather dubious," observed Mr. Bob Allen . . . "This business was capitally described in the advertisement, Ben. It is a practice, a very extensive practice—and that's all." (p. 762)

Bob Sawyer, having obtained his surgery from an advertisement advising readers of the death of the previous occupant, Doctor Nockemorf, is forced to concoct a variety of bizarre advertising practices in order to keep the practice afloat. His ads are largely staged scenarios, a physical kind of advertising intended to make his presence known in the neighborhood. Mr. Winkle, a Pickwickian, comes to call, and compliments Bob on his apparently thriving business. "All appearances," is the reply—Bob has created false props and stock to disguise his lack of supplies. He employs his young servant as advertiser:

> He goes up to a house, rings the area bell, pokes a packet of medicine without a direction into the servant's hand, and walks off. Servant takes it into the dining-parlor; master opens it, and reads the label: "Draught to be taken at bed-time—pills as before—lotion as usual—*the* powder. From Sawyer's, late Nockemorf's" . . . Next day, boy calls: "Very sorry—his mistake—immense business—great many parcels to deliver—Mr. Sawyer's compliments—late Nockemorf" The name gets known, and that's the thing, my boy. . . . Bless your heart, old fellow, it's better than all the advertising in the world . . . (p. 624)

The inadequate "advertising" Bob Sawyer is negatively comparing his own advertising performance to was the outmoded circular form, a virtual newspaper listing only names, addresses, and changes of venue. For instance, the lawyer Pell gives his condolences to Samuel Weller on the death of his stepmother on the basis of having read of her death in the *Advertiser,* since her demise meant a possible sale of her public house. Bob Sawyer's creativity in making himself visible extends to other public performances:

> "The lamplighter has eighteen pence a week to pull the night-bell for ten minutes every time he comes around; and my boy always rushes into church, just before the psalms, when the people have got nothing to do but look about 'em, and calls out, with horror and dismay depicted on his countenance. 'Bless my soul,' everybody says, 'somebody suddenly taken ill! Sawyer, late Nockemorf, sent for. What a business that young man has!' " (p. 625)

Pickwick himself, despite his former career as a businessman, remains oblivious to the need for advertisement, and to its reordering of social relationships. One of the most damaging pieces of evidence against him in the Trial of Bardell v. Pickwick for breach of promise is that in becoming one of Mrs. Bardell's lodgers, he answered an *advertisement.* While to the innocent, ingenuous Pickwick this document was no more than a bill posted in the Bardell window, soliciting "a single gentleman" to take on a room, in the convoluted reasoning of the court, he failed to perceive that he, an eligible bachelor, had been advertised for, and should follow through on the assumptions thereof (p. 560). Pickwick cannot believe that he should be susceptible to a suit like Mrs. Bardell's; beyond the maniacal comedy of the courtroom scene a world is beginning to be skewed by the interpositioning of advertising in the exchanges between people, property relations mediated by advertising and adjudicated by the Law.

The lower-class group in the novel is also conversant with advertising, although their counterparts of thirty years previous could not have been. Sam Weller, his father Mr. Weller, and Arthur Jingle, the itinerant actor and poseur, are all familiars of advertising and incorporate it into their speech. Jingle's strange, discontinuous disquisitions often include advertising phrases, in rather arbitrary juxtapositions; making his way through a dense crowd Jingle cries out in salute "Ah! Regular mangle—Baker's patent—not a crease in my coat, after all this squeezing—might have 'got up my linen' as I came along—ha! not a bad idea that—queer thing to have it mangled when it's upon one, though—trying process—very" (p. 287). Jingle's protean language has assimilated the cadences of early advertising perfectly (and his name is less than coincidental); he drops its public messages into his speech as he does fragments of language from the melodrama, the courtroom, and the colonial government. Sam Weller takes an acerbic stance toward advertising language; he generally prefers to speak in long periphrastic similes derived from modern proverbs, but he can counter with the sarcasm of the inflated advertising ploy, knowing he is being sardonic. In a commanding retort to an insinuation by Serjeant Buzfuz at Pickwick's trial, " 'Yes, I have a pair of eyes,' replied Sam, 'and that's just it. If they was a pair o' patent double million magnifyin' gas microscopes of hextra power, p'raps I might be able to see through a flight of stairs and a deal door; but bein' only eyes, you see, my wision's limited.' " Buzfuz is momentarily silenced and humiliated, the outlandishness of an advertising claim subtly linked back to his own question (p. 573).

Sam and his father Tony perform a stark "deconstruction" of both advertising language and narrative composition in their collaboration on Sam's valentine to his future wife Mary. Sam is initially reminded of Valentine's Day because he sees valentine cards advertised in the window of the stationer's, where a "written inscription in the window testified, there was a large assortment within, which the shopkeeper pledged himself to dispose of, to his countrymen generally, at the reduced rate of one and sixpence each" (p. 537). Valentine cards were printed in mass runs only when color lithography became a cheap process; Sam responds to the ad because the valentine will be a serious token for Mary, as proven by the efforts needed to search shop windows for it and purchase it. Sam still needs to supply the message, and his father intervenes in the creative process.

> "Lovely creetur," repeated Sam. "Tain't in poetry, is it?" interposed his father. "No, no," replied Sam. "Werry glad to hear it," said Mr. Weller. "Poetry's unnat'al; no man ever talked poetry 'cept a beadle on boxin' day, or Warren's blackin', or Rowland's oil, or some of them low fellows; never let yourself down to talk poetry, my boy. Begin again, Sammy." (p. 540)

Mr. Weller identifies poetry with the advertising jingles created by a younger Dickens, among other writers, and is adamant that Sam not lower his own literary production by adopting them as models. The suggestion here is that poetry is excess, superfluity—either it is incomprehensible and false ceremonial eloquence, or it is a devious, low language practice designed to obscure its real purpose. Sam sets down a complex compliment in prose, and Mr. Weller further elaborates on his suspicion of poetry—it makes false comparisons. "What's the good o' callin' a young 'ooman a Wenus or an angel, Sammy?" But despite being vigilant about eschewing poetry, for its low associations with advertising, Sam inadvertently creates a miniature advertisement.

> "So I take the privilege of the day, Mary, my dear—as the gentleman in difficulties did, vein he walked out on a Sunday,—to tell you that the first and only time I see you, your likeness was took on my heart in much quicker time and brighter colours then ever a likeness was took by the profeel macheen (Which p'raps you have heard on, Mary my dear) altho it *does* finish a portrait and put up the frame and glass on complete, with a hook at the end to hang it up by, and all in two minutes and a quarter." "I am afeerd that werges on the poetical, Sammy," said Mr. Weller, dubiously. (p. 542)

Mr. Weller's doubts are again well-founded, since Sam has rewritten a typical advertisement for the miraculous profile machine, a silhouette device that made instant "portraits" at popular profile parlors.[26] The encroachments advertising is making on the common stock of language, especially when pressed into the artifice of representation, makes its unbidden appearance almost unavoidable. Advertising has crossed over the line of poetry and begun its infestation of narrative as well; while Sam's valentine escaped the hyperboles of advertising metaphor—the Wenus stage—it has ultimately succumbed in comparing Mary to the silhouette likeness; advertising's eloquence wins out over Sam's at the end of the comparison.

Pickwick contains this careful, if unwitting, critique of the proliferation of advertising, yet the book itself was launched with an advertisement Dickens himself wrote, a delicious parody of vaunting advertising language, but an advertisement nonetheless. A sample paragraph reads:

> It was reserved to Gibbon to paint, in colors that will never fade, the Decline and Fall of the roman Empire—to Hume to chronicle the strife and turmoil of the two proud houses that divided England against herself—to Napier to pen, in burning words, the History of the War in the Peninsula—the deeds and actions of the gifted Pickwick yet remain for Boz and Seymour to hand down to posterity.[27]

The immediate enthusiastic response to the green-covered editions made it clear that the book was being read by all literate classes, and that others were finding ways to have it read *to* them. This reading market was held in suspension, as it were, from month to month, and as the magnitude of its popularity became evident, *Pickwick* became one of the first books to contain a regularly printed advertising insert, a set of pages sewn directly into the copy, constituting the first widely disseminated "family" advertising.[28]

The incident with the Guiness Stout illustration had shown that there was a mysterious alembic involved in this text; it had such a strong hold over its audience that whatever was contained within it could be separated out and treated as a discrete, advertised entity. Sam expresses this "magic" quality in the book itself; suspecting that he and his master are being mocked, he calls Mr. Pickwick's attention to the writing on the door of the cab they are about to enter.

> "Our names is not only down on the vay-bill, sir," replied Sam, "but they've painted 'vun on 'em up, on the door o' the coach." As Sam spoke, he pointed to that part of the coach door on which the proprietor's name usually appears; and there, sure enough, in gilt letters of a goodly size, was the magic name of PICKWICK!

"Dear me," exclaimed Mr. Pickwick, quite staggered by the coincidence; "what a very extraordinary thing!" (p. 582)

And there *was* magic in the name of Pickwick; instead of trusting to shop windows, trade cards or stray newspapers, a shop owner placing an ad in the paper edition of the book could know that the sine qua non of advertising, the act of reading, was being performed simultaneously, and with extreme enjoyment, by a quantifiable majority of the public. *Pickwick* is, of course, first and foremost a text; it also served as an advertising primer of extraordinary power. Dickens had taken Pickwick's name from the "Moses Pickwick" cab company; after the publication of *Pickwick*, Weller cabs were plying the streets. *Pickwick's* name *was* written in gold; versions of it were soon affixed to the most popular penny cigars and a writing pen, and Pickwick toby mugs, Sawyer cough drops, Weller boot polish, and candy tins printed with Pickwickian revels began to be sold.[29]

The ads printed inside the paper-covered copies had none of the energy of Dickens' own comments on or textual forays into advertising. Since there were neither advertising agencies nor advertising writers, except for the despised poetasters, most ads were written by the owners of shops and companies, and their early efforts are usually confined to two to three pages of microscopic print, detailing in every particular the items they had for sale. Evidence seems to indicate that Dickens tried to give counsel to these amateurs.[30] His later efforts on behalf of the fledgling advertising industry will be documented at another point in the chapter. The success of *Pickwick* was decisive, however; Dickens was never abandoned by advertisement, and his texts were inexorably linked to the "social reading" that was allowing advertising to expand.

PERFORMATIVE GESTURES

The Old Curiosity Shop[31] is perhaps the Dickens text that approaches advertising most directly. It engages with advertising on the thematic and organizational level, one that seems to have little to do with the manifest fairy-tale plot of innocence betrayed and redeemed. *Pickwick* had to remain set in the countryside to preserve the illusion that urban advertising had not happened; *The Old Curiosity Shop* develops explicit theories of advertising from within that formerly privileged pastoral realm. Continuing the discussion of social invisibility, and making the strongest connections between advertising and writing, the book both predicts and invents an advertising culture.

In a return to the settings of the *Sketches by Boz*, *The Old Curiosity Shop* is centered on a store. While Nell and her grandfather are cast out into the fast disappearing English countryside, and Quilp and the Brasses draw the action to dockside and Cheapside, the old curiosity shop itself is set as the nodal point of this novel's London. It is arrived upon as the first discernible landmark in the shifting panoply that is the city at night, because the novel begins in an unusual first-person narration of the nocturnal traversals of the London streets made by the solitary "old gentleman." The shop is the "character" who remains at the imaginary point in London. Although Dickens changed his mind about the book in midstream, abandoning the narrator and jettisoning the omnibus quality of the tale in order to concentrate on Little Nell's story, the opening is nonetheless germane to the later prominence given the shop. The old gentleman's experience of his night walks in London is one of obliquity, of shadows cast in streets and of the "glimpse of passing faces caught by the light of a shop window" (p. 23). Commerce has halted for the day and contact with other people takes place through their refraction in what would be, in daylight, the nonreflective and mesmeric store window displays.

This description fragments London into a night world of instability and reflection, so that when the narrative arrives through the circumambulations of its crippled narrator at the portrayal of the shop, it is the first building to have loomed out of the indistinct darkness. Cast in this narrative twilight, the shop is personified as "one of those receptacles for old and curious things which seem to crouch in odd corners of this town and to hide their musty treasures from the public eye with distrust. There were suits of mail standing like ghosts in the corners, fantastic carvings brought from monkish cloisters, wood and iron and ivory: tapestry and strange furniture that might have been designed in dreams" (p. 53). While other shops and stores are characterized here by their specular nature—the glimpses of sign, display, and glass that become separate phenomena at night—the old curiosity shop is delineated as a place, an oneiric realm in the heart of London.

The shop has no marker, no sign, no advertisement of itself. In that sense it can only be discovered at night, having been rendered invisible to the city because its lack of advertisement makes it literally without custom, a hidden place which does not announce itself. That a shop should not normalize itself by calling attention to its existence makes the old gentleman refer to it as "a kind of allegory" (p. 56), specifically one settling around Little Nell. Nell's grandfather superintends a store whose curios are chiefly the relics of the past, in an "atmosphere of dust and rust and worm that lives in wood." The curiosity shop is a shop still existing in a pre-advertising mode of exchange, before the museum and the antique store have come respectively into existence to regulate the transaction between relic, spectator and consumer. It is not only the odd merchandise of the store that sets Nell and her grandfather apart, but that they choose to live in it as if it were a home and no more.

The two must flee London and the shop, seemingly because the machinations of Quilp against them have become so ominous. They are expelled into an England whose folkways have been transformed; this section of the text begins Dickens' inspection of the performative and theatrical folk world as it gradually comes to be absorbed by and into the forms of advertisement. The "pure" world of entertainment now requires its own advertising apparatus, since it has become a business and is especially prey to the problem of invisibility. In addition, the reliance of all cultural productions, whether literary or otherwise, on accompanying advertisement is revealed to be total, with immense political repercussions as well.

Nell and her grandfather enter a middle ground which is neither city nor country—they are caught up in a series of traveling performances that blend the rural and the urban, from Punch and Judy shows to trained dog acts and acrobatics. In the *Old Curiosity Shop* life behind theatrical scenes is grimly, desperately competitive. The Punch and Judy show operators, Short and Codlin, who seize on the wandering pair in hopes of making a fortune from them, are also philosophically alert to all the problems besetting their livelihood. "Unless we get the start of the dogs and the conjurer, the villages won't be worth a penny" (p. 201), Codlin observes dourly. He is the self-appointed businessman, the advertising strategist, of their puppet business—and the Pickwickian pastoral is decisively over.

At the Jolly Sandboys, the tavern where the incongruous group spends a rainy night, the talk turns to an incisive strategy session on advertising methods and shared wisdom about its uses. The discussion Dickens constructs is the first instance of the system of advertising coming into cultural self-awareness—as he creates the scene, the motley band of performers thrash out the kinds of advice and nostrums advertising agency heads (as yet a nonexistent group) were later to write books about. Vuffin, of the freak show, is worried about the possible weakness of his giant. "Once a giant get shaky on his legs, and the public care no more about him than they do for a dead cabbage stalk, they're usually kept in carawans to wait upon the dwarfs." This expenditure is called for by an exquisite bit of advertising reasoning, explained by Vuffin to Short of the Punch and Judy show.

"It's better than letting them go upon the parish or about the streets," said Mr. Vuffin. "Once make a giant common and giants will never draw again. Look at wooden legs. If there was only one man with a wooden leg, what a property he'd be! Instead of which, if you was to advertise Shakespeare played entirely by wooden legs, it's my belief you wouldn't draw a sixpence. This shows the policy of keeping giants still in caravans, where they get food and lodging for nothing, all their lives, and in general very glad they are to stop there. There was one giant—a black 'un as left his caravan someyear ago and took to carrying coach bills about London, making himself as cheap as crossing-sweepers. He died, making no insinuations against anybody in particular, but he was ruining the trade; and he died." (pp. 204–205)

The elision Vuffin makes between the giant's previous career as a freak show performer and his ultimate trade as a walking advertiser is highly significant in this context. Vuffin explicates the link between the mysterious cachet of gigantism, which occasions the advertising ploy of sequestering giants, and the annexation of giants' sensationalism to an unrelated object—the coach firm whose name the giant exhibited. Whereas in a performance, even on the Punch and Judy, freak-show level, an interesting quality like dwarfism can be made essential to the spectacle, advertising was seizing on rare and/or striking qualities and juxtaposing them with unrelated commodities such as coaches for hire, creating a representation whose very "visibility" threatened the hidden, secretive mysteries necessary for an effective aesthetic performance. Mr. Vuffin *must* now use advertising knowledge to keep his traveling dwarfs and giants objects of eager interest in the countryside, but his bitter enemies, and closest aesthetic heirs, are the advertisers who would cavalierly exploit the intimacy and surprise of the shocking performance by attaching its *frisson* to coach bills. The troupers of the middle section of the *Old Curiosity Shop* are hyperaware of the careful framing now required around a representation, and of how rapacious advertising has been in appropriating that framing device. They view the public as so jaded it has to be induced and seduced, i.e., advertised to, to be entertained. They have forged a compendium of performative advertising devices around this reality—from locking up giants in a van to sending out false playbills. Their implication that even Shakespeare needs his canny impresario, that aesthetic representations must be made visible and thus competitive through advertising techniques, reflects back on Dickens' own texts, making their public way by being touted through advertisement. The danger for these itinerant showmen is that advertising is becoming predatory on their realm—giants, dwarfs, Punch-and-Judy are being cannibalized to create an aura around a product. The permeability of Dickens' texts to advertisement is hugely ironic here, for the force that ruins Vuffin's show, what makes his drama *less* "saleable," was contributing to the success of Dickens' representations: many proliferations of Pickwick on cigars, candies, and mugs only enhanced *Pickwick* as a book. Dickens confronts these tensions in the *Old Curiosity Shop* by revealing the close cousinage of representation and advertising, and predicting the triumph of the latter in setting up the conditions of aesthetic, as well as social, visibility.

The book also contains the portrait of an early advertising genius, in the person of Mrs. Jarley, the waxworks show owner who takes Nell and her grandfather into her care, after they have fled the suspicions of Short and Codlin. Mrs. Jarley rides through England in her caravan, and her circuit through the text epitomizes this early performative world of advertising. Using techniques that were not to be employed in the advertising industry until twenty years after Dickens included them in this text, Jarley proceeds to run her itinerant show with scientific skill: she creates textual narratives for her demonstrations, she realizes she must direct her ads at all classes, and she can adapt performative gestures to narrative requirements. In her case, the physical advertising element of performance and spectacle that concerned Vuffin and the other traveling players, itself a relation to Bob Sawyer's "physical" advertising scenarios in *Pickwick*, becomes a narrative, textual technique, a story about historical personages she can modify at will.

Mrs. Jarley has been so close for so long to the demands of advertising it has invaded her ordinary language and conquered it. Even her sincere offers and kind requests are clothed in the language of promotion she is so adept at. She convinces Nell to stay with her as a companion and helper by lauding the waxworks in her incantatory advertising style:

"It's not a common offer, bear in mind, . . . it's Jarley's waxworks. There is none of your open-air wagrancy at Jarley's remember, there is no tarpauling and sawdust at Jarley's recollect. Every expectation held out in the handbill is realized to the utmost, and the whole forms an effect of imposing brilliancy hitherto unrivalled in this kingdom. Remember that the price of admission is only six-pence, and that is an opportunity which may never occur again!" (p. 271)

Despite her flair for grandiloquence in declarative speech, Mrs. Jarley has hired a poet—Slum is his name—to produce verse in service of her wax tableaux, because she must reach out to captivate a literate public in the towns she visits. Her poet had also penned a range of verse, including the handbills sent around to the tavern audience only, and these poems "speak" in that lower-middle-class voice: "If I knowed a donkey what wouldn't go, to see Mrs. Jarley's waxworks show" (p. 270).

Jarley's understanding of the complex demands of advertising narrative ultimately puts her at odds with her poet in the final phasing out of the Warren's poet figure running through the novels from the *Sketches* on. Jarley had once been affianced to Slum, but she even breaks off this connection. Musing on the efficacy of his poetry, she ponders, "It comes so very expensive, and I don't really think it does much good." Slum's final expulsion comes on the heels of Mrs. Jarley's having talked down his price for an acrostic he had written for Warren's, but claimed was "convertible to Jarley." When she refuses his hand, too, Slum perorates on the powers of his vision of advertising:

"Ha, ha!" cried Mr. Slum, "you're giving way, you're coming down. Ask the perfumers, ask the blacking-makers, ask the hatters, ask the old lottery office keepers—ask any man among 'em what my poetry has done for him, and mark my words, he blesses the name of Slum. If he's an honest man, he raises his eyes to Heaven, and blesses the name of Slum—mark that! You are acquainted with Westminster Abbey, Mrs. Jarley? Then upon my soul and honour, ma'am, you'll find in the Poet's Corner a few smaller names than Slum." (p. 282)

Mrs. Jarley finds a complex, class-differentiated narrative technique to substitute for the primitive advertising "poems" she had once used. She seeks out the public audiences she knows she can entice on different grounds; Miss Monflathers' girls school, for example, is brought around to the waxwork show by an ingenious reworking of some of the costumes and their description:

Mrs. Jarley had been at great pains to conciliate, by altering the face and costume of Mr. Grimaldi as clown to represent Mr. Lindley Murray as he appeared when engaged in the composition of his English grammar, and turning a murderess of great renown into Mrs. Hannah More . . . Mr. Pitt in a nightcap and bedgown, represented the poet Cowper with perfect exactness; and Mary Queen of Scots in a dark wig and white shirt-collar was such a complete image of Lord Byron that the young ladies quite screamed when they saw it. Miss Monflathers, however, rebuked this enthusiasm, and took occasion to reprove Mrs. Jarley for not keeping her collection more select. (p. 288)

The waxwork figures cooperate fully in Jarley's market segmentation.

One of the greatest Jarley triumphs is her use of Nell as a living advertisement, an irony that reverberates through this text, since Nell and her grandfather had been "proprietors" of a shop that, in its assemblage of historical periods and past curiosities, resembles a version of the waxworks show, but had been incapable of discovering any "advertisement" for it. Mrs. Jarley sets up Nell in an attractive cart to drive through the towns sitting above a placard for the show. Nell's allure and innocence make her a "living waxwork," an advertisement for a wholesome and yet compelling show, and she is taught to give the ever-variable narration tour, describing the waxwork figures according to whose class interests are being "represented" back to them at the time of the tour. In her trek through a revisionary England, Nell has become an actual advertisement. The art of shop-window display was revolutionized by the introduction of mannequins, inspired directly by the waxworks shows in vogue at the time. Mrs. Jarley's effort to display a passive Nell as a representation of her spectacle, undertaken before such mannequins appeared, nonetheless serves to make a mannequin of a real girl, who is scorned when she visits a friend at Miss Monflathers' boarding school by being dubbed "the waxwork child."[32] Performance is allied with narrative here—Nell's appearance and speech connected to the stories about the historically mutable wax figures creates a *system* of advertisement, a cultural totalization.

Once the novel is seen to be imbued with this complex treatment of advertisement it can be rescued from critical scorn on the grounds of its sentimentality, or from interpretation as a latter-day fairy tale. The text energetically dismantles the "innocent" country world of show and folktale, indicating that this performative space is being rearranged by the dictates of advertisement; moreover, that the strict distinction between rural, folk culture and urban, commercial, mass entertainment has been destroyed. A mass, popular culture is in the making. Nell's caravansery through this world *is* strongly marked with irritating Victorian and Dickensian emblemata—her girlish purity yielding to a death we all laugh at since Oscar Wilde pointed out its humor to us. In the dialectic of advertisement and narrative, however, Nell is a disquieting figure, not a sentimental angel. Associated with the curios and relics of a preindustrial past, and simultaneously with the mutable, waxen mannequins of the new representational system of advertisement, she can be read as an extreme point of pressure in this text, at once a marker of the loss of the historical past and an exploited victim of the malleable "history" of the present. Her doom is not brought on by advertising per se, nor does the text vilify its extraordinary advertisers: on the contrary. Nell's pertinence to the subject of advertising and cultural transformation lies in being such a readily adaptable symbol and simulacrum, whether for her grandfather's ancien régime shop in the heart of a changing London, for itinerant carnival and gypsy acts, for the breezy efforts of Jarley's waxworks to turn all history into spectacle, or for the cathedral quiet of an obsolescent English village.

The vigorous Mrs. Jarley, termed an "inventive genius" in the text, is a miracle of advertising because, in describing her and then analyzing so precisely the levels of her representational world, Dickens has invented advertising methodologies and simultaneously performed their critique. In the *Old Curiosity Shop* the earlier, and simpler, textual dichotomy of social visibility and invisibility as mediated by advertising is made more nuanced: in his later work, advertising is taken as having blurred this distinction, producing representations that make it impossible to be sure *what* is being represented, and hence, made visible.

Martin Chuzzlewit[33] is a transitional text in this process, contrasting advertising entrepreneurs with entire systems of publicity. The systematic use of advertisement is still portrayed, in this work, through the "performances" of a series of individuals, although the second part of the book, with its American scenes, gives a foreshadowing of a society driven by advertisement with no particular conspiracy of villainous individuals responsible for this circumstance. The prior strand of investigation is represented by Pecksniff and by Montague Tigg (Tigg Montague), both of whom cover their inherent emptiness by lavish entertainment; they are private avatars of advertisement.

Pecksniff, a middle-class version of Mr. Squeers, summons students to his architectural school by means of fraudulent advertisements. Once ensnared, the students receive no useful training, and if they are so fortunate as to stumblingly design a building, Pecksniff takes immediate credit for their work. Pecksniff is such a benighted hypocrite that he and his daughters can compose the advertisements *en famille*, without a trace of embarrassment. His advertising rhetoric is derived from his hypocritical piety and intellectuality, although, again like Squeers of Dotheboys Hall, his only "product" is the economic welfare of his family. In *Nicholas Nickleby*[34] Squeers writes an hilariously inaccurate printed advertisement for his school. He also uses his son, Young Wackford, as a "living advertisement" (p. 528), touting the (needless to say) false benefits of his school. "Look at that fat—his tears are pure oil! That's the best advertisement on Dotheboys there's ever been!" (p. 604). Pecksniff is more sinister, if less sadistic, in his keener awareness of the power of advertisement to attract wealthy families to his school—of course his downfall is similarly predictable.

Montague Tigg takes advertisement into a more complex economic realm—his genius for self-representation, and his chameleonlike personal changes allow him to build a huge financial empire on the basis of advertisement alone. The Anglo-Bengalee Assurance Company he forms is only an advertising front, since it has but two shareholders and no capital backing its life insurance policies. Tigg is able to make himself and his company socially visible or invisible at will.

> Publicity! Why, Anglo-Bengalee Disinterested Loan and Life Assurance is painted on the very coal-scuttle. It is repeated at every turn until the eyes are dazzled with it and the head giddy. It is engraved upon the top of all the letter paper, and it makes a scrollwork round the seal. . . . It is repeated twenty times in every circular and public notice and advertisement wherein one David Crimple, Esquire, Secretary and Resident Director, takes the liberty of inviting your attention to the accompanying statement of the advantages offered by the Anglo-Bengalee Disinterested Loan and Life Assurance Company, and fully proves to you that any connexion on your part with that establishment results in a perpetual Christmas Box and constantly increasing bonus to yourself . . . (p. 500)

When Jonah Chuzzlewit balks at the insolent boldness of his huge company, so apparently solid with its marble and footmen, Tigg laughs, "He's bold as brass who gets gold in exchange!" Tigg resembles earlier Dickensian counterparts like Ralph Nickleby in his fraudulent scheming, but his flamboyant capitalizing is made possible, unlike Nickleby's, by his genius for manipulating advertisement, and thus registers a cultural and economic shift. The text demonstrates that the shifting narratives Tigg has built around his life, through his constant disguises, allow him to perceive the power of *social* narrative. The ads he makes for the company flesh out a complete, but completely insubstantial, international business dream.

Young Martin Chuzzlewit and Mark Tapley find a society dominated by this kind of advertisement when they get to America. The reification of society into diverse advertising publics had been accomplished there more fully than it yet had in England. Reading P. T. Barnum's autobiography in 1855, Dickens commented on what *Chuzzlewit* had already predicted:

> There is one comfort in all this. We English are not the only victims of that other Public. It is to be heard of, elsewhere. It got across the Atlantic, in the train of the Pilgrim Fathers, and has frequently been achieving wonders in America. Ten or eleven years ago, one Chuzzlewit was heard to say, that he had found it on that side of the water, doing the strangest things. The assertion made all sorts of Publics angry, and there was quite a cordial combination of Publics to resent it and disprove it. But there *is* a little book of memoirs to be heard of at the present time, which looks as if young Chuzzlewit had reason in him too. Does the "smart" showman, who makes such a mermaid, and makes such a Washington's nurse, and makes such a Dwarf, and makes such a singing Angel upon earth, and makes a fortune, and, above all, makes such a book—does he address the free and enlightened Public of the Great United States: the Public of State Schools, Liberal Tickets, and Universal Education? No, no. That other Public, down somewhere or other, whose bright particular star and stripe are not yet ascertained, which is so transparently cheated and so hardily outfaced.[35]

Martin and Mark are seduced and deluded by these publicities at every turn—thinking they are witnessing politics, they find themselves caught up in advertising; believing they are reading newspapers, they see only networks of publicity and promotion; they are lured nearly to their deaths on the blighted American frontier by clever advertisements from the Eden Land Company, whose glowing narrative depiction of a promised land sends them out on the first riverboat. The book charts their chastening exposure to the mass society of advertisement and publicity, and the two flee it for an England that, in retrospect, seems not to have lost itself quite so fully. Tigg Montague, Montague Tigg, will, after all, be unmasked.

DIRECT MAIL

If Dickens' early work celebrates the aesthetic and performative roots behind individual self-representations, even those constructed in the advertising mode, and his transitional texts grapple with the social stratifications and the petrifactions of language occasioned by advertising styles, his later novels articulate a total social world of advertisement, its ineluctable invasion of the body politic and of social discourse in general. I will touch on two major texts of Dickens' later, or floruit, period, using advertising as the wedge to gauge their elaborations on the inexorable cultural changes of modernity.

Both *Bleak House*[36] and *Our Mutual Friend*[37] exhibit striking textual organizing principles—the juridico-political whirlpool that is Chancery, the excremental dustheap that is synecdochic of the filthy bonds of lucre—and the best commentators on those texts, among them J. Hillis Miller, John Carlos Rowe, Jonathan Arac, Steven Marcus, Eve Sedgwick, and Edward Said, have explored the manifold implications of these forces, mapped out over the realignments of the second phase of British capitalism, its high finance period. It is important also to show the ongoing textual investment in advertising and its incipient institutionalization these works demonstrate, because both books illuminate features of advertising that take finance capitalism into the precincts of language and narrative. Consequently, in discussing them I will move along the outskirts of their most salient textual machinery, on the grounds that this stage of Dickens' writing career marks a crucial augmentation of his texts' dialectic with advertising—our mutual friend, as it were. The two works have lost confidence in the prospects for any individual retaliation against the engulfing and systematizing social powers of advertisement; *Bleak House* registers a world whose elite is a veritable construct of advertisement, and whose political horizons are regimented by advertising parameters, while *Our Mutual Friend* resurrects Dickens' earlier concern with social invisibility to starkly contrast the worlds of those who can afford to advertise with the utter invisibility and consequent neglect of those who cannot make themselves seen.

Bleak House offers us such an invisible one in Jo, the totally destitute boy whose job is to sweep at the crossings of the desolate Tom All-Alone's neighborhood, who is outside the circle of social functioning because he cannot read. The depth of his illiteracy is indicated, however, by his inability to penetrate the codes of shop windows and signs—he is unable to participate in any form of social reading. "To shuffle through the streets, unfamiliar with the shapes and in utter darkness to the meanings of those mysterious symbols, so abundant over the shops, and on the doors and the windows!" (p. 274). The figure Jo leads through the ghastly streets at night is his polar opposite, Lady Dedlock, who is portrayed as being so immersed in the system of social reading that she cannot see anything else; her life is predicated on fashion and artificial, advertising-induced desires. Her susceptibilities are sardonically described:

> "If you want to address our people, sir," says Blaze and Sparkle the jewelers—meaning by our people Lady Dedlock and the rest— "you must remember that you are not dealing with the general public; you must hit our people in their weakest place, and their weakest place is such a place." "To make this article go down, gentlemen," say Sheen and Gloss to the mercers, to their friends the manufacturers, "you must come to us, because we know where to have the fashionable people, and we can make it fashionable." (p. 89)

Jo is blind to the readings he is meant to see, while Lady Dedlock and her group are immersed in the images, the representations, of advertising at its most lustrously encapsulating.

Standing between these class poles is the mediated public voice of bourgeois society, now itself trasmogrified by an advertising discourse. The literal hectoring in the text comes from Mrs. Jellyby; her "philanthropic" campaign for the settlement at Borrioboola-Gha seems to be the first published mention of a direct mail advertising campaign. Mrs. Jellyby spends all her time writing, with her daughter as amanuensis at her side; Caddie is described as "one big ink blot." In a constant flood of advertising letters, she solicits either contributors to or potential settlers in the African colony. The text is indignant over the hypocrisy of the venture, partly because Mrs. Jellyby's family and by extension all of England is being sacrificed, but also because the solicitation letter is a thin altruistic scrim over an economic project. Mrs. Jellyby may not fully realize it, but she has been enlisted to sell a certain ideological reading of Africa in order to sanitize the larger cultural project of empire. The emanations of this direct mail approach—the notion that the public is now only to be reached through an advertising apparatus even in their capacity as citizens—marks the transition to a consumer society, and to a systematized advertising.

> "Africa at present occupies my whole time . . . I am happy to say that project is advancing. We hope by this time next year to have from a hundred and fifty to two hundred healthy families cultivating coffee and educating the natives of Borrioboola-Gha, on the left bank of the Niger." "If my memory does not deceive me, Mrs. Jellyby, you once mentioned that you had sent off five thousand circulars from one post-office at one time?" (p. 150)

The vast circulatory apparatus of advertising structures social discourse even as it destroys the Jellyby family, almost in passing.

Our Mutual Friend extends the direct-mail society tentacles to domestic political and social fronts. The Veneerings, a "new" family in town, are shown making their way in society and politics by manipulating the direct-mail technique. Sending letters to a host of people they would like to become known to, they invite them to meet other prominent people, described as already being Veneering's "very dear friends." Only the frail Mr. Twemlow somehow senses that he is not now, nor has he ever been, an old friend of Veneering's. The machinations are so effective that Veneering is able to stand for Parliament, and to win, in a triumph of self-advertisement.

It is interesting to contrast the bitingly critical presentation of the Veneerings and their contaminating superficiality—a veneer of self-publicity that is so powerful and virulent a social interface that the language of surface so apt for the Veneerings is papered over all their interactions—with the affectionate treatment given Veneering prototypes like Mrs. Leo Hunter in *Pickwick*. For the latter, it is still possible to harness the nascent possibilities for self-advertisement with the innocent bravura of the theatrical showman, and the requisite language of hyperbole employed to achieve this has a glorious, distorted connection to creative rhetoric. The Hunters and the Jingles, the Crummies and even the Squeers of the earlier texts are agents provocateurs of advertisement in solitary or even sordid splendor; the Veneering "principle" is a secret agent pervading all social discourse. Advertising itself is fast becoming a kind of decorporealized Veneering—or, within the discourses of politics and class, a veneering. The almost fearful intricacies of Dickens' plotting in these two massive novels inscribe patterns that are revelatory of the interconnections of class, money, power, and sexual hierarchy informing nineteenth-century British society. But sharing a place in these texts is also Dickens' creation of an interstitial network of advertising sites, or spaces; advertisement is extruded into all the surfaces of social relations, a veneering that, to use a homely metaphor, resembles the volatilized foam forced into wall openings to make a layer of insulation.

A tension that plays over the inscription of advertising as a system in these later texts derives, it would seem, from the privileged relation of all Dickens' work with advertisement itself, and nowhere more so than in the linguistic blend of voices that subtends the Dickens style. It is a short leap from "he do the police in different voices" to the monologizing individual narratives that advertisement was learning, from literature, to construct. The perfervid linguistic emanations that make his characters so "distinct," so "visible," also offered clues to advertisers in their attempts to foreground and frame, to make (commodities) visible. One way that Dickens' texts manifest this tension, or ambivalent reciprocity, with advertisement is in the inclusion of characters who possess the extraordinary linguistic distinctiveness that makes them blindingly visible within the text, who are in that regard virtual advertisements for themselves, but who are shown in the textual material itself to have fallen through the cracks of the advertising system. *Our Mutual Friend* offers a galaxy of characters embodied by Silas Wegg, Jenny Wren, and Mr. Venus who inhabit this textual interspace. They are at once preternaturally "visible" to readers, but within the texts exiled to fringe areas mapped by advertising styles, and their relations to their social others are demarcated by their position with regard to advertisement.

Existing in the margins of the advertising society are those who, like Mr. Venus, Silas Wegg, and Jenny Wren, are forced to engage in custom without the benefit of advertisement. Venus' shop is distinguished by its virtual invisibility from the street; a dark garret with an almost medieval stock of bones, fetuses, and crocodiles, it is a mysterious haven from the ever-present demands of consumption and exchange. Silas Wegg has tried to operate a sidewalk store with a few old junk items for sale; he is forced to use an imaginary narrative tie to the "great ones" in the adjacent house as a way of encouraging others to buy his wares. Jenny Wren uses the old singing and traveling fair methods to sell her dolls, but she needs to look at the most fashionable store windows to find out what merchandise she should copy in selling to her modern clientele. And *Our Mutual Friend* lavishly reports on the contents of shop windows, as do many other Dickens' texts before it. Bella Wilfer, eponymous heroine, is seen absorbed in the secular world winking out at her from the best London shops; the book is evidence of the hold on the imagination these shop-window representations had—reminding one of the confrontation with desire Walter Benjamin wanted to describe in his unfinished *Arcades* project, a record of the Parisian shopping arcade of the nineteenth century.[38] Bella Wilfer is ultimately given the contents of those store windows at the end of the novel; her consumptive frenzy is made acceptable by her moral renewal as a bourgeois housewife. On either side of her, though, stands the invisible contingent, and the powerful public manipulators, the Veneerings, who manage, always, to make it to center stage. Advertising is portrayed in its most attenuated sense in this novel, as so totalizing a system that it is palpable in the streets, in the shops, in the great houses, and over England, generally.

READING ADVERTISEMENTS

Despite the dark diagnoses of the later novels, which presciently anticipate the coruscating effects of advertising, Dickens' career continued to be furthered and consolidated by advertising. He helped write the advertisements for his books, he chose advertisements for inclusion in the monthly editions, and as editor of *Household Words* he both chose *and* wrote ads for the magazine.[39] Yet beyond this biographical data is a more intimate, textual liaison between the books themselves, as commodities, and the burgeoning textuality of advertisement. The way the novels both adumbrate and analyze advertising as a narrative, representational system has been traced out; an extension of this is the "corporealization" of the books as advertising objects of a unique kind.

At this juncture in my analysis, an historical excursus is necessary, if not sufficient. As has been mentioned, advertising agencies and advertising writers in their modern incarnation did not exist when Dickens began writing—the "poets" and the intrepid entrepreneurs created what ads there were. It was Dickens' close friend Edward Mitchell who founded the first advertising agency in 1847.[40] He had been a coffee-house owner famous for his exacting system of organizing informal advertising exchanges before it occurred to him that there was a bona fide profession about to be born, merely by setting up an agency to handle the placement of ads in newspapers and books.

Initially his agency did not create any ads; its function was to prepare an intricate itemization of newspapers and books and their regional circulation figures, in order to make discriminations about the effectiveness of ads in particular places. The calculations this required, in a prestatistical period, were staggering, but Mitchell put out his magnum opus, the *Advertising Register*, shortly after founding his office. Suddenly, the "publics" to whom ads had been addressed became quantifiable and real; their profiles could be discerned in the circulation data of their reading matter. The *Register* operated as both a library and a publication circuit, until it added the next inevitable step, by providing the writers of ads with quantifiable information based on its greater knowledge of who the public was.

The practice of using outside advertising writers did not catch on universally for some time, not until the advertisers had succeeded in establishing their special role through a vast flood of books and pamphlets on the "art of writing advertising."[41] Dickens was able to advise the early agencies on techniques for making their function respectable and professional; the efforts he had expended in helping rewrite the prolix and dull lists passing for advertisement within his books he now directed toward assisting the fledgling industry. Dickens may even have given money to help set up an agency, or have held shares in one; the fact remains that, alone of major writers of his period, he saw something in common with his work in the formulation of advertising as a system.[42] His books were essentially biweekly suspended solutions of all the reading classes and the leveling middle-class interests found in England, and consequently crystallized a mass market that advertisers were seeking as well. Dickens himself made direct overtures to that market when he began to promote his own books through his reading tours; here advertising feeds off its own textual corpus.

Dickens' obsession with the readings he gave during the last decade of his life, almost to the exclusion of his writing career, has been investigated as evidence of a psychopathology, or of his unbreakable tie to amateur theatricals.[43] The reading career can be placed within the dialectic with advertisement for my purposes as well, without requiring such strenuous hypotheses. When Dickens excerpted his work for the public readings, he was performing a dissection of his own texts, but this dissection had already been accomplished in the raiding of his books and characters for advertising purposes, in their corporealization. In order to set up the reading tours, a vast web of publicity and advertisement had to be created; an exhibit at the Berg Collections of the New York Public Library reveals the hand Dickens had in using his own material as the basis for ads designed to promote the reading of that material—i.e., using Pickwick to sell *Pickwick*.[44] The wide currency Dickens' texts had, both in England and America, had partially come about through the dissemination of characters and incidents in the form of penny pamphlets, cigarette cards, public readings, and products named for them. The step to closing the hermeneutic circle of publicity was not a large one—old ads for the books became new ads for the readings, while the readings were themselves ads for the books, sold outside the reading hall. Dickens, seen not as an author but as a collection of books, was apotheosized as an advertising vehicle when his own novels were pillaged to become ads for public performances.

The corporealization extended to the creation of products, as has been mentioned in connection with *Pickwick*, but this soon came to spread to the entire corpus. Sairey Gamp umbrellas, Dolly Vardon aprons, Mr. Turveydrop shoe polish, Captain Cuttle tobacco, Micawber pens, canes, gaiters, hats, chintz fabrics imprinted with Dickens scenes, and even corduroy trousers came out with some variety of Dickens' imprimatur.[45] This flood of goods continued unabated in the nineteenth century, and to some extent in the twentieth; Dickens remained as a marketing force of unalloyed appeal, because he *made* a market visible. In past years Cutty Sark and Smirnoff both capitalized on Dickens in their advertising; Cutty Sark used "A Christmas Carol" to associate its whiskey with the quintessential secular Christmas story, and Smirnoff punned on a text by captioning a glistening martini photo "Oliv'r Twist." Dickens remains thoroughly legible within the advertising realm, his texts almost encoded as advertising symbols.

There was something in the Dickens *ouevre* for everyone—just as the success of *Pickwick* as a book was one of the first markers of the existence of an eager mass public for fiction, the books could continue to be mined for their built-in public appeal, and their representations could create second-order fictions for products. Using Dickens allowed an advertiser to skip a difficult stage in the production of an advertisement—if ads were gradually becoming a system of social narrative, the books had already provided the narration and the first reading. What Dickens had discerned, and had made so central a feature of his books, was also a pedagogy for advertisers. The face on the cigarette card continues to stare out at us today, transcending advertisement but framed by it.

What I have been calling the corporealization of Dickens' texts, the tendency to extract from their vivid portraits of class languages and styles the "body" needed to assign that vividness, that visibility, to a commodity on the market, is a process with a concomitant, and opposite, movement. Dickens' work lent itself to the hypostatizations of language so critical to the formation of an advertising language, while at the same time the works produced an audience, already attuned to the act of reading, metonymically sliding from the Dickensian text to the advertising text that accompanied it. The countervailing movement finds advertisement decorporealizing itself, in that, over the course of Dickens' career and its coincidence with the forming of the advertising institution, advertising became less and less tied to the physical, gestural, speech-based procedures of its early incarnations. In some ways, the dialectic of advertisement with Dickens' work shows us a return to the floating space of "avertissement" characteristic of the early printed book, but made highly different by advertising ties to corporate manufacture and to commodity capitalism. One point of this investigation is to reveal advertisement as a complex event in language, a concatenation of cultural forms, particularly literary ones, that then are translated as the language face of social relations. Throughout the nineteenth century, advertising battens on the discursive spaces literature provides; it is equally true, as Dickens' literary career emblematizes, that modern literature, and particularly the novel, has its reading parameters defined by the linguistic horizon of advertising— a language that emanates from everywhere and nowhere. Dickens is the nineteenth-century Shakespeare in so fully circumscribing the competing voices of modernity, while giving them voice. Amongst these voices is advertisement, soon to be a virtual metadiscourse in its social inclusivity and its linguistic omnivorousness. The collection of Dickens' texts assembles these voices when they are yet an alternating current, when those texts can still produce and engender advertisement, rather than the other way around. Dickens' textual body is vast enough to be both the host and the guest at the sumptuary feast of advertisement.

2 • Spectacular Authorship: American Advertising Authors

"And above all, circulate documents, always circulate documents!"
P. T. Barnum to M. Kimball, 1843

ADVERTISING BEGINS ITS NINETEENTH-CEN-
tury genesis in England, but it achieves its full momentum as an industry and inseparable partner of capitalism in America. The Dickensian moment of advertisement in England demonstrated the mutual interpenetration of literature and advertising, with the conditions for Dickens' fiction shaping an enlarged space and engendering an audience for advertising alongside it. The critical concerns of this chapter center on writing a genealogy of American advertising by differentiating the historical modes of authorship avaiiable to advertisers themselves, when the meteoric success of American advertising stems from their adaptation of literary models. In this analysis, the first generation of American advertising is exemplified by the paradigmatic authorship of P. T. Barnum, who as a solitary advertising author rivals Dickens in the popularity and dissemination of his work. The second stage of this genealogy will be read through the writings of an advertising agency founder and copywriter, George Rowell, where the spectacular literary showmanship of Barnum gives way to a system of authorship that resembles a centralized factory of language production. In its germinal stage advertising had to feed off literature, borrowing the cachet of this already established mode of writing. The final section of the chapter explores the extraordinary parasitism of advertising on the body of literature, reversing the direction set out in the study of Dickens' work. The last generational phase of advertising develop-

ment, in which advertisement abandons literature as a source in order to form its own erotically charged narratives, will be discussed in the investigation of the iconic American girl in the work of Henry James, and of the erotic mythology of advertising as unfolded in *Ulysses*.

BARNUM AND SPECTACULAR DISCOURSE

This genealogy of American advertising is anchored in the problems of authorship and of social reading. If American advertising owes its momentum to its imitations of literary texts, then all the aspects of that borrowing must be scrutinized: the question of authorship, the treatment of reading, the displacement of literature or its absorption and transformation, and the implications of advertising as a discourse on the real social relations of American society. The career and work of P. T. Barnum provides a starting place, since he is universally acknowledged to be the father of American advertising and its most famous representative. Just as Dickens was read in the preceding chapter as the initiator *and* the merchandised product of a new textual confluence between literature and advertising, so Barnum needs to be apprehended simultaneously as an individual creator of advertisements, and an author of advertising in the broadest cultural sense. Barnum the historical figure will be read as "Barnum," a force-field of advertisement.

Phineas Taylor Barnum is acknowledged by nearly all the major historians of advertising as the indubitable creator of American advertising and, as Frank Presbrey puts it, "the first great advertising genius and the greatest publicity exploiter the world has ever known."[1] Forging into advertising from a humble background as the operator of a Connecticut general store, Barnum became a revered and somewhat awesome figure whose autobiography, *Struggles and Triumphs*, first published in 1855, sold more copies in the nineteenth century than any book except the Holy Bible. Richard Herskowitz places Barnum in advertising history by contending that:

> Barnum's contribution to modern advertising was his elaboration of methods of making misrepresentation tolerable to the consumer. The friendly, ethical way that Barnum permitted his "suckers" to see how they were being conned makes him a precursor of the dignified advertising of late capitalism. The obviousness of many of

his deceptions, however, with their glaring falsehoods in the service of profit, roots him in the patent medicine tradition. Barnum, therefore, can be seen as a transitional figure. To modern advertising, he is a beloved and embarrassing founder.[2]

Viewed through the lens of his sensationally popular autobiography, his manifold writing, and his advertising empire, however, Barnum must also be seen as a central author of his time. Barnum was creating a peculiar form of writing that demanded a very specific mode of reading, one which he was prepared to decode for the public, until it became proficient at it on its own. And this style of writing, this larger text comprised of all his multifarious ads, posters, newspapers, and books, became the predominant aesthetic mode, if the productions of American advertising are judged purely quantitatively. Traveling with his circus in his old age as an added attraction, Barnum was preceded by an ad (self-composed) that read "Wait and See the Old Hero about Whose Name Clusters So Much of Romantic Interest and Whose Brilliant Deeds are Themes of Poetry and Prose."[3] At that point, this encomium hardly qualified as hyperbole. Barnum stalking into his circus arena, trailing clouds of advertised glory, is humorously analogous to Hegel's image of Napoleon as the Zeitgeist on horseback, especially when the nineteenth century is defined, as Henry James terms it, as "the age of advertising."

To read Barnum as an author, not merely as a flamboyant figure who carved out an advertising and entertainment empire in the nineteenth century, requires a realignment of the concept of authorship probably best grounded in the terms of Michel Foucault's essay, "What is an Author?"[4] In this article Foucault outlines the problematic meanings of what he calls the "author-function," tracing the modern insistence on establishing the parameters of authorship and the boundaries of individual authors' texts to the transgressive nature of writing in the late eighteenth and early nineteenth centuries. He argues that the question of an "author" represents a privileged moment of individualization in the history of ideas and the proliferation of private property, contrasting this with earlier ages' lack of concern for authorial originality and indifference to exhaustively cataloging the products of an individual author. Foucault concludes that in the absence of any psychological or intentional definition of the author, "the name of the author remains at the contours of texts, separating one from the other, defining their form, and characterizing their mode of existence."[5] In other words, the author functions as a deliminator of certain discourses in society, allowing certain texts a status as property, offering authentication of certain modes of discourse, and providing a means of assigning values to individual texts—e.g., this is a work of philosophy because it is by Nietzsche, this is a profound poetic commentary because it is a letter of Keats. A critical point in the development of this notion of the "author-function," in Foucault's theorization of it, is the ability of an author to establish a discursive practice, a realm of discourse over and above any individual texts that the author has produced.

Foucault carefully distinguishes the formation of a discursive practice from, on the one hand, initiating a genre or type of work, and, on the other, launching a scientific area of discovery. The chief characteristic of a genuine author of a discursive practice is that all subsequent work in that discourse of necessity becomes a rereading of the initiating work of that author.

The distinctive contribution of these authors is that they produced not only their own work, but the possibility and rules of formation of other texts. . . . Marx and Freud, as "initiators of discursive practices," not only made possible a certain number of analogies that could be adopted by future texts, but, as importantly, they also made possible a certain number of differences. They cleared a space for the introduction of elements other than their own, which, nevertheless, remain within the field of discourse they initiated.[6]

The "author-functions" Foucault considered here and in his earlier works *(The Order of Things, Archeology of Knowledge)* are restricted to very hallowed figures we already know as major "authors," like Freud, Marx, Darwin, and Diogenes Laertes. My justification for somewhat playfully distorting the cultural pantheon in order to make a case for Barnum as an "author," in the enlarged sense of the initiator of a discursive practice, comes in the pertinence of Foucault's criteria for mapping out a discourse. The key questions he would have us ask of the more traditional discourses such as mathematics, science, politics, and psychoanalysis must be asked of advertising as well: "What are the modes of existence of this discourse? Where does it come from; how is it circulated, who controls it? What placements are determined for possible subjects? Who can fulfill these diverse functions of the subject?"[7] The discourses Foucault recognizes are all analytic in some way, while advertising, since it is manifestly devoid of intellectual content, cannot be assimilated to the major disciplinary categories he considers. In advertising, paradoxically, we are confronted with a non-transgressive and noncumulative yet utterly pervasive mode of writing that (1) gradually determines a path of circulation, through book, newspaper, poster, television, etc.; (2) possesses an institution of formalized controllers, the advertising agencies; and (3) defines a group of subjects, modern "consumers," who are articulated by their relationship to this discourse. Advertising answers all Foucault's criteria for a discursive practice, yet remains functionally authorless and undesignated.

Barnum's power as an author-function, beyond this being the literal author of innumerable books, newsletters, and documents, lies retrospectively in his having transmogrified a fragmented set of cultural practices and performances into a systematic, generative, and inexhaustible literary machine. To be able to penetrate modern advertising critically, beyond labeling it "ideological" (which it certainly is, but in the more fruitful Althusserian sense) and/or "oppressive," requires an assessment of the conditions of advertising as a discourse, conditions which are initiated by Barnum. Despite great breaks in its development, and historical discontinuities that radically alter it, advertising since its nineteenth-century inception remains within the boundaries set by Barnum's "authorship." Since Barnum the man did not consciously set out to systematize advertisement, nor to define it, the "Barnum" who constitutes this discourse is the collocation of ads, autobiography, spectacle, legend, and memory invoked to explain the "Barnumization" of American society.

The best source for a taxonomy of Barnumization is Barnum's autobiography, *Struggles and Triumphs*.[8] The textual nature of Barnum's "triumph" is underscored by all the levels of textual affiliation embedded in his early career. He mentions all these steps without particular reference to their relevance to his advertising success, although he includes them as stops along the way, a Pilgrim's Progress of the advertiser's consciousness. Reading his career in retrospect is almost like finding an encapsulated version of the histories of American advertising—the progressive changes that George Foster and Frank Presbrey, Henry Sampson and John Head all chronicle as its decisive stages exist in miniature in Barnum's own life, a palimpsest of advertising practices. I rehearse the events of Barnum's biography not for their intrinsic interest, but because they bear material witness to the traffic between and among books, newspapers, theatrical performance, and early sales techniques responsible for the emergence of a practice, advertising, that collocated these cultural modes. The unstable congeries of practices that begins to take the form of advertising is foreshadowed in the extraordinary oscillations and influences of Barnum's business careers—we can trace out advertising's affiliations along his often checkered path.

He worked first, as a young boy, at a country general store in Connecticut. General stores were America's commercial outlets at the time; merchandise was sold unlabeled in large bins, while the proprietors attracted customers not by advertising these goods, but by holding lotteries and contests in their stores. Barnum initiated several successful, although illegal, lotteries, nascent forms of the spectacles he later made his central activity. When he abandoned the store he became first a book auctioneer, and secondly a newspaper publisher.

As an auctioneer, Barnum had a chance to experience books as commodities that had to be sold like the goods in the general store, but with the advantage of having unique title "labels," both a connection to the larger world of books and an inside copy that gave these commodities a differentiation not available to bulk flour and tin pans. He then moved from discrete books to the fluid world of newsprint. Barnum's newspaper, *The Herald of Freedom*, was linked to political action against the conservative power structure of the state of Connecticut, and Barnum's editorial policies caused him to be jailed on several occasions. His exposure to newspaper work placed him again in a proto-advertising milieu, because the newspaper was the natural bedfellow of the advertisement, with Benjamin Franklin himself having founded the first newspaper advertisement agency. Barnum subsequently saw the newspaper as a pure instrument of promotion, because he made no invidious distinction between "news" and "ads." When his own paper failed, Barnum came to New York and wrote for a variety of city newspapers, eventually using his access to the newspaper columns to provide a stage set for acts he had decided to manage. "I wrote a notice of [Signor Vivalla's] wonderful qualities and performances, printed it in one of the Albany papers as news, sent copies to the theatrical managers in New York and other cities, and went with Vivalla to the metropolis. . . . By the potent aid of printer's ink the house was crammed" (p. 84). Barnum discovered the permeability of newsprint to advertisement early on: he launched all his triumphant exhibits through "news" articles planted in the press, and apotheosized this method in producing his own imitation newspaper, called P. T. Barnum's *Advance Courier,* distributed at his circuses.

When Barnum's second dry-goods store failed he became a drummer in the countryside. This position, described by Foster as a signal one in the history of advertising, involved going out to the same country stores and attempting to inculcate a kind of "brand awareness" into the small store owners.[9] Drummers often became a conduit for the presentation of a wide variety of novelty items and luxury goods, because these were easier to define as "special," and these men had a strong impact on rural life and its modes of production since their visits often imparted the only product-cum-cultural news a small town would be likely to receive. Drumming was a theatricalization of both sales and information. And building on the performative expertise drumming had given him, Barnum became an independent showman for traveling novelty acts, a circus manager, a writer of advertisements for the Bowery Amphitheatre, and the main seller of the Sears Edition of the Bible. These disparate activities were linked together by their dependence on print and on the avenues of newspaper or book circulation.

Barnum's career really rocketed when he amalgamated these professions and took over Scudder's Museum on Broadway. The first museum in America was Peale's Museum, containing the paintings of the Peale family artists, Charles Wilson Peale and his sons Rembrandt, Rubens, and Raphaell, along with assorted tusks and fetuses.[10] Barnum outbid the Peales in the race to purchase Scudders by complex maneuvers in print, an arena of mastery for Barnum, given his strategic relation to print and sales. He wrote a whole series of "articles" for New York newspapers ostensibly critiquing the new social institution of the museum by ridiculing them and their puny, eclectic contents and cautioning the public that buying stock in a museum, as per the Peale public offering, would be "more ridiculous than investing in Dickens' Giant United Metropolitan Hot Muffin and Crumpet Baking and Punctual Delivery Company" (p. 99). Killing the value of the Scudder stock through this polemical ploy, he was able to buy the museum himself, and promptly published a stream of articles chronicling the construction of the museum, its redecoration, the future importance of museums in American life, and the fabled exhibits soon to be encountered there. The arrival of the museum was a distinct and decisive watershed in the culture of modernity and in the ideological procedures of capitalism, as theorists from Walter Benjamin to Jean Baudrillard attest. The significance of Barnum's purchase of a prototypical museum as the arena of his ideological productions resides in the consequences for advertising—advertising became, in addition to other things, a site for cultural display, a museum arcade of cultural production.

Barnum's multiple, even overdetermined, exposures to a spectrum of aesthetic productions, from juggling acts, circus tours, and Biblical rhetoric to "serious" reviews, gave him a promiscuous vision of aesthetic boundaries:

> The show business has all phases and grades of dignity, from the exhibition of a monkey to the exposition of that highest art form in music or drama, which entrances empires and secures for the gifted artist a world-wide fame which princes might envy. Such art is merchantable, and so with the whole range of amusement, from highest to lowest. The old word "trade" is as manifest here as it is in the dealings at a street-corner stand." (p. 79)

His own advertisements set up an equally capacious continuum for future advertisers, from his photographs of pinheads to the "serious" prose and poetry he lavished on the marketing of Jenny Lind.

To merchandise aesthetic experience, or to create narrative scenarios that define themselves as art, Barnum resorted to writing, to a literature of advertisements calculated, as he put it, "to extort attention." "I thoroughly understood the art of advertising, not merely by means of printer's ink, which I have always used freely, and to which I confess myself so indebted for my success, but by turning every possible circumstance to aesthetic account" (p. 103). When Barnum established his museum, he crystallized a procedure of writing that opened the horizons of advertising as well. Barnum's Museum on Broadway became the site of America's tutelage in a new kind of reading, one that, as Barnum complained, could never be grasped by "the literal."

Neil Harris, Barnum's biographer, describes the requirements of Barnum's Museum reading as an operational aesthetic, "a form of art as problem-solving in relation to questions of authentication, illusions, and the working out of spectacle."[11] Reading the ads for the museum, as well as visiting the showplace itself, placed the reader (or visitor) within an ambiguous aesthetic space—the texts and exhibits posed both the problem of how "real" they could be ("see Joice Heth, George Washington's slave nurse"), and of how the illusion of their "reality" could be accomplished through sleight-of-hand ("view the actual mermaid for the first time"). The museum, like the ads for it, problematized the nature of appearance and announcement. An aesthetic spectacle was set forth that could not be "read" without decoding the advertisement that accompanied it, since this too was part of the spectacle. The ads promised an alluring "real" event, like an "authentic buffalo stampede," but then became a fiction when the stampede proved to be the setting loose of an ordinary calf. "Readers" who had learned from Barnum not to be literal were able to enjoy the anticlimactic exhibition as the unmasking of the spectacle provided by the ad, as deeply satisfying a hermeneutic procedure as seeing a "stampede" might be exciting. One complex example of the operational aesthetic at work on stage, and also an uncanny echo of James' *The Bostonians*, to be discussed in the next chapter, is taken from the autobiography:

> It devolved upon me to open a rival to Peale's mesmeric performance, and accordingly I engaged a bright little girl who was exceedingly susceptible to such mesmeric influences as I could induce. That is, she learned her lesson thoroughly, and when I had apparently put her to sleep with a few passes and stood behind her, she seemed to be duly "impressed" as I desired; raised her hands as I willed; fell from her chair to the floor; and if I put candy in my mouth, she was duly delighted. (p. 133)

At this point in the act, however, Barnum would turn to the audience of duly convinced mesmeric believers, those who had crowded the museum because of ads promising just such a spectacle, and would offer to cut off the fingers of the little girl, without her evincing any pain. He made a solemn and dramatic turn back to his mesmerized subject, only to find her fleeing behind the curtain, in a display of the operational aesthetic—first the fictional lure, followed by an open revelation of how the representation had been achieved through sheer trickery, which gave the audience both illusion and the delight of knowing disillusionment. Barnum's textual mystifications cut both these ways as well; his ads were purportedly devoted to airing a scientific fact or to glossing a deep social mystery ("see the albino violinist whose parents are coal-black savages"), while they equally blatantly called for a distancing from the spectacle, a reading at a remove to a complicit realization that the aesthetic spectacle was a successful call for money, a theatricalized moment of economic exchange.

Barnum was also able to funnel events at the Museum back into the representational circuit of the advertising he did for it. For example, he set up baby contests with entrance fees, because "while they paid in a financial point of view, my chief object in getting them up was to set the newspapers talking about me, thus giving another blast on the trumpet which I always tried to keep blowing for the Museum. . . . I gave prizes in the shape of medals, money and diplomas and the whole came back to me four-fold in the shape of advertising" (p. 246). The rigorous use of all money made by advertising to generate more advertising resulted in a kind of phenomenal acceleration of profit, a surplus value, unanticipated even by Barnum. His vocabulary is unable to account for these magical increases, so new in the economics of capitalism, so he falls back on metaphors of fertilization, manuring, harvesting, and planting.

> I was careful to keep up the excitement, for I knew that every dollar sown in advertising would return in tens, and perhaps hundreds, in a future harvest, and after obtaining all notoriety possible by advertising and by exhibiting the mermaid at the Museum, I sent the curiosity throughout the country, directing my agent to everywhere advertise it as "From Barnum's Great American Museum, New York." The effect was immediately felt; money flowed in rapidly and was readily expended in more advertising. (p. 111)

Barnum had unwontedly become the author of a labyrinthine discourse, a textual infinite regress, where every item of publicity worked to create new items, and every ad or performance was given value not for its content, but for its role in an exploding series. The perfect ad, according to Barnum, performed a species of rope trick: its words so lacked referentiality that they turned back upon themselves, content at the vanishing point in favor of a self-reflexive aesthetic loop far more akin to poetry. Barnum's oeuvre, if one can so generalize it, instantiates the poetics of advertisement, almost despite itself. The extraordinary economic fecundity of advertisement was, obviously, not a matter of Barnum's doing; he was as nonplussed as anyone else by the uncanny profitization of this new form. Advertising could dramatically swell

profits at this period because advertising was still a species of performance as well as a framing of performance. Neil Harris cites the praise
given to one of Barnum's circus press agents, Tody Hamilton, in an
encomium that speaks to this strange self-reflexive quality discernible
in the aesthetic of advertisement: "Tody Hamilton is a verbal conjuror,
whose language is so polysyllabic that an Oxford professor would have
found it difficult to understand. His rich words traveled to the threshold
of trembling tautology."[12] The tautological threshold gives a name to
the uncanny space produced by advertising, stealing its procedures
from literary self-commentary and from the theatricality of words on
display—as display. Marx's famous discussion of the magical quality
of money in *Capital* is apt with reference to the advertising realm
Barnum virtually stumbled upon by accident of history—advertising
had a magically self-engendering aesthetic economy, a "magical" discursive relation to economic production itself.

Advertisement imitated the aesthetic economy of established literary
modes to work its productive magic. In answer to Foucault's query of

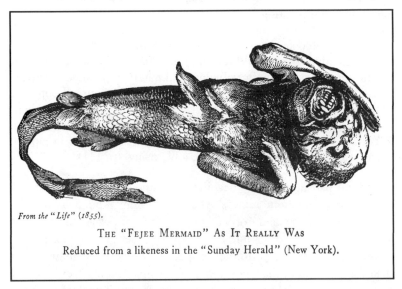

From the "Life" (1855).

THE "FEJEE MERMAID" AS IT REALLY WAS
Reduced from a likeness in the "Sunday Herald" (New York).

A demystifying, yet thoroughly remystifying, social reading.

"The Fejee Mermaid as it Really Was"
Wood engraving by an anonymous engraver, originally published in the *Sunday
Herald*, New York City, 1855.

Courtesy of The New-York Historical Society, New York City

how a discourse circulates, a study of Barnum's ads reveals that their proximity to so many established literary forms of circulation was the key to their prominence, and to Barnum's preeminence among American advertisers. The ads replicated simple type-face and then more complex features of newspapers, pamphlets, illustrations and books in their encroachment on methods of writing.

Early in his career, Barnum's ads managed their tautological sleight of hand through a somewhat primitive graphological, or typographic play—possible chiefly because having words "perform" in print was a novel translation of the medicine show and other homely performances. A specimen hieroglyphic:

After months of unwearied labor, and spending
NEARLY TEN THOUSAND DOLLARS
NEARLY TEN THOUSAND DOLLARS
NEARLY TEN THOUSAND DOLLARS
in capturing and transporting them from that
part of the Gulf of St. Lawrence nearest
Labrador, the Manager is enabled to
offer his visitors
TWO LIVING WHALES
TWO LIVING WHALES
TWO LIVING WHALES
TWO LIVING WHALES
TWO LIVING WHALES
TWO LIVING WHALES, etc.[13]

Barnum's ads, then, became a more specular kind of advertisement he related to magazine practices. Setting oil paintings of animals in all the window niches of the Museum, facing outward, Barnum transmuted art works into ads, merely on the basis of their contextual placement. This redoing of the building he described as "a complete transformation in the appearance of an edifice [which] is seldom witnessed." What he had done was to turn the building skin inside out, to invest the outside with a hint of the wonders of the inside. Barnum called this spatial elaboration a "pictorial magazine," in another reference to the sui generis kind of social reading his ads were proposing. The circulation of this "magazine" was furthered by handing out lithographs and advertising handbills depicting the building wearing its painterly garb, a miniaturization of the act of reading the whole structure (p. 120).

The imitation of writing reaches a pinnacle in the newspaper si-mulacrum Barnum published and had distributed at his circus shows. The *P. T. Barnum Advance Courier*, subtitled "Something for Every-one to Read," involved its readers in a veritable vortex of advertise-ment.[14] The "news articles," densely detailed and profuse with quotes and verifications, told of his forthcoming circus plans; the editorial columns were written by and about himself—one sample topic: "In many instances, not only has my own language been stolen, my ideas appropriated, but my advertisements have been copied entire." Barnum the "newspaper" editor crusades for a fair deal for Barnum the injured advertiser, whose private language property has been vio-lated. Inspirational pieces in the newsletter really serve as advertise-ments for the high moral character of Barnum's circus, as for example in the "Colored Brother's Plea," an as-told-to written by Barnum and purporting to record the recovery from alcoholism experienced by a black circus employee under the influence of Barnum's uplifting tee-totalism. The educational and "scientific" columns refer readers to the sideshow exhibitions of the circus; eminent scientific authorities con-tribute pieces on the automaton bell-ringers, the live Modoc Indians, the centaur child, and the equestrienne goat. Since no newspaper is complete without its ads, the "Advance Courier" also devotes columns to more typical advertisements, where the moral hectoring of the teetotaler and the patient wisdom of the professor can give way to a blunt "View the Relics of a Living Cannibal Family." The false newspaper totalizes advertisement by making all the discourses it commands—religious, scientific, political, etc.—fall under its rubric, becoming meta-advertisements in disguise. The effect on readers is analogous to what Dickens achieved with the paperbound copies of his novels, where the advertisement copy seemed to proceed naturally and inevitably out of the text. Barnum's authorship, however, presses all writing surfaces into the service of advertisement, creating a honey-comb of hierarchically linked and embedded advertisements.

The paramount example of Barnum's authorship at its most "liter-ary" is his own autobiography, *Struggles and Triumphs*. Barnum wrote a variety of other textual works, among them several under the pseu-donym Pedro Velasquez: *Dollars and Sense, or How to Get On; The Whole Secret in a Nutshell;* and *Humbugs of the World*. The autobiography became America's most widely read nonsacred book, partly due to a promotional system more ferocious than that for any typical book campaign. Barnum summoned all his past repertoire of advertising techniques in order to sell a book that was in itself a mimetic spectacle of advertising. The various editions it went through were accompanied by textual changes all designed to further promote the work. Carl Bode describes some of these promotional stages:

> Barnum aided in advertising the 1855 version of the book and the publisher did his part—with handsome results but not handsome enough. To put out the 1869 version Barnum chose a new publisher with experience in the newly popular subscription method of merchandising books, as opposed to the older method of using bookstores. Hartford happened to be a center of subscription selling and the smooth-tongued agents of Burr & Company journeyed through towns and villages to sign up buyers for the book. Armed with an ornate brochure that Barnum had commissioned, they peddled cop-

The aestheticized panorama of Barnum's museum.

Wonders of Barnum's Museum, trade card, circa 1860, drawn by Edward S. Hall, Waters & Son, engravers on wood, New York City. Thomas McIlroy, printer.

Courtesy of The New-York Historical Society, New York City

ies at a great rate. After they had marketed all the copies they could, Barnum purchased the plates, and from then on promoted the book beyond anything previously attempted by American publishers. Gradually he both lowered the price and widened the means of distribution. The 1869 version cost at least $3.50 a copy; he kept whittling away until the 1889 version could be had for as little as fifty cents. Although he reduced type size as well as cut down the contents, buyers rarely complained. . . . Barnum's channels of distribution, above all his circus, must have been the envy of many another author. He inaugurated the circus only a year after the 1869 version of the book came out and increasingly exploited it as a place to sell *Struggles and Triumphs*. Customers at the circus simply could not avoid the book. It was hawked inside and outside the tent; copies lay piled at the entrances. . . . To those who had not seen the circus he offered a free ticket with each book. . . . The consequence was sales of an astronomical order.[15]

The autobiography was unprecedented in being a book about advertisement sold through advertisement, for the purpose of advertising Barnum's career, tautologizing the tautological threshold of resistance. Barnum had "Barnumized" the book, realigning traditional techniques of authorship and book circulation to carve out an independent advertising space. Even his most spectacular entertainments, the circuses, were spectacles meant to teach his audience how to read his book, displays attendant to an act of social reading.

Barnum's autobiography normalized a discourse of spectacle for those who read it, providing them with a lexicon of advertising as an indigenous American episteme. Barnum's jokes, his self-deprecations, his career decisions and his triumphant successes all enlarged the meaning of "advertising," a term that did not have a legitimate currency or such locatable meanings until the various versions of the book "taught" them anecdotally and encoded them in its circulation. In fact, a friend of Barnum worried that the book was too blatantly a manual of advertisement and the cold-blooded manipulation of it, trying to redeem Barnum as another type of author altogether, who deserved a less literal reading: "The soberer, matter-of-fact public did not see the Pickwickian sense of humor and the Orientalism of statement that pervaded it. The cold type could not carry with it the twinkling of the author's eye."[16] The book promulgated a theory of advertising as it monumentalized the life of America's most celebrated citizen, a creation of the technologies of reproduction, a man whose final good-bye to his public was recorded on the first gramaphone records made by Thomas Edison. The theory remains implicit in the text, overtly appearing only in Barnum's frequent asides about the "miracle" he has wrought. When he takes the young boy he had promoted as General Tom Thumb back to his country town to visit his parents, one of the townsfolk tells Barnum, "We never thought Charlie much of a phenomenon when he lived among us, but now that he has become "Barnumized" he is a rare curiosity!" (p. 159). The spotlight of Barnumization, "gilding Broadway with unaccus- . tomed glare," as the poem "Barnumopsis" would have it, converts the ordinary into the spectacular through its magic arresting light, a nimbus of words.

As an author, not as a historical personage, Barnum "wrote" spectacles. Viewed in advertising terms, he was the author of spectacular ads about spectacles, another version of the tautological threshold. Barnum's notions of the immense circularity of advertisement are of course nonepistemological. Rather primly, he notes in the autobiography the absence of spectacle he had discerned at the site of the former Scudder's Museum, and links this to the absence of words: "Only 'American Museum' to indicate the character of the concern; there was no bustle or activity about the place, no posters to announce what was to be seen; the whole exterior was as dead as the stuffed skins and skeletons within" (p. 316). Understatedly, he assures us, "My experiences had taught me the advantages of advertising. I was prodigal in my outlays to arrest or arouse public attention." Words are decor for Barnum; text is an impasto to apply with determined excess.

Barnum remains resolutely on the operational side of his theory of advertising, insisting that advertisements are things one uses, not a system in their own right. His own book has to be decoded for a sense of the epistemology which lies behind such an embrace of the specular and the spectacular. In the closest he can come to reverie, hearkening back to what the Museum meant to him (now that it has burnt down for the final time), Barnum uses the theatrical and literary vocabulary so essential to his authorship of the spectacular framework of advertisement, and a clue for us to the power of advertising's mimesis of print modes. "My mind's eye recalls the less solid, more showy edifice which once occupied the site [his Museum, now a warehouse] and was covered with pictures of all manner of beasts, birds and creeping things, and in which were treasures to be read that brought treasures and notoriety and pleasant hours to me" (p. 113). The building is conceived of as a theatrical event, housing spectacles (plays, exhibits, shows, waxworks, a band) that point to and are pointed at by a literature of the spectacular, i.e., advertising. The insubstantial surfaces he created to be read were more than the fronts of buildings he owned, or the physical presences of the artists, like Jenny Lind, he engaged, or the complex presentation of his circus shows. Barnum, as the author of a discursive practice, had discovered a blank scrim within modern culture—an empty cultural space—poised in front of what his advertising had taught him was now a mass *public*. "I work for the millions, and they give me millions." This blank space concretized public, mass discourse, and was the space for Barnumization, a kind of spectacular halo that Barnum's ad network was able to call into being.

The discourse was so successful that even when it became annexed to industrial corporate capitalism in the late nineteenth century, Barnum would be recognized as the progenitor of it. He looms largest in American advertising partly because circumstances permitted his exploitation of the pure, self-reflexive poetics of advertising before industrial advertising had realized it in such monumental form. Under his hegemony, advertising came to be a form of social literature distributed to fashion an aesthetic space around products, which in Barnum's case were all theatrical and "aesthetic" spectacles, but for later advertisers were such nonspectacular goods as shoes, inks, machines, and plumbing tools. Barnum is a modernist of advertising, as well as the transitional figure Herskowitz labels him, because seen as an "author-function" his roots in entertainment and spectacle immediately provided for a seamless loop from ad to entertainment and back to ad, a niche Disney was to occupy in the twentieth century. The cultural images Barnum sold in his museums and circuses coincide with the imagery engendered by his advertising style. As an author, and especially as the author of a wildly best-selling book that taught the public to recognize advertisement where it had previously seen spectacle or "literature," he was able to carve an aesthetic space around commodity images that could truthfully be known as the zone of "Barnumization." *Fraser's Magazine* commented at his death, "Barnumism will drive all true artists from the profession." And the *Christian Examiner* mournfully added, "He seemed to have regarded his conscience as a kind of magic lantern, and his lies as analogous to optical illusions."[17]

The material conditions that allowed Barnum to launch a spectacular reading of the social world, at such great personal profit, are complex, but the reciprocal role of advertisement in the political and economic changes of the nineteenth century is central. Guy Debord, in his *Society of the Spectacle*, sets out, in possibly too Manichean a manner, the way in which political economy comes to align with spectacular consumption:

> Whereas in the primitive phase of capitalist accumulation, "political economy" sees in the *proletarian* only the worker who must receive the minimum indispensable for the conservation of his labor power, without ever seeing him in his leisure and humanity, these ideas of the ruling class are reversed as soon as the production of commodities reaches a level of abundance which requires a surplus of collaboration from the worker. This worker, suddenly redeemed from the total contempt which is clearly shown him by all the varieties of organization and supervision of production, finds himself, every day, outside of production and in the guise of the consumer, seemingly treated as an adult, with zealous politeness. At this point the *humanism of commodity* takes charge of the worker's "leisure and humanity," simply because now political economy can and must dominate these spheres *as political economy*.[18]

Barnum's magic lantern flickers in the service of this enlarged field of political economy, aggregating and training a mass public for entertainment, while producing the style of advertisement that will broaden into a literature of consumption.

Despite operating for and by himself, Barnum's ad empire was teaching an entire population how to consume advertisement. In an article he included in his highly sophisticated circus newspaper simulacrum, Barnum writes, under the heading "Popular Amusements a Necessity," that:

> Men ought not to live through work alone. They are but children of a larger growth, with the child's inborn and healthy playfulness and craving for amusement, directed by the sobering years into calmer channels of recreation. I am a faithful disciple of that enlightened school of political economy.

As penned by Barnum, in his entrepreneurial and unformalized way, advertising prepared the mass public for its later push into consumerism, and outlined the spectacular political economy newly ripe for formation. Even during Barnum's authorial reign, the urgency of establishing systematic advertising circulation grew up alongside his home-made efforts, so that a self-aware advertising institution came into economic prominence, although not into public visibility, while Barnum was still putting on his magic lantern show of words.

THE WRITING FACTORY

An index of the increasing sophistication and capitalization of advertising, and an exposition of its continuing displacement of and dependence on literature, is George Rowell's 1870 *Men Who Advertise: An Account of Successful Advertisers Together with Hints on their Methods.*[19] The book, though written by Rowell, is listed under the authorship of his company, George Rowell & Co., and it is this collective entity that takes credit for the pieces appearing in the book, modeled on a gazette. The convolutions of authorship and the textual subtleties of the book are evidence that the flagrant exhibition of "authorship" proclaimed by Barnum was being rapidly corporatized, just as the earliest advertising agencies in America were coming into existence. (The first agency was founded by J. Walter Thompson, a Civil War veteran, in 1865.) The "author-function" is taken over by an anonymous collectivity, only revealed to those in a position to procure its services, just as even now J. Walter Thompson Inc. does not "sign" its ads in public, but claims authorship in the privacy of its clients' boardrooms. Interlarding the short biographies of the men who have succeeded—in each case because they were able to use advertising as a pivotal professional force—are testimonials to the Rowell company as a model advertising agency, reprinted from various newspapers which are then included in the last section of the book, itself a listing of the prominent newspaper advertising outlets to serve as a guide to manufacturers. Thus one set of covers binds a purportedly serious biographical work, an argument for advertising, an advertisement for the Rowell company, and a useful advertisement for the newspapers who act as the liaison between advertisers and manufacturers. The agency produces a text which is the simulacrum of a real book (the popular success-story collection), is distributed like a real book, and is authored like a real book, but whose purpose is to become a textual advertisement. Rowell's text is a palimpsest of the textual modalities advertising conjoined in modeling itself on the paradigm of the book, and can be read against Barnum's to explicate the second genealogical stage of advertising as a literature in nineteenth-century America.

The pervasive theme of *Men Who Advertise* is that advertising is a new kind of writing, with its own corps of writers who have mastered the arcane secrets of literature and have gone beyond them, constructing a rigorous monastery of words lodged in the abyss between literature and technology. Rowell's images of tireless advertising writers who toil around the clock, even before Gramsci's Fordism, turning out words as an industrial product, spinning the invisible webs that form a nerve center for capitalist enterprise, is a dystopian vision almost the reverse of William Morris's *News from Nowhere* (1891), where writing does not and cannot contribute to economic and cultural centralization. While Rowell's book never directly speaks of the supplanting of literature, all the metaphorical descriptions of the advertising agents are taken from literary endeavor and book publication. The text itself has the Borgesian quality of a vertiginous advertising library, where the possibilities for advertisement are so vast that even the book itself cannot escape being encompassed by them.

All the articles in the collection refer to advertisement, and set between the life sketches are Rowell's thoughts on how to impart the knowledge of advertising, a problem he sees as a textual one. His preface begins by invoking literary books, and arguing for advertisement's need to become more like one: "An advertisement is in its nature transitory and perishing. It is not preserved in archives and libraries except by accident, and when so connected to news and literature that to dissever it is impossible." Writing is the matrix from which advertising needs to be "dissevered" in order to appropriate for it an independent plane of knowledge, especially the realm of literature, which has established its right to be preserved in archives and libraries. Rowell & Co. chafe at the supplementarity of advertising, at its deferential and ephemeral position vis-à-vis literature.

Consequently, *Men Who Advertise* stakes out its domain on the familiar turf of literature, to normalize advertising as an activity, while illustrating the chief difference between advertisement and literature: advertising narratively produces *money*. "Liberal trade is good scholarship popularized, and commerce is literature on a signboard," Rowell begins. The new world of commerce that advertising articulates takes place, as Rowell sets it out, not in the relations of manufacturer to seller to buyer, nor in a circuit of financial exchange, but as the instantiation of a new form of social *reading*.

> The signboard, literally considered, is essential, and a matter of course, but there is still another, fully as efficacious, and almost as generally adopted—the columns of the newspaper. This is the signboard of which we would speak, recommend, and endeavor to persuade our readers to avail themselves of. . . . A notice of any kind, to be read, must be readable; to be readable, it must have been properly compiled, and to be properly compiled requires no little skill and labor. (p. 23).

Writing the advertisement becomes the province of a new model of expert writer, and Rowell subtly makes clear that the days of handmade or simple bills and posters are over. "We have also endeavored to set forth in our pages the superiority of advertising in newspapers over that of other kinds. The handbills are thrown away and the posters not read, and it is safe to say that an advertisement costing five dollars will reach twice as many people and be read by twice as many as the same money put in a handbill" (p. 24). Only an advertising institution can offer proximity to the vast network of newspapers.

Rowell displays the expertise of the new cadre of professional advertising writers, of which he is one, by performing a critical reading of a variety of advertisements. Advertising is a style with its forbears in poetry, literature, and newspaper reporting, and Rowell notes the overlapping of these styles in the ads he exhumes. Where earlier advertisers have failed is in either foregoing literary stylistics altogether, or inadvertently creating strange textual hybrids, inept admixtures of advertising's textual models. Rowell gives an example of an ad that, while crude in its handling of the problems, displays in bold relief the archaeological traces of the other writing styles advertising needs to master. He ironically asks his readers to consider this textual conundrum, a generic miscellany:

> After vain endeavors on our part we must leave it to our readers to class this either as an "obituary," a "token of affection," or a "puff extraordinary":

> "Died on the 11th ultimo, at his shop in Fleet Street, Mr. Edward Jones, much respected by all who knew and dealt with him. As a man, he was amiable, as a hatter he was upright and moderate. His virtues were beyond all price, and his beaver hats were only £1 4s. each. He has left a widow to deplore his loss, and a large stock to be sold cheap for the benefit of his family. He was snatched to the other world in the prime of his life, and just as he had concluded an

extensive purchase of felt, which he got so cheap that the widow can supply hats at a more moderate charge than any other house in London. His disconsolate family will carry on the business with punctuality." (p. 55)

Rowell also alludes to Dickens in his historical survey of advertising methodology. He quotes a successful barber, one Packwood, who once answered a query about his singularly powerful advertisements with the explanation, "La, sir, we keeps a poet." In an echo of *Sketches* and *Pickwick* Rowell emphasizes that advertisement *is* related to the poetic style, but he ultimately sides with Dickens' Mrs. Jarley, who had decided to dispense with her poet and write her own advertising. The poetic journeyman may occasionally work wonders, but only the professional can mimic literature in a truly effective way. Rowell is cheered by finding that many ads "now have a truly rhythmical and rhetorical ring, such as people like, and are most influenced by. It is an unmistakeable fact that novelty in a manuscript attracts attention, and this is one secret of the success of so many of our advertisers." He advocates a style of advertisement he calls "literary," but one that is careful to use literary methods only if they are supplemented by the newer, and more recognizable, advertising voice, a heightened framing of literary aesthetics, literature within advertisement's quotation marks.

An ad for the medicinal tonic Plantation Bitters is held up as a model of the new kind of writing, although Rowell is somewhat disingenuous in his analysis of it, since it later appears he himself wrote that pithy and effective document.

They made her grave too cold and damp ·
For a soul so honest and true.

(Picture of tombstone surrounded by mourners)

If they had been wise the dire necessity of opening the grave for one so lovely might have been averted, since 'Plantation Bitters' if timely used, are sure to rescue the young and lovely, the middle-aged and ailing from confirmed sickness. (p. 49)

Rowell notes the rhetorical effectiveness of the opening couplet, a snatch of poetic lyricism that sketches out in elusive poignancy a protonarrative of early death for a lovely and virtuous damsel. We are not required to agree that those lines are poetry to nonetheless see that advertisers were struggling for a niche in the poetic economy. "The first two lines insure the reading of the whole article, and the following paragraph is more certainly remembered from its connection with what precedes," Rowell assures us—advertising is here still an architecture composed of bona fide "reading" matter (i.e., literature) grafted to what follows, the advertising pitch. The poetic couplet is a space which installs a reader within the advertisement. Rowell encourages the popular equation of advertising with text, in particular with poetry, and intends advertising style to exploit its identification with text and rhetoric. Previous advertisers, since they were usually ordinary shop-keepers or manufacturers acting in their own interest, had produced "curiosities, and evidence of the eccentricities the human mind is subject to"; the advertising professional would strategically employ a cross-fertilization of text, news, and advertisement to establish a sci-entifically grounded literature of effects. "The idea we would convey is simply that more attention should be paid by the advertiser to the preliminary steps, that success may more surely crown his efforts." Advertising is a poetics of regulated attention.

Rowell's actual biographical sketches of "the men who advertised" offer embedded portraits, where each life is comprised of the various early stages or aspects of advertising, or can be seen to point beyond itself at the gradually emerging industry. In every instance, "advertis-ing was the foundation stone" of the success of the men who *did*. "The whole matter resolves itself to this: Decide to introduce some one thing to the American people, and then 'push things,' " Rowell says rather baldly. Nonetheless, most of these careers are connected to either the print media advertising was aping, or to the vestigial remnants of theater and medicine show, not to mere "pushing." The longest and most detailed of his biographical sketches (which include, not surprisingly, the careers of newspaper publishers, book salesmen, medicine salesmen, and authors) is that for P. T. Barnum, who is apostrophized as "the author of his own success," and as the creator of "a new way of reading the world through advertisements." All the portraits of these advertising mavens are written in such a way as to normalize and legitimate what seemed to some to be a dubious profes-sion and a specious branch of knowledge. Thus, a majority have "quiet demeanors," intellectual gravity, wide learning, and/or "serene, manly brows" that ratify their innocence.

Mr. Bonner, under the nom-de-plume of Dr. Chalmers, has created a legendary literary paper, built on his pseudonymous identity, and offering "queer and unusual advertising," like blank sheets inserted in the newsletter, type-face displays tucked into a corner, and ads masquerading as parts of the articles they are inserted in. Ads exfoliate out into information and seep into margins and empty corners. Here advertising directly mimes print and particularly newsprint, highlighting the way they have blurred into one another. Dr. Jayne was a patent medicine seller who took to national pamphleting and made a fortune. "He was a wonderful man; his faith in the efficacy of newspaper advertisement was never shaken. Peace to his ashes," Rowell eulogizes, underscoring this first union of the individual medicine seller with a national professional network in his wryly sympathetic tribute. Other key mavens were similarly bound up in the book/advertising nexus: Packard created *Packard's Monthly*, one of the first self-advertised magazines; Holloway, a druggist, went to London and saw there that "the system of advertising has been carried to a far greater extent than here," thereupon exhibiting at the Crystal Palace exposition and writing a best-selling monograph about that for United States consumption—advertising his "ad." G. W. Childs, a newspaper man, created a fictional and preposterous page that claimed to be the record of "Dr. Kane's Arctic Explorations," which he then advertised by reviewing Dr. Kane's travails in his newspaper copy. Rowell celebrates the boldness of these individual self-reflexive advertising enterprises, tempered by the warning insinuation that the salad days of private advertising are no more; the illustrious past has been streamlined into modern approaches like those taken by Rowell & Co. We shall not see the like of the "men who advertise" again.

The advertising scene no longer accommodates the singular practitioner nor the haphazard, sportive advertising sensation. The reader is treated to a fanciful, monitory description of the interior of Rowell & Co., adjacent to the *New York Times* offices, employing two hundred writers (a seriously inflated figure—perhaps twenty actually worked there), with a vast library, an instant link to the nation's newspaper network and its own presses operating day and night. "It is the greatest workshop of brains and type in the world" (p. 270). Rowell and his company were in the first generation of advertising agencies in America, which began forming after 1865 and the decisive economic victory of the capitalist North. While the agency concept still needed to be argued for, and Rowell's text as a whole has a hortatory air, nonetheless the notion that advertising is a sui generis mode of writing, and one that distinguishes itself from other forms in a self-conscious way, is salient in this specimen text of the period of advertising's consolidation.

An illustration of the Rowell offices accompanies the text, and it can be read to represent an eerie writing factory. Laid out in overlapping circles, with legions of (imaginary) copywriters bent over their tasks, runners whisk the fresh copy down spokelike corridors to the central hub of information distribution, the eye of the storm. The panoptical organization of the room itself underscores the corporatization of advertising as a writing force within the newly centralizing corporate economy.

The concentration of money and power in the hands of the neophyte advertising agencies occurred as a response to the difficulty of making economic and communicative connections in a society newly opened up to industrial enterprise. A knowledge vacuum existed that the advertisements themselves were forced to fill. Rowell analyzes the need for a centralization of national information:

> Advertising is founded upon the great, fundamental truth that he who desires to sell the most must have the widest acquaintance and be the best known. When society is aggregated in a Robinson Crusoe or in the cabin of the Mayflower it is practicable for any man to know everybody, but when civilization advances into complexity it can no longer be done. In our own country this is especially true. There is no common centre. (p. 119)

A network of texts, of advertisements, "floats" throughout the country and accomplishes the supreme task of creating a center where one has never existed. Ads provided a way of charting this unfathomable, centerless world, and the newspaper was their particular territorial domain. Rowell is confident enough of advertising's prowess to give us an apocryphal anecdote about an Eastern sage versed in "all the wisdom of the Persian orient," and presumably a virginal reader, who, when given a newspaper to read, chanced upon the advertising page, the fourth one. "The fourth page," says Rowell's wise man, "cannot be understood except by a sage. He who invented it was a benefactor to humanity. In a singularly narrow space he has contrived to collect the most valuable information." To this extent, the sage agrees with Mallarmé, who said that in a newspaper with two facing columns, the advertising column "leaps out like a bolt of electricity."

Moreover, this discursive terrain, poised between aesthetics and economy, is clearly a cultural battlefield, with the new copywriters as shock troops in a war over a new kind of reading. Advertising fabricates itself out of literary contexts, but places an emphasis on the *eye* that does the reading, on the reading subject. Just as current film criticism speaks of the visual creation of subject positions within a film, so too advertisement proferred a radically different "subjectivity" of reading than literature had required. Rowell provides us with a record of this address to the subject eyes, in unsettling martial terms:

> The eye is the sentinel of the will. An advertisement assaults, first and last of all, the eyes. Customers do not reason, do not arrive at a purchase by the slow method of military "approaches," impelled by an elaborate ratiocination, but carry the coveted commodity by a sudden assault pricked up to it by the indomitable bayonets of the artists in advertising. No monarch's slaves ever scattered at his bidding so fleetly or faithfully, or in such bewildering numbers, as the literary messengers that bear your individual word to the people of this great nation. (p. 246)

Advertising reading is, then, an assault on the eye, in which every permutation of reading has its military counterpart: the customers are bayoneted, the artists are indomitable soldiers, and words become slaves, literary messengers attacking a nation's eyes. The gap that opens up between traditional notions of reading, of book and print and literature, and their advertising counterparts is dizzying.

It may help in mapping this rivalry to set the interpenetration of literature and advertising within an archival context, to underline the extent to which advertisement played off literature and worked through a phase in which it still deferred to its rival's textual power. A survey of representative advertisements from the Landauer collection displays the ingenuity of advertising and the extent to which it was a parasite on literature in the nineteenth century. Advertising as a center of ideological production mined literature for its sources, and in a reversal of the Dickensian roles, where the book supported the advertisements, it even became literature's patron.

JUMBO AESTHETIC

Literature can be shown to be the primary thematic allusive system used in nineteenth-century American advertising until approximately 1900, when, as Bella Landauer describes it, "the bathing beauty" took

The family at attention, at the modern scene of instruction, courtesy of the
advertising institution.

Advertisement for N. W. Ayer & Son, Newspaper Advertising Agents, printed
in *Harper's New Monthly Magazine*, Philadelphia, July 1896, p. 336.

Courtesy of The New-York Historical Society, New York City

predominance over literary glamour. Advertising used literature indiscriminately, appealing to no special (supposedly elite) groups of readers, and not restricted to any special range of advertisers. The literary spectrum from Mother Goose to Shakespeare formed a plenum along which advertisers plucked at will.[20]

Other than specific references within an ad, advertisers created books and marketed literature, miniature books, advertising copies of classic works with interleaved ads, premium illustrated versions of the same for presentation to libraries, so that ads could be read in that hallowed environment, broadsides and trade card series of authors and poets, and a variety of giveaways and literary artifacts like pens, mock scrolls, and spectacles.

Advertising practiced different modes of incorporation of literature. These ranged from the reproduction of an entire story or poem, leaving the cover, end paper, and fly-leaves for ads, to the use of mere titles of famous works. Occasionally anthologies of diverse genres were produced, offering ads for more than one product. Parodies were particularly popular; one of the most famous was written by Bret Harte early in his career, mimicking Longfellow's *Excelsior* to sell a soap:

> The shades of night were falling fast,
> As through an Eastern village passed
> A youth who bore, through dust and heat,
> A stencil-plate, that read complete—
> SAPOLIO
> (presented by Enoch Morgan's Sons)[21]

Ads rendered literary work into fragments of raw material, trading on an author or a character's auratic prestige, sometimes without evoking any of the surrounding text. The cigar bands made for a variety of tobacco companies were most typical of this approach—these wrappers spun out a drum-roll litany of names: One such band indiscriminately reads: "Shakespeare Gorki Macbeth Maud Muller Sancho Panza Harriet Beecher Stowe." Cigarette packs carried authors' portraits and lists of their work, with Charles Dickens as a favorite choice. Companies made trade cards featuring pictures of authors, their homes, or scenes from episodes in their works. As Landauer puts it: "Naked irrelevant names of the laureled men of words or of their creatures were considered magic enough to overcome the stiffest sales resistance: Emerson, Goethe, Don Quixote: Wear Irish Linen!"[22]

Naturally enough, classical authors were relied upon to provide this magic. Shakespeare was chosen as the overwhelming favorite—it is salutary to remember that although he re-achieved critical popularity only in the early nineteenth century, the melodrama versions of Shakespeare's works had been perennially popular, and there were trade cards depicting, for example, Cordelia and Edgar marrying in the Nahum Tate tradition. Mother Goose rhymes often appeared on soda cards, while Sea Foam Baking Powder produced a 16-page Humpty-Dumpty pamphlet. The indisputably "high" classics were most often used, generally reworked into a variety of new and surprising scenarios. Merrick Thread Company had a novel series of ads, in both senses of the word, when it depicted Gulliver tied down by Lilliputians using the remorselessly unbreakable Merrick thread, or offered readers the sight of Robinson Crusoe making extensive use of Merrick thread in his attempts to forge a solitary civilization. Fairbank Lard framed poems and scenes by Shakespeare and Byron with its dignified company name; the Wilson Packing Company put out a set of Don Quixote-based cards, the Don tilting at windmills under the subtle blazon of a meat-packing plant.

Possibly the most imperialist forays into literature's territory were made by the tobacco industry. In addition to the trade cards and literary cigar bands already mentioned, the companies decorated their packs and their cigar boxes with quotations and pictures of or from *Ivanhoe*, Ruskin, Plutarch, Cooper, Schiller, and Shakespeare. The publisher George Rutledge issued Dumas' *Count of Monte Cristo* in a special edition for "presentation to the lovers of the most exquisite Havana cigar by P. Pohalski & Co." This deluxe volume, merely one example among the many such that were published, has the Monte Cristo cigar label as illustration on its front cover, and on the back a picture of the cigar factory in Key West, circa 1889. Dumas' novel is the bold staging ground for the representation of the desire structure of the Havana cigar; all the romance and excitement that is meant to inhere in the novel is "quoted" and brought to the cigar, in this case pictorially made to surround and cover the literature it invokes and is evoked by. Egyptienne "Straights" and Sovereign cigarettes launched new stories with each package run. Inserted inside the wrapper was an installment of a story from, among others, Kipling and O. Henry. Many stories, including those by well-known writers like O. Henry, were only published in this cigarette format, a sub-rosa form of circulation and exclusivity. Advertisers brought out many of their own volumes, and major writers like Ambrose Bierce published in advertising volumes for years before their work came out in more orthodox publications. The 1872 *Buyers Manual*, an omnibus volume including many different advertised products, had exclusive stories and poems by Bierce, Harte, Twain, Lowell, and Holmes.

A *locus classicus* for the confluence of advertising and literature in this period is the bizarre intersection of discourses built up around the figure of Oscar Wilde. Advertisers suffered a virtual Oscar Wilde epidemic for a period of ten years in the penultimate decade of the nineteenth century, a kind of advertiser's fin de siecle movement. Two factors contributing to Wilde's literary celebrity at the time were his having been parodied in Gilbert & Sullivan's popular *Patience*, as "The Sunflower," and his own hectic tour of America. These elements came together for advertisers in a strange mosaic construction of Wilde as ultimate aesthete, extremist litterateur, wearing a velvet suit and lace collar, carrying a sunflower, brought into captivity within the ads like the unicorn in medieval tapestry. This motif was played upon in endless versions; a particularly acute specimen is the 1882 large-size trade card in full color issued by Ehrich Brothers Dry Goods Store of New York City. On the reverse side of the picture a poem entitled "The Lily's Avengers" is printed, reading

> I love the Golden Sun no less
> Than e'er I did before,
> But oh! but oh! but oh! oh! oh!
> I love my Oscar more.

The advertising moment recedes behind the face of this highly artificed representation of Wilde, used here like a literary totem capable of conjuring up a fervent world of celebrity and aesthetic rapture. The dry goods store need affix no more than its name to the card; this acknowledges that the actual items in the dry goods store are not really central to the enterprise of advertising for the store. Rather, the advertising is used to create an ambience, an aura that aesthetically unfolds around the act of purchase. In the prototypical Wilde trade card, reference to the world of literature is sufficient to invoke that aura, and to put the actual act of commercial exchange under a unique form of erasure. Ultimately advertising would no longer need to borrow the referential system of literature as its model for representation, but until the early twentieth century, literature, as evidenced by the Wilde card, was still the necessary wild card to hold in the game.

Advertising is, however, not just *borrowing* literature in these fetish associations; the ads express how intimate a connection was felt to obtain between the respective "spaces" of literature and advertising at a point where commodities lacked their own narratives. No sense of incongruity prevented the most disparate advertisers from availing themselves of literary treasure, nor did advertisers question the link between poem, story, and book on the one hand, and package, poster, and advertising volume on the other. A prime example of the spatial blurring brought about, and one still within the Oscar Wilde examples discussed above, is an ad that parades the similarity of literature and advertisement on its surface. This placard features a picture of Oscar Wilde, fey and velvet-suited, walking the street arm-in-arm with Jumbo the elephant, who has been adorned with a sunflower in his grey, wrinkly buttonhole area. Their uncanny conjuncture bears the title "Jumbo Aesthetic" rampant on its surface. Jumbo the elephant was himself a pure totem of advertising. He had been brought to America from a British zoo by P. T. Barnum in 1882, and although there were other elephants in America at the time, Barnum managed to surround Jumbo with such a mystique that he was met by huge crowds on his arrival to these shores, was the source of thousands of ads, especially those for thread and soap, and after a mourned death was finally stuffed and mounted for display at Tufts University, with tributes to his "wonderful sagacity and moral character." The pure creature of advertising cavorts in tandem with the ultimate representative of the world of literature; Wilde lends his "aestheticism" to the supercolossal wondrousness of Jumbo, who returns the favor by commodifying the literary persona.

The existence of one or even a multitude of such ads does not "prove" that advertising had set itself on a continuum with literature, but the free-associative quality of all these ads (and there are thousands of them) does indicate that literature became a kind of "dreamwork" subject, or fetish system, for advertisement as it was crystallizing into a discursive system. Any combinations or permutations, fragments or symbols of literary discourse are permitted to appear without question in the ads dreamed by these early advertisers, whose repertoire of images still comes from the body of literature. "Jumbo Aesthetic" is a striking instance of the leveling logic of these dreams, when Wilde is

The discourses of advertising and literature meet and take a promenade down the social street.

Jumbo Aesthetic, from a collection of Jumbo trade cards distributed through merchants, in *Jumbo's Influence on Advertising*, Bella C. Landauer, in the *Quarterly Bulletin* of The New-York Historical Society, October 1934.

Courtesy of The New-York Historical Society, New York City

made to walk with the elephant whose fame has arisen strictly from its advertising connections. As in a dream, all the strangeness of their friendly encounter evaporates in the equivalency made between Wilde's "aesthetic" literature and the aesthetic life Jumbo has had as a wild creature lodged within advertisements. Both are paragons of a literature, and can take their promenade through the same representative space.

3 • "The Age of Advertising": Henry James & the Advertising Scene

> Thence back into the throng, until we reach,
> Following the tide that slackens by degrees,
> Some half-frequented scene, where wider streets
> Bring straggling breezes of suburban air.
> Here files of ballads dangle from dead walls;
> Advertisements, of giant-size, from high
> Press forward, in all colors, on the sight;
> These, bold in conscious merit; lower down
> *That*, fronted with a most imposing word,
> Is, peradventure, one in masquerade.
>
> William Wordsworth, *The Prelude*, Book VII

HENRY JAMES' WORK IS PARTICULARLY AP-
posite as a lens for reading nineteenth-century advertising.
Despite his unlikely candidacy, given the supposedly mandarin concerns of his fiction and his criticism, James' engagement with advertisement and his texts' struggles with the nature of the incipient
consumer culture is formidable and thoroughgoing. Until recently,
James has been difficult to capture in this historical, material light.
Leaving aside another tradition content to tend to the formalist fences
set up around the Jamesian oeuvre, more politically oriented critics
have had their problems with Jamesian realism. Raymond Williams,
for example, is at great pains to write James out of his countertradition
of the English novel, *The English Novel From Dickens to Lawrence*,[1]
splicing together a chain of writers to counter Leavis' *The Great Tradition*,[2] which bypasses James in favor of Thomas Hardy. Williams
describes his dissatisfaction with James: "At a crucial moment in the
evolution of the novel, he leads toward a preoccupation with the
processes of the spectacle and with the process of observing the spectacle. That may be connected with certain ideological blockages, which
prevented him taking his characteristic insight right through."[3]

While Williams has now come to believe, as evinced by interviews
in *Politics and Letters*, that what James says about money is very
important, he still allies James with Flaubert and with a stultifying
formal sterility that derailed an historical evolution. This critical picture

of James chastises him for being dégagé where it does not ask him to refine his insights into a Weberian analytic system. A corrective to this manner of reading James is to take the question of "spectacle" seriously, along the lines laid out in the previous chapter, where the introduction of a new spectacular discourse poses major shifts in material life. James' fixation on spectacle becomes a nodal point for examining the confluence of money, image, and social mystification, and his "ideological blockage" a fertile tension in the correlation of narrative with social change.

Another major political critic, Fredric Jameson, unfavorably compares James to Conrad on grounds of modernism, where James appears less assailable than in progressive political theory.[4] Jameson claims that Conrad's apparently old-fashioned concern with story-telling actually places him in a postmodernist category, while James remains in a beautifully wrought vacuum, incapable of leap-frogging ahead to engage our present critical concerns. Regardless of how this may revivify Conrad, James' concomitant relegation to the backwaters of the modern novel is less helpful. James' acute social importance and the prescience that allowed him to dub the nineteenth century "the age of advertising," with its echoes of display, consumption, publicity, and propaganda, has come under renewed scrutiny. In what follows, I will be primarily concerned with establishing the importance of James' work in its observance of and interlocutory dialog with the forces of modern advertising. Read in this fashion, James' texts become registers of a complicated struggle to isolate and name the features of a nascent consumer culture, as well as to enact the changing social orientation toward the spectacle. James' work relates the advertising spectacle to the aesthetic and moral concerns of literature, while in its own thematic and structural arrangement it records a developing narrative spectatorship. The history Raymond Williams finds lacking in James may be translated into the search for the origins of a powerful cultural hegemony, advertisement.

I have been accompanied in my exploration of the material and historical vectors of James' work by a rich new body of scholarship. Much attention is now being paid to James' own fraught relations with the literary market, as in Marcia Jacobson's *Henry James and the Mass Market*, which discusses the effects on his work of his desire for market success. Two recent studies are particularly relevant to one placement of James' work within other discursive practices. Mark Seltzer's *Henry*

James and the Art of Power questions "just this radical distinction between the aesthetic and the actual," writing with the thesis that Henry James' texts must be read in their alignments and alliances with the tactics of power. "Power" remains rather unspecified in this New-Historical investigation, which nonetheless excitingly argues for the relation of the Jamesian style to hegemonic cultural strategies, especially in a reading of the hegemonic spaces of the city revealed in *The Princess Casamassima*. Jean-Christophe Agnew provides a brilliant interpretation of Henry James and consumer culture, with special reference to *The Golden Bowl*. Writing in "The Consuming Vision of Henry James," Agnew notes:

> The consuming vision implants itself at the heart of James' fiction in the years after 1886. An appetite once thematised within the novel now thematises the novel as one of a variety of its representative forms. What was once a problem within the novel is now its problematic: its defining set of questions and motives. . . . Such redemption as occurs within the novels becomes the redemption not of characters but of form, the commodity form.

As a cultural historian, Agnew argues for the relevance of James' work to any material analysis of the conditions of consumer culture, presumably by other historians as well as by literary critics. My assessment of James' texts up against the body of late nineteenth-century advertisement will follow these critical interventions in also insisting on the significance of Henry James for understanding the formation of American advertising, and on the crucial relevance of rival discourses to the critical appraisal of James' own work. Rather than tracing the more abstract shapes of power traversing James' work, or focusing on the multiple valences of consumption, my analysis is restricted to watching the chemical reaction of the Jamesian corpus set up against advertisement per se—not a case of elective affinities.[5]

Like Agnew's essay in its treatment of the mechanics of commodity consumption (an area that cannot neatly be divided off from advertisement), I am more eager to use James' literary work to situate the procedures of advertising than to plump up the material pillows of James criticism; that literature and advertising are on a two-way street is as amply clear for James as for the other writers in this study. I will touch on *The Bostonians*, *The Ambassadors*, and *The American Scene* to give a convenient, if fictive, chronology to this analysis, but also because each text accomplishes its interpenetration of and by advertisement at a deepening level of engagement, a trajectory from the thematic to the stylistic.

James' work is pervaded by the scenic; its reliance on a metaphorical and even metaphysical system of theatrical representations inserted into the novelistic frame has been given excellent elaboration by Richard Poirier and Peter Brooks. The loose net of my argument in this chapter rests on extending that theatrical nexus until it intersects with advertising discourse. The "scene" in Henry James acquires two signal sources of energy, often overlapping in the embedded metaphors of his prose—the epistemological and the sexual. This is hardly surprising news, and, moreover, questions of knowledge and the fluid scenarios of intrasubjective desire are thoroughly entangled. (Leo Bersani's chapter on James in *A Future for Astyanax* is perhaps the best exploration of this entanglement.) That scenic economy is brought to bear on advertising in James' work, since advertisement has a theatrical, spatial form for James, as well as an uncanny erotics. In the three works I will explore, the scene of writing that is James' battleground with advertisement undergoes a shift from a mise-en-scène of performance, to a primal scene of violation, to an allegory of theatricalized erotic struggle over the conditions of social knowledge.

THE WALKING ADVERTISEMENT

P. T. Barnum makes a natural bridge from the precincts of advertising theory discussed in the previous chapter to the narrative web of James' novels. *The Bostonians*[6] records the cultural Barnumization of America and reverberates with a critique of P. T. Barnum himself. James never vilifies nor anathematizes Barnum, as even Charles Dickens had done; rather, his texts skirt the career of the great advertiser, analyzing how the flair for theatricality, spectacle, and writing segues into the hermetically sealed cultural world of mass images. He is far from immune to the charms of Barnum, and in fact credits him with having provided his first aesthetic experience: it happened during the Saturday afternoons that he and his brother William spent at Barnum's Museum on Broadway. Among other plays, the two boys saw *Love, or the Countess and the Serf*, featuring the actress Emily Estayer. "I forget everybody but Miss Estayer. . . . She had a hooked nose, a great play of nostril, a vast protuberance of bosom, and always the crop of close, moist ringlets. . . . She had a rusty, raspy and heaving authority of which the bitterness is still in my ears." As Constance Rourke describes this thralldom in her biographical sketch of Barnum:

> In superabundant measure Miss Estayer seemed to possess precisely those brave seductions which made the theater an abomination. The little Jameses were enchanted; doubtless other young people enjoyed a similar wedge of dubious pleasure. The little Jameses, indeed, were restrained by no narrow axioms; the only irony which hemmed them round lay in the fact that the elder Henry James politely and exquisitely detested what he called "flagrant morality." Flagrant enough it was at Barnum's, the mere blazing word and the adroit admixture covering the uproarious fact.[7]

The serious aesthetic seduction undergone by James in Barnum's parlors and the incorporation of much of that aesthetic into his own views of "writing," can be read in his autobiography in the effusion regarding those museum visits. The afternoons were "flushed with the very complexion of romance," and in that "stuffed and dim little hall of audience" he "plucked somehow the very flower of the ideal."[8] If America's premier advertiser was able to engender this paean, it is overly simple to dismiss either Barnum or James' diagnosis of him. In that critique are embedded the aesthetic canons that shaped the work of James himself, and an acknowledgement that the visual theatricality he imbibed from Barnum continued to inform the staging of his own fictions.

James' *The Bostonians* registers all the changes advertising was to undergo in its meteoric American development. Nominally a book about a "Boston marriage," a platonic lesbian relationship and its connections to the feminist movement and other "crank" developments of the time, i.e., phrenology, temperance, homeopathic medicine, and women's suffrage, it is in fact the delineation of the Barnumization of America. The narrative of Verena Tarrant and her family telescopes the rudimentary processes of early American advertising, its eventual link to the newspaper, and its ultimate ties to spectacle, deracinated history, and the sexualization of the advertising image.

The Tarrant family includes Selah Tarrant, a hapless mesmerist living in extremely straightened circumstances in a backwater Cambridge house, his wife, the dissatisfied daughter of an old Boston

abolitionist family, with its roots in American mass political movements, and their daughter Verena, an extraordinarily beautiful girl
whose specialty is undergoing a genuine trance during which she
releases a stream of fluent and automatic language persuading her
listeners of the rights of womankind. A rich Bostonian bluestocking
called Olive Chancellor, who has devoted her education, her money,
and her time to the feminist cause for some time, encounters Verena
at one of her impromptu showings, where she has taken the place of
the scheduled speaker on feminism. Olive "adopts" Verena in order
to free her from commercial exploitation by her father, and to educate
and develop her as a signal beacon in the feminist movement. A
complicated nest of suitors descends on Verena as she widens her
popularity; a rich Harvard graduate vies for her, Olive attempts to keep
Verena for herself and the cause, and an adamant reactionary and
misogynist, Basil Ransom, ultimately takes her from the very stage, to
rescue her from publicized feminism by marrying her. These plot
strands entwine to expose the dynamic effect of American advertising
on the cultural, political, and sexual spheres of American life, beginning
with a portrait of the early history of advertising embedded in the
character Selah Tarrant.

Verena Tarrant's father is an avatar of the advertising age, combining
in his own person all the early versions of uncodified advertising practices. He initially began his career as the itinerant seller of patent
medicines, traveling throughout New England in a cart and providing
his own potion, his own labeling, and his own advertising commentary.
The historian of American advertising George Foster traces America's
earliest ads directly back to the patent medicine milieu—and of course
the residue of this cultural practice survives in the appellation of
"snake-oil salesmen" to even modern participants.[9]

Patent medicines were a natural category for early advertisement,
in part because of the system of distribution of goods. Most Americans
shopped in the rural country stores, the "general stores" of reknown,
where under one roof were barrels and shelves filled with undifferen-
tiated and unnamed bulk goods. Patent medicines eluded the general
store system and remained unrecognized by it, so that the creators of
these "medicines" necessarily had to create traveling theaters for their
presentation. Since there were as yet no mass events which a large
public audience could be depended upon to attend, with the exception
of the primitive circuses traveling through the Eastern states as early

as 1700, the arrival of the medicine cart became its own advertising event. Into the space hollowed out by the untoward appearance of an itinerant salesman (because tinkers and gypsies were rare at this period, and America had no tradition, as did England, of buying bulk goods at traveling fairs of the kind depicted in Hardy's *The Mayor of Casterbridge*), an advertising theater had to be invented.

Medicine carts relied on perfunctory narratives and stark cultural images in their attempt to teach the public how to "read" these medicines: the narratives ranged from the story of inspiring and poignant cures, often acted out by assistants, to the creation of archetypal figures like the professor or the wise, taciturn Indian. While patent medicines were not mass-produced until later in the nineteenth century, when Lydia Pinkham's et al. flooded the market, paradoxically the merchandising efforts created by the medicine peddlers remained the most powerful *image* of the reception of advertising in a society that was new to this imperative. Consequently, the selling methods and the narratives produced on these advertising journeys, as well as the rearrangement of cultural space they evoked, were ultimately borrowed by the more structured promotional schemes for the original mass-produced goods—and the "medicine show" was a synecdoche for advertising in toto.

The patent medicine carts traced out a path over the American landscape, which was to have superimposed over it the next stage in the American advertising aesthetic, the Chatauqua lecture/performance circuit. The Bella C. Landauer Collection of American advertising gives ample testimony to this burgeoning phase of advertisement.[10] The theater was still frowned upon and even banned in some states, so the "educational" panorama provided by these spectacles touched a ready market. Many medicine vendors entered the Chatauqua shows or their ilk, where the skills honed in solitary wandering advertisements could be translated into full-scale performances. Exemplary of these performances are some of the following ads: "Reids' Popular Dime Recitals—the elocutionists—Every Selection a Gem!" Or South Ryegate's extravaganza: "Mrs. Jarley's Wax Work, tableau played by actresses. Other tableaus include Queen Elizabeth, Columbus, Alexander, Topsey, Father Time and George Washington." The Honorable Wm. Parsons offers as "my best effort" a lecture series on the "Story of the Golden Age," the Liliputian Opera Co. of midgets offers Cinderella—"we imitate none, but excel many," while in Wells

River, Vermont, the topic is "The Czar and Nihilism." Selah Tarrant climbs on this bandwagon as well; as his wife imagines it, "she had gone of an evening to a *seance* or a lecture as regularly as she had eaten her supper. Her husband always had tickets for lectures; in moments of irritation at the want of a certain sequence in their career, she had remarked to him that it was the only thing he did have" (p. 65).

James moves Selah Tarrant on beyond the lecture room to the next phase of his, and advertising's, career—in Selah's case, to mesmerism, and in advertising's, to the marketing of mass-produced urban novelties. Selah's esoteric practice of magnetotherapy, really patent medicine in a marriage with science and technology, is given distinctly erotic connotations by James. Selah spends so much time closeted with his neurasthenic lady clients, the group to whom the "electricity girdle" and the "spirit cap and scalp restorer" were directed, that he is in danger of having to stop his therapeutic practice, as he had to relinquish spiritualism, despite being "an extraordinarily favored medium," for reasons "of which Mrs. Tarrant had her own version" (p. 68). Nonetheless, "she knew that he was very magnetic (that, in fact, was his genius), and she felt that it was his magnetism that held her to him." These insinuations of exotic sex color all James' textual reflections on advertisement; the attraction of audience to ad, whether that ad is a person like Selah or Verena Tarrant, or a more abstract entity, is conceived of as erotic. Selah, Verena, even Chad Newsome and the advertised American girl spread out a magnetic canvas of desire, holding their audiences in the thralldom of sexualized spectacle. Selah's extramarital closetings point to the sexual energy released in cultural/commercial exchanges, especially since so much advertisement was directed at middle-class women new to the delights of consumerism.

Mesmerism, or magnetotherapy, seems so arcane that it is difficult to realize that James has set Selah Tarrant squarely into the mainstream of incipient American advertising, although the halcyon days of mesmerism were gone before the tardy Selah ever got involved in it. Mesmerists and others like them had their own impromptu advertising network, arising out of the lecture tours, home-made posters and handbills, and newspaper announcements of their work as matters of "intellectual curiosity."[11] The fraudulence and sleaziness of the Tarrant model was typical, but James is not directing animosity toward this shabby backstreet world of advertising entrepreneurs; the critique is reserved for sophisticated systems of modern advertisement. The

COME ONE AND ALL
GREAT AND SMALL.

Those who are sick and afflicted and given up by all Medical Doctors.
DON'T FAIL TO GIVE THE WONDERFUL
MEXICAN INDIAN CLAIRVOYANT
Healing Medium a Call.

THE   THE

SEVENTH   SEVENTH

SON   SON.

OF

Who can tell you all your troubles and difficulties at a glance of the eyes from the time you can remember, and can inform you of your future life, and inform you of the deaths of friends, and if friends have deserted you will tell whether they will return, and tell of distant friends who are gone. Can tell ladies if they have a love whether he will be true to them, and tell the same to gentlemen in regard to the ladies, whether they will make good companions in life as husband or wives. Do not be afraid to come and have your life told.

For each incorrect answer I will forfeit ten cents. Will tell about complaints and diseases of the system, whether they can be cured or not. Tell you if you will be successful in your business undertaking or not. If you cannot come, send your children if you have them, let me tell them of their future lives. I will write a chart so they can take it home and show it to their parents if they wish.

Ladies, 75 cents.   Gentlemen, $1.
Children under 12 years, 25 cents.

Who Heals by using Water and Magnetism ; by use of the Hands ; by Wetting and Bathing ; and doctors by the Indian style. He will forfeit TEN THOUSAND DOLLARS to any one who can beat his Wonderful Powers. He can tell by looking at you the troubles of the system ; whether you can be cured or not. If I see you are not curable I will tell you so, and if I see you are I will also tell you. Those who are sick and afflicted and DON'T BELIEVE WHAT I SAY, come and give me two or three trials, and let me show you how much better I can make you.

Ladies, if you have Little Children

Afflicted you must try all the Medical Doctors in this city, and after trying them come and give me a call. I have cured people in Lockport who have doctored for several years with our leading physicians, without finding relief. I don't say this for you to believe me, for I can prove it to be the truth. Those who have long been afflicted with Cancers give me a trial, as I have cured people who have suffered for sixteen years with the disease. I treat the following diseases :

BAD COUGHS, CONSUMPTION, STAMMERING OF SPEECH, KIDNEY COMPLAINT, RHEUMATISM, FEMALE WEAKNESS, PILES, PALPATION OF THE HEART, MILK FEVER, FLOODING AND FAINTING, SECRET COMPLAINTS, CORNS, INGROWN NAILS, SORE EYES, WORMS, DROPSY, FELONS, GRAVEL, HEARTBURN, JAUNDICE, BALDNESS, CHILLS and FEVER, AGUE, REMOVING BOILS FROM THE FACE, ETC.

My wife is also a good Healing Medium. Ladies, call and witness her wonderful Healing Powers. CHARGES $1.00 A VISIT. MAKES A SURE CURE. To those who are afflicted and can not call on us, it will put them come and board with me and we will send you home with health restored. That is, as good as the world can expect. Board and Doctoring per week $7, and have a good back to take them out riding once a week, and have everything pleasant. Now you had better come and try what virtue there is in our wonderful Healing Power by laying on hands and bathing. Send or bring your children and have them cured.

TESTIMONIALS.

Here is a list of a few persons who have called on me to be cured after they have been doctored by leading physicians without finding relief for several years :

Detroit, Mich., May 29, 1876.
KIND FRIEND :—I am very glad to say that I am feeling as well as I ever did. I had much given up to die with the consumption, but I can say I thank God for I am well and do not feel any pain in my lungs. I thank you have cured me. I will say when you first took my case in hand I did not think I could live long, and I am not think you could cure me. Don't you remember me saying so, and you said there was nothing impossible to die. I thank you now and can say I will say that I did not believe in your way of doctoring, but my husband told me to go and see what you could tell my complaint, and you described how I felt better than I could have told you still I thought that I could not be cured with magnetism, No more at this time.
From MRS. ELIZA JONES.

New York City, July 5, 1875.
DEAR SIR :—I take my pen in hand to write you a few lines to let you know how I am feeling. I am not help telling you the truth. You have saved me from death, for I was almost dead when I called on you with the Asthma. Now I hope that God may bless you for you have been the means of curing me, too-d-by. This letter is from your friend.
GIDEON FATH, West 30th St., Lot. 39th and 10 avenue.

DEAR SIR :—I thought I would write you a few lines to let you know how my father is. I am glad to say that the swelling has all left his legs and the water is all gone out of them, and there is no sign of dropsy about him now. He can eat thing the is glad that he is well. He is going to send you $20 as a present for curing him, and my mother is going to send you $5 for curing her. No more at this time. From your friend.
MISS LUCY THOMPSON.

Address your letters to Suspension Bridge, Niagara County, N. Y.

Lockport, N. Y., Oct. 1877.
DEAR FRIEND :—I take pleasure in testifying that through you my child is now as well as ever, after being given up by some of the best physicians in Lockport.
MRS. NETTIE WILLOX.

Lockport, N. Y., Oct. 14, 1877.
DEAR SIR :—After treating with you the second time I found myself much relieved from my very severe illness.
CHAS. A. SHIELDS.

Those who are afflicted and have not much means to employ me, can get a receipt from me with which they can cure themselves much cheaper than I can afford to do. If any one is not able to call on me, and want me to call and see them they can notify me by letter addressed to

DR. VERNETT, LOCKPORT, N. Y.
At Medina House, on Wednesdays
and Thursdays of each week only.

The intersection of the print medium with the advertising medium, in and through the "healing medium" of the traveling medicine circuit.

"Give the Mexican Indian Clairvoyant Healing Medium a Call," an advertisement from the Bella C. Landauer collection, circa 1877.

Courtesy of The New-York Historical Society, New York City

novel underscores the natural procession from the patent medicinemen and the mesmerists to the more serious, relentless encircling of publicity and advertisement; Selah, in his own impotent way, has helped to fashion this noose, but is really outside the power center of the process. He salvages some scraps of dignity by never letting down his guard, even *en famille;* his wife reluctantly admires him for knowing "he was a humbug, but he had never admitted it." The subtle reference to humbuggery would have flashed Barnum's name across any contemporary reader's mind, but where that worthy made a career of baring his humbuggery, explaining it and exorcising it, Selah tries to remain within morally and intellectually respectable limits. The mesmerist performance Barnum delightedly exposes in his autobiography is the reverse of Selah's, who professes a belief in it and even takes credit for the power to "bring out" his daughter Verena's trances, until it becomes apparent that she can induce them on her own.

The bravado of this portrait of the Tarrant family, American advertising past, present, and future, is as bold as the posters turned out by those in Selah's world. Even the family physiognomy contributes to the layers of historical analysis accreted in James' description of them: Mrs. Tarrant is portrayed as a "figure of wax," looking like one of the omnipresent imitations of Mrs. Jarley's waxworks show that became such a feature of American theatricals, a star of her own domestic tableau. Verena is constantly remarked as looking like a poster or a theatrical celebrity; Mrs. Tarrant hopes she will make a good match to a suitor in public life, "which, to Mrs. Tarrant, meant that his name would be visible, in the lamplight, on a colored poster in the doorway of the Treamont Theater" (p. 86). Verena, a figure on a poster, is affianced in imagination to a name also inscribed on an advertising bill.

Selah realizes he inhabits a backwater, and that the wilder shores of publicity will pass him by. The all-important connection with the newspaper spelled out by Barnum and by Rowell still manages to elude him.

In reality he had one all-absorbing solicitude—the desire to get paragraphs put into the newspapers, paragraphs of which he hitherto had been the subject, but of which he was now to divide the glory with his daughter. The newspapers were his world, the richest expression, in his eyes, of human life; and for him, if a diviner day was to come upon the earth, it would be brought about by copious advertisements in the daily prints. He looked with longing for the moment when Verena should be advertised among the personals, and to his mind the supremely happy people were those of whom there was some journalistic mention every day in the year. . . . The vision of that publicity haunted his dreams. . . . Human existence to him, indeed, was a huge publicity, in which the only fault was that it was sometimes not sufficiently effective. (p. 89)

The most striking evidence of Selah's immurement in the world of publicity is in his wish to be bodily incorporated in it. During one of his daily visits to the newspaper office, or to the hotels whose lobbies were full of reporters and "famous" people,

[W]riting letters at a table inlaid with advertisements, Selah Tarrant made innumerable contemplative stations. He could not have told you, at any particular moment, what he was doing; he only had a general sense that such places were national nerve centers, and that the more one looked in, the more one was "on the spot." The *penetralia* of the daily presses were, however, still more fascinating, and the fact that they were less accessible, that here he found barriers in his path, only added to the zest of forcing an entrance. . . . He hung about, sat too long, took up the time of busy people, edged into the printing rooms when he had been eliminated from the office, talked with the compositors till they set up his remarks by mistake, and to the newsboy when the compositors had turned their backs. He was always trying to find out what was "going in"; he would have liked to go in himself, bodily, and failing in this, he hoped to get advertisements inserted gratis. The wish of his soul was that he might be interviewed; that made him hover at the editorial elbow. Once he thought he had been, and the headings, five or six deep, danced for days before his eyes; but the report never appeared. (p. 91)

Selah's desperation to be at the heart of the "national nerve center," and preferably to be lodged in those nerves, recalls Rowell's description of an America that had no center at all except that provided by the giant advertising-cum-newspaper combine of his own company. James' text expresses the social invisibility, in the terms used to discuss Dickens' work, inherent in mass culture, and the pain of being exiled to the periphery of knowledge and visibility. Selah's pathetic yet understandable desire to be placed bodily into the newspaper exhibits the early symptoms of a more pervasive cultural disease. De Tocqueville was struck by America's infatuation with news and ads; James'

Selah represents a longing for public verification only advertisement could offer, with a hint that Selah's genuflections before publicity are a parody of the stations of the cross.

The desire to be taken up bodily by advertisement, to enter into its space and to constitute, for once, its message, is literally enacted not by Selah Tarrant, but by his daughter, Verena, the child on whom all his hopes of publicity come to rest. Verena belongs to the long line of Jamesian American girls, but where *Portrait of a Lady* and *The Golden Bowl* obliquely relate their heroines to consumer culture, Verena's portrait is explicit. "She looks," disdains Mrs. Luna, "like a walking advertisement" (p. 113). Verena's "gift," her exploitable commodity, is her trancelike fluency in arguing for women's rights from the stage, in combination with her striking beauty and her "consummate innocence." The first newspaper editor who sees her casual and unheralded first performance murmurs, "There's money for some one in that girl; you see if she don't have quite a run!" (p. 56). Verena stands at an advertising crossroads, all unwittingly, because her flair for performance and theatricality, her parental past in the byways of self-promotion, and her nullity as a quintessential American girl construct her as an advertising emblem. When she first appears, there are those in her audience who take her for a prophet of the nascent women's movement, chiefly Olive Chancellor, a wealthy Bostonian who is wedded to the cause and also erotically drawn to Verena's charms. The masterstroke of *The Bostonians* is that Verena is pinioned on the verge of being two mutually exclusive and self-contradictory things: the leader of a woman's movement, whose roots are tainted with advertising humbug, and the incarnation and objectification of femininity, to be used in commercial guise. She can operate as either a false visionary or a piece of advertising currency. Matthias Pardon, the newspaperman, is determined that Verena shall be played for the latter.

> He thought there was too much hanging back; he wanted to see her in a front seat; he wanted to see her name in the biggest kind of bills and her portrait in the windows of the stores. She had genius, there was no doubt of that, and she would take a new line altogether. She had charm, and there was a great demand for that nowadays in connexion with new ideas. . . . She ought to be carried straight ahead; she ought to walk right to the top. There was a want of bold action; he didn't see what they were waiting for." (p. 110)

The excitement that Verena arouses derives from her free-floating currency as an advertisable image. Newspapers vie to absorb her because she is a pure token of publicity, a figure to be used in an infinity of promotions. James shows Verena being courted by the power elite of New York as well; Verena can "stand for" any consumable public message, and the rich New Yorkers who hold salons to display Verena are uninterested and indeed antipathetic to her "feminist message." They too want to assimilate Verena to cover their estrangement from the social movements of the day; Verena will "mesmerize" their critics.

Matthias Pardon is one in a series of newspaper men appearing in James' work, and an earlier version of George M. Flack, the journalist in *The Reverberator* whose relentless quest for promotional material horrifies Paris. Pardon represents the new writer, a type just visible on the horizon and a genuine threat to literature:

> His appearance was perfectly reconcilable with a large degree of literary enterprise. It should be explained that for the most part they attached to this the same meaning as Selah Tarrant—a state of intimacy with the newspapers, the cultivation of the great arts of publicity. For this ingenuous son of his age all distinction between the person and the artist had ceased to exist; the writer was personal, the person food for newsboys, and everything and every one were every one's business. All things, with him, referred themselves to print, and print meant simply infinite reporting, a promptitude of announcement . . . he was a thoroughly modern young man. (p. 107–8)

Throughout the text Pardon is waiting in the wings to promote Verena, and his most sublime hope is to marry her, a marriage which would make him the author of Verena as a public advertisement. Pardon forthrightly desires to manipulate Verena, to marry her and then, as Selah puts it, "to produce her in public; . . . [to be] a husband who was at the same time reporter, interviewer, manager, agent, who had the command of the principal dailies, [who] would write her up and work her, as it were, scientifically—the attraction of all this was too obvious to be insisted upon" (p. 210). Verena becomes an object to be produced, a blank whose aesthetic surface allows nearly any representation to be imprinted upon it. Just as Gilbert Osmond chose Isabel Archer for the malleable innocence that allowed her to "reflect off his surface and become a piece of gilded art," so Pardon's ideas for Verena are those of advertising toward the American girl, the iconic figure who was to become the incarnate spirit of American advertising.

James installs a challenger on this field of cultural battle; in opposition both to the "crank" feminism and, as he sees it, the possessive sexuality of Olive Chancellor, and to the advertising predators drawn to Verena, looms Basil Ransom, a Confederate Civil War veteran and an aristocrat fallen on hard times. Choosing a figure from the defeated, poverty-stricken and agricultural South to wage battle against the primary thrust of Eastern cultural hegemony, James ironically allows Ransom to win. His own assessment of the struggle to control and define cultural images, increasingly to be identified with advertising, must have made clear that the American girl could no longer be vanquished and returned to a docile, domestic symbol, simply because she was such good business.

James complicates the duel for Verena, the American advertising girl, by playing it out across cultural, regional, economic, and sexual lines. He pits the romantic and atavistic Southerner, Ransom, the representative of a defeated cultural style and an earlier mode of production, against the industrial wealth of a Vanderbilt-style heir, the cultural values expressed by the Bostonian, Olive Chancellor, and the publicity-mongering of the urban North. All compete for control of Verena in a miniaturization of a larger cultural war, with literature the odd man out.

The world of *The Bostonians* is already beginning to be the world laid out by advertisers; James clearly limns the different nodal points of this "national nerve center": capitalist production, urbanization, mass publics, newspapers synonymous with advertising features, and the cultural predominance of the East. The first systematic consolidation of advertising in the United States, with the creation of advertising agencies and writers, and regularized ties to business, occurred immediately after the Civil War, when Union war veteran J. Walter Thompson came upon the idea of providing a service to newspapers by writing advertisements for them, and selling them to manufacturers. This watershed in consumption took place only after the commercial future of the United States had been decided squarely along the model of the Eastern and Northern industrial complex, and it flourished out of the climate of theater/lecture/performance/medicine show that constituted a cultural style there. The superannuated advertising world of Selah Tarrant is brought into harsh conjunction with the superannuated cultural model presented by Basil Ransom: the latter hopelessly quaint and reactionary, yet chosen by the novel because no other cultural field existed that had not already been mined by advertisement. Selah stands on the cusp of organized advertisement and can only admire it from afar, despite having overlapped with the era, while Ransom stands back from it and decides to retreat into magazine writing—itself coming to be dominated by advertising, especially when, in 1875, J. Walter Thompson's Agency placed the first magazine ads in the *Atlantic Monthly*.[12] Even Ransom, despite having rescued the sublime Verena from her iconicity, will depend on the structures of advertising to see him through his writing career.

In the climax to *The Bostonians* Basil Ransom spends a summer trying to woo Verena away from Olive Chancellor and her lovingly made plans for Verena's triumphal feminist lecture tour. Verena falls in love with Ransom, but remains in Olive's orbit because of her gratitude to her benefactor. At the finale, Ransom arrives at the Boston concert hall where Verena is to make her tour debut. The auditorium is packed and expectant, and Olive has staked her entire reputation on Verena's success, but Ransom breaks Olive's hold over her and whisks Verena out a back door before the recital begins. To make their surreptitious getaway Ransom literally covers Verena in a huge cloak sufficient to mask her beauty; in advertising terms, he has to blot out the spectacle entirely to make it invisible. Verena as American icon is not restored to any semblance of independence; she has to be completely immured in order to disappear. If Ransom "saves" her from being a walking advertisement, he does so only by entombing her. The final image of the novel is of a veiled, effaced Verena, in tears beside Ransom. "It is to be feared that with the union, so far from brilliant, into which she was about to enter, these were not the last she was destined to shed" (p. 390). There is something ominous about the melodramatic lilt of these last lines, an uncomfortable sense that the sexualized advertising icon has been destroyed in order to save it.

Its quasi-optimistic narrative closure aside, *The Bostonians* renders a Barnumized world, one whose interstices are already penetrated by advertisement, whose political, economic, and cultural worlds revolve around it, and whose heroine, saved from "Barnumization" though she may be, is merely a locus of the new determinants of cultural imagery. And even melodramatically sly moral triumphs become moot when moral outrage can be circulated in the vast cycle of promotion, publicity, and advertisement. Matthias Pardon asks Olive Chancellor's sister Mrs. Luna, in an interview, whether she is leaving town because she disapproves of the feminist movement and Olive's promotion of it:

> "Ah, but do protest, madam; let us at least have that fragment! A protest from this house would be a charming note we *must* have— we've got nothing else! . . . I should be so delighted (I see the heading from here, so attractive) just to take down 'What Miss Chancellor's family Think about It!' " . . . Mrs. Luna sprang up again, almost snatching the memoranda out of his hand. "If you have the impertinence to publish a word about me, or to mention my name in print, I will come to your office and make such a scene!" "Dearest lady, that would be a godsend!" (p. 332)

Mrs. Luna's "scene" or tantrum would be recuperated into an advertising scene, a sexually charged encounter whose sexual energy would "write" it on the pages of the newspaper. Verena, feminist or no, has been scenic in just this way, eroticizing her political scene until it becomes advertisement, eroticized by her inscription as an advertising currency. Advertising is a mobile, fluctuating sexual subject position within writing, erotic above all because advertisement puts commodities of all kinds into sexualized narrativity, makes them labile sexualized counters.

THE GAZE: ADVERTISING AS CULTURAL FRAMING

The Bostonians gathers its advertising metaphors from the world of the stage; the novel deploys theaters, posters, performances and stages as textual correlatives for the scene of advertising, and differentiates fictional composition from the more limited horizontal field of the staged spectacle. This aggregation roughly corresponds to the conditions of authorship ascribed to Barnum in the previous chapter. As a specimen case, *The Ambassadors*[13] (1903) can be read as addressed to the problematic of the "assault on the eye" Rowell implied in his description of advertising as a mode of reading. James' fictional techniques bear a confessed kinship to the melodramatics of advertising style, as if he had tamed a Barnum within his midst, but the corporatizing authorship of the agencies proves less amenable. Rowell's writers competed aggressively with literature, and saw words as weapons hurled against the eye. *The Ambassadors* probes this rift by battling with advertising, instead of parodically absorbing it. Long revered as a pinnacle of James' late style, the book is more concretely a tissue of the implications inherent in the rapidly dawning "advertising age." Both its formal features and its "subject" contribute to the unfolding of this complex aesthetic and material web. The text clearly senses the portents heralded in Rowell's, as well as other writers', advertising texts, and marshalls a field of battle against the usurpation and displacement of literature that loomed on the horizon. The book maps out its terrain on economic, social, aesthetic, and moral grounds, simultaneously playing out its "international" theme and its bravura narrative technique. To walk gingerly over the advertising terrain involves letting those latter features of the book recede somewhat into the surrounding landscape; this enterprise also requires casting *The Ambassadors* in a material and ideological light.[14]

The Ambassadors begins with a definite mission: Lewis Lambert Strether, editor of the review out of Woollett, Massachusetts, is despatched by his patroness, Mrs. Newsome, to rescue her son Chad from the coils of Parisian society and its womanhood in order to resume his place in the family business. Once "Parisianized" himself, and aware both of the seemingly salutary changes wrought in Chad and of the urgency and importance of "living while you can," especially since it is too late for him, Strether counsels Chad against the business and against Woollett as a sort of fifth columnist. Brought up short by the sudden revelation that Chad and Madame de Vionnet are having a physical as well as spiritual affair, Strether accommodates this to his newfound intellectual and moral freedom, sees Chad abandon what he, Strether, has come most to value, and returns to America, to live with the new "difference" between himself and his cultural past. This encapsulization of the manifest content of the novel obscures its equally powerful latent subtext; the strands of money and consciousness, appearance and reality, fiction and fact are placed in the crucible of advertising.

The novel is situated at a critical time in the development of American capitalism, and the Newsome family factory and fortune is representative of this. The family now superintends "a big brave bouncing business," a large industry, and, as Strether puts it, "a manufacture that, if it's only properly looked after, may well be on the way to becoming a monopoly." While the factory is a large workshop, almost a "little industrial colony," the essential crux is what is produced there.

"It's a thing. The article produced." Strether's temporizing over what the article *is* is legendary. Under relentless questioning from Miss Gostrey—"Rather ridiculous? Clothes-pins? Saleratus? Shoe-polish?"—he refuses to give way. "No—you don't even 'burn.' I don't think, you know, you'll guess it." Miss Gostrey's exasperated rejoinder is at least partially shared by the reader: "How, then, can I judge how vulgar it is?" (pp. 48–49).

Strether's reluctance to reveal the item arises out of a powerful truth about the stagnation of "gilded-age" American business and its turn to advertisement. As makers of a very common household item the Newsome family was in danger of seeing its profits shrink in the competing welter of similar items being produced. Although Strether argues that the factory makes this product "better than other people can, or than other people, at any rate, do," he also makes clear that the business trembles at a watershed point. The actual product is indeed meaningless, not because vulgar but because it takes on its meaning only in *relation* to its distinction from its perfectly similar imitators. As Stuart Ewen points out in his *Captains of Consciousness*,[15] the last quarter of the nineteenth century found manufacturers in their first wide-scale *need* for advertisement, since America's economy had not previously been one of consumption. With markets saturated by ordinary necessities, and production reaching great heights through more efficient factory techniques, the thrust of American buying patterns had to be transformed. Items that had once been bought in anonymity in bulk quantities at general stores now had to be given a minutely differentiated identity; moreover, individuals had to be taught preferences and wants in order to assimilate the surplus of goods rolling out of the factories. In addition to being a piquant narrative surprise, the silence surrounding the source of the Newsome wealth is also paradigmatic of the nature of the common household item at this point in the development of consumer culture. The invisible, if humble and trivial, product stands in need of the auratization, the narrative halo, that only advertisement will be able to provide. It is literally unnamed until Chad can come back and work that alchemy upon it.

Strether refers to the business as poised on the verge of becoming monopoly capital, and even here the text provides a scrupulously careful material history. Mrs. Newsome's private fortune, which we can assume was melded to her husband's as he built the Woollett empire, derived from her own father's primitive capitalist accumulation. Speaking of Chad, Strether is quite clear on the geneaology of this dubious fortune:

> "The source of his grandfather's wealth—and thereby of his own share in it—was not particularly noble."
> "And what source was it?"
> Strether cast about. "Well-practices."
> "In business? Infamies? He was an old swindler?"
> "Oh," he said with more emphasis than spirit, "I shan't describe *him* nor narrate his exploits." (p. 49)

Nor has Mr. Newsome senior created the factory in any "happy" capitalist spirit. When asked whether the late Newsome had emulated the grandfather, Strether describes him as being "the other side," and as therefore "different." "Better?" Miss Gostrey asks. "No." Nonetheless, this Mr. Newsome was a prophet of sorts, having laid out the plans for the furtherance of his capital ten posthumous years. When Strether has his first meeting with Chad, and is still hot for persuading him to come home, he expounds these plans and expatiates on how lucrative they will be; at the end of the book, when Chad explains his interest in advertising to Strether, he indicates that this was precisely what his late father, and Strether as his emissary, had told him needed to be done. The crisis in capital, reflected in miniature in the Newsome factory fortune, issues at this point in the urgent imperative to advertise, for which Strether was the unwitting spokesman at the beginning of the book. The fluctuations in capital and the presaging of the demise of the Newsome funds without the support of a new aesthetic system, advertising, are clearly demarcated in the ostensibly desultory chat of Strether and Maria Gostrey.

As Strether uncovers the outlines of monopoly capital in the Newsome family, he undergoes a shadowy revelation of his own position as a writer within that capitalist structure. In his abashedness at the seamier side of the factory wealth, despite his brave "they did as everyone does; and (besides being ancient history) it was all a matter of appreciation," with the uneasy pun on "appreciation," he is forced to argue for the moral superiority of Mrs. Newsome as a redemptive fact. Mrs. Newsome is a philanthropist and a cultivated woman, standing outside the sordid circle of her money by virtue of the beneficent use she makes of it, he argues. Strether tiptoes around the disclosure, but acknowledges that the review he edits is entirely subsidized by Mrs. Newsome, and by extension, by the "practices" he had declined to name. In James' appendix to *The Ambassadors* he reveals that Strether is modeled on the writer William Dean Howells, but that he had decided not to make Strether a straightforward author for fear of making the parallelism too close. Instead, he describes Strether as having been a journalist, with "hankerings of serious study, for serious literature, for serious journalism, [who] threw himself, with characteristic intensity, into experiments in that direction" (p. 377). So if Strether is not quite a novelist, he is clearly a writer *manqué*, and as such, his patronage by Mrs. Newsome sets up a clear internal parallel with Chad. Both are writers subsidized by the Newsome fortune; support for writing, in the larger sense, always comes from one of the two faces of capitalism. Chad is to be rewarded for producing a form of literature that will keep a factory on its way toward monopolization; Strether works on the other side, where the profits generated by Chad's kind of writing need their expiation into a "purer" kind of writing.

> ". . . Is it [the Review] her *greatest* fad?" she briskly pursued. "The Review?" He seemed to wonder how he could best describe it. This resulted however but in a sketch. "It's her tribute to the ideal."
> "I see. You go in for tremendous things."
> "We go in for the unpopular side—that is so far as we dare."
> "And how far *do* you dare?"
> "Well, she very far. I much less. I don't begin to have her faith. She provides three-fourths of that. And she provides, as I've confided to you, *all* the money." (p. 50)

The tightrope set up here stretches across another of the abysses of the conversation, with Strether in the position of having to claim that Mrs. Newsome speaks entirely for the "ideal," and for the unpopular side, while it is the very preconditions of the factory system that have created the abuses to which the unpopular side is addressed. Mrs. Newsome's Review allows for a kind of writing that penetrates just so far beyond the veil over the conditions of its own subsidy. Capital wrests control over writing out of the hands of authors and places it into the hands of those in the marketplace, as surely for literature as for advertising. The grim warfare emerges in Strether's analogy for the magazine. Pushing his analysis all the way, to the "very secret of the prison-house" (p. 50), he reveals that they, the unholy alliance that is the Review, "don't sell."

So much a prison house of language is the Review that when Strether is first asked what kind of magazine it is, he replies "it's green," green being the color of the cover. The emphasis falls on the cover because the magazine is a play of surfaces, and in no instance more than in what is printed on that cover. Lambert Strether's name is emblazoned across it, but far from bestowing the Review with a signal of authorship, it gives him his "poor little scrap of identity." "His name on the green cover, where he had put it for Mrs. Newsome, expressed him doubtless just enough to make the world—the world as distinguished, both for more and for less, from Woolett—ask who he was. He had incurred the ridicule of having to have his explanation explained. He was Lambert Strether because he was on the cover, whereas it should have been, for anything like glory, that he was on the cover because he was Lambert Strether" (p. 63).

The pitiful reflection off the green cover is contrasted repeatedly with another wonted stance toward books, symbolized by the lemon-covered editions that proliferate in Paris. Strether has a reverence for these authorless, titleless yellow volumes that bespeaks his nostalgia for books he can imagine are produced in another way, books de-commodified, as it were. In their perfect objectness they are like rare jewels. Strether had once attempted to take some of this essence of the book back with him to America:

> He remembered for instance how he had gone back in the sixties with lemon-colored volumes in general on the brain as with a dozen—selected for his wife too—in his trunk; and nothing had at this moment shown more confidence than this invocation of the finer taste. They were still at home somewhere, the dozen—stale and soiled and never sent to the binder; but what had become of the sharp initiation they represented? They represented now the mere sallow paint on the door of the temple of taste he had dreamed of raising up—a structure he had practically never carried further. (p. 64)

The bookstall, with its "array of literature classic and casual," reminds him of nothing more than an open-air cafe, a place to consume books, which he refrains from buying. He merely wants to *look* at them—"he wasn't there to dip, to consume—he was there to reconstruct." Strether has a flash of this certainty again when he shops a Parisian bookstall and buys himself a seventy-five-volume set of Victor Hugo, this time garbed in imperial red and gold. When he can purchase books, he buys a massive installment, more as a bulwark against losing his newfound insights than anything else. Books outside the market system are his little totems of reassurance. His ultimate epiphany about books, and apparently a sort of *cri de coeur* in the text itself, comes as he waits in an anteroom of Chad's Paris house, a house that Chad is leaving to become an advertiser.

> The novel half uncut, the novel lemon-coloured and tender, with the ivory dagger athwart it like a dagger in a contadina's hair, had been pushed within the soft circle. . . . The night was hot and heavy and a single lamp sufficient; the great flare of the lighted city, rising high, spending itself afar, played up from the boulevard and, through the vague vista of the successive rooms, brought objects into view and added to their dignity. (p. 297)

The unspecified novel is romantically personified as it dances in the center of an island of light, a vista onto the city, a spot of recherché light in reciprocity with the great insubstantial palace of light that is the night city. The butler lays the book out like a gourmet meal or rare bijoux. Reading the book flirts on the edges of a seduction scene.

At one point in the novel Strether is convinced that Chad is a book too, in this same voluptuous sense. He discusses the inscrutable Chad with his artist friend Little Bilham, and the two of them build an extended metaphor about Chad that teases out a comparison to knowledge and sexuality combined in books. Bilham tries to account for the improvement Strether discerns in Chad:

> "I'm not sure he was meant by nature to be so good. It's like the new edition of an old book that one has been fond of—revised and amended, brought up to date, but not quite the thing that one knew and loved. . . . I believe he really wants to go back and take up a career. . . . He won't then be my pleasant well-rubbed old-fashioned volume at all . . ."
>
> "Ah there you are!" Strether exclaimed. "That's just what I want to get at. You speak of your familiar book altered out of recognition. Well, who's the editor?" (p. 115–6)

Reading is again analogous to a warm bath of comfort and familiarity, rather than to the shock and assault of reading in advertising. The irony implicit here is that Chad *cannot* be "read" like a book—he will finally be seen in an unnerving spectacle.

If Chad appears to be altered out of recognition even to the more prescient characters in the book, his reasons for remaining in Paris are more pungently theorized by Jim Pocock, his brother-in-law and an "awful" example of Woollett in action.

> "Well, hanged if I would if *I* were he!"
> "You mean you wouldn't in Chad's place—"
> "Give this up to go back and boss the advertising!"
> There were things in this speech that Strether let pass for the time. "Don't you then think it important the advertising should be thoroughly taken in hand? Chad *will* be, so far as capacity is concerned," he went on, "the man to do it."
> "Where did he get his capacity over here?" Jim asked.
> "He didn't get it over here, and the wonderful thing is that over here he hasn't inevitably lost it. He has a natural turn for business, an extraordinary head. He comes by that," Strether explained, "honestly enough." (p. 225)

This exchange makes clear the expectation that Chad is going back to Woollett revolves around his perceived advertising ability, and the importance of its being taken in hand. As yet, Chad himself has not pronounced on the world of advertising, so thematically it may appear as if advertising twinkles only occasionally across the novelistic firmament. Rather, advertising has all the more presence by being virtually suppressed as an explicit topic after this conversation between Jim and Strether, a taboo both aesthetic and sexual, only to reappear in a very long, climactic interchange toward the end of the book. That interchange leads back to all that has gone before it, a reading that reshapes the contours of the novel.

The preceding chapter contains the famous recognition scene, where Strether accidentally encounters Chad and Madame de Vionnet in a rural park, unmasking them as lovers. The metaphorical system employed in the writing revolves around painting, rather than money or boats or stage sets, other Jamesian stalwarts. In this tightly constructed piece, Strether steps almost literally onto a painted canvas, replicating, in his excursion to the countryside, the scene of a Lambinet landscape painting he had been unable to buy many years ago. The illusion of having walked into a painting is so acute Strether can almost see the gilt frame around what he is experiencing. Into this hyperpictorialized universe come the two lovers floating downstream in a rowboat, adding the perfect complement to the composition. At this juncture the aesthetic metaphors begin to blur back to staging; "Is this fiction or farce?" Strether asks himself. The framing devices, the way of seeing, Strether had been coming to rely upon during his stay in Paris derive from or are analogous to eighteenth-century painting, backed up by the constant textual references to eighteenth-century medals, coins, medallions and friezes. Strether is arrested in the midst of an eighteenth-century gaze, frozen in a superannuated mode of cultural recognition that underscores just how "late" it is for him indeed. The moment of rupture is more than moral, more than characterological; an intruder has stalked onto the cultural field of vision and has halted it, just as advertising eludes the aesthetic lens that would seek to define it.

The text plays with Strether's *frisson*, and the reader's as well, to give us a picture of Strether in his moment of knowledge as a virtually castrated observer of a cultural fiction. His attenuated conversations with Madame de Vionnet, and his more baffling encounters with Chad have actually subjected him to a stage set, a performance directed by Chad that he can only unveil by the shock of recognition. Strether's fictions deceive only himself, while Chad's are manipulated for the deception of others. If Chad and Strether are accordingly set up as rival authors of a sort, Chad, as the advertising writer, is invested in a kind of fiction-making that can penetrate back out into the world, one that can actively make things happen. Strether, in his eighteenth-century guise, must suffer the shock of encountering an unknowable or at least unpredictable style of art. He had come over to France to urge Chad to adopt his advertising career; as the text makes clear, Strether had no idea of the deep naiveté of his knowledge of advertising, a sexual, economic, epistemological ignorance. The two men talk their way around this abyss of vertiginous advertising practice at the end of the novel, when Strether has advised Chad never to give up Madame de Vionnet.

But to no avail. Suddenly abandoning his lover, and with her, presumably, the cultural connotations of classically eighteenth-century European framing, Chad confuses the textual metaphors by profusely praising advertising. Advertisement had been an erased or suppressed term between Chad and Strether, but it erupts here when Chad is on the verge of casting off all the vestiges of Europe. The two men hold their colloquy with Strether's knowledge of the sexual relationship between Chad and Madame de Vionnet as the newly suppressed term. Initially, Strether had felt free to allude to illicit sex and to caution Chad against it; now advertising is the obscene topic Chad insists on discussing.

> [Chad] had been getting some news of the art of advertisement. He came out quite suddenly with his announcement, while Strether wondered if his revived interest were what had taken him, with strange inconsequence, over to London. He appeared at all events to have been looking into the question and had encountered a revelation. Advertising scientifically worked presented itself as the great new force. "It really does the thing, you know." They were face to face under the streetlamp as they had been the first night, and Strether, no doubt, looked blank. "Affects, you mean, the sale of the object advertised?"
>
> "Yes, but affects it extraordinarily, really beyond what one had supposed. I mean of course when it's done as one makes out that, in our roaring age, it *can* be done. I've been finding out a little; though it doubtless doesn't amount to much more than what you originally, so awfully vividly—and all, very nearly, that first night—put before me. It's an art like another, and infinite like all the arts." He went on for the joke of it—almost as if his friend's face amused him. "In the hands, naturally, of a master. The right man must take hold. With the right man to work it *c'est un monde*." (p. 359)

This extraordinary tête-à-tête under the street lamps utterly reverses the gradual progression of Strether's coming into consciousness. Chad's vision of a new world is a violent usurpation of Strether's, a pantomime rivalry. First, Chad traces his revelation of the artistry and infinitude of advertising back to Strether, in what must be for Strether a counterrevolution. The infinitude that has opened up for Strether in Paris, his recognition of the fatal finitude of Woollett and all it stands for, is translated by Chad into the play of an infinitude of appearances, an infinite textual world that only a master can manipulate. Money as a magical object is often invoked in James' texts, both for what it can make visible in the world, and what it can make invisible. What Chad has discovered is that advertising is the infinite, insinuating art that *makes* money, an aesthetic with the erotic twist of consummating itself, discharging itself directly as money. "My interest's purely platonic," Chad avers. "There at any rate the fact is—the fact of the possible. I mean the money in it."

On the other side of this fountainlike literature of money Chad now perceives death. Although claiming he will cling to Madame de Vionnet "to the death," he counterpoises that romantic, European death-in-life to the resurrecting power of the tumid money in advertising, the force that gives it an erotic charge sufficient to supplant his relationship with Madame de Vionnet: advertising will substitute for Madame de Vionnet in Chad's erotic economy. Strether watches Chad mouth his denials, but all the time sees him on the verge of doing some peculiar autoerotic dance-step, "an irrelevant horn-pipe or jig." Chad can hardly suppress the intoxication of advertising, the erotic promise it holds for a master. Artistry always commands a sexual staging ground for James—see "The Figure in the Carpet" and others—and Chad here dances the crude, somewhat blatant dance that mimes the sexual stratagems of advertising. Strether is privy to yet another primal scene.

Strether's final indignity is to suffer being told he is the panderer, the seducer, who has brought this enticement to Chad. "You're exciting," Chad says, as a parting shot, making it obvious that in some measure the de-eroticization of Strether has enabled Chad's tumescent triumph. Their discursive rivalry has its strict erotic economy as well. If, as claimed earlier in this argument, advertising is a mode of reading that assaults, envelops, seduces the eyes, then Chad's ability to "assault" Strether's eyes, to force Strether to be a voyeur at a framed scene of sexuality, is similar in kind to the energy released by the reading of an advertisement, in which all consumers become hapless, voyeuristic readers. Strether certainly has experienced something of a moral sea-change at novel's end, a glimpse of what it means to "live," but it is also undeniable that he ends frozen, acquiescent and resigned, characterological metaphors for the impossibility of stopping the juggernaut of advertising, inmixed as it is with all the aesthetic and epistemological referents of the novel.

Strether ends by observing the spectacle, in Williams' phrase, but the observation brings about the inexorable collision of two kinds of writing. The collision takes place in Europe, where Chad's new commitment to advertising stands out more sharply against the European scene, under James' harsh, raking international spotlight. In *The American Scene* James reverses its trajectory, turning his Europeanized sensibility toward the now alien American landscape, an abyss of advertisement.

THE AMERICAN GIRL

Henry James' late work, *The American Scene* (1907),[16] can be read as the structural analysis of the social conditions in America allowing the advertising society to come into being. His book commemorates the trip he took in 1904, after returning from twenty years in Europe, a "pilgrim" come to see his own native land. The patchwork of places and sights—St. Augustine, Newport, the Waldorf-Astoria, Hoboken— may seem impressionistic renderings of his journey, but above all the text explores explicitly the phenomenon of a capitalist culture that has come into its own since his departure, and that is a striking harbinger of modern life to come. While the text fetishizes place over any other analytic touchstone, James never merely records place *per se;* each stop becomes a site of investigation, and what the text is doggedly alert to is the establishment of an image-based economy, a political economy already operating along the lines later discussed by Gramsci, Weber, Barthes, and Debord.

James' text is able to discern these contours partially due to the sheer biographical fact of his long absence—after a self-imposed exile he has a measure of critical distance. But in addition those features of his style that often relegate him to the high cultural antipodes of criticism—the extreme valorization of sight and the emphasis on spectacle—make his textual discernment paradoxically more cogent. During his years away, America had become a mass culture, and James' language can "see" it, *in flagrante.*

He found a "conception of publicity *as* the vital medium organized with the authority with which the American genius for organization, put on its mettle, alone could organize it." His trip is a "magic lantern show" of the workings of publicity, of the changes it has wrought. Everywhere James looks actively for history, but finds it has been usurped by the fictions of publicity. The "restless analyst," as he calls himself, tries in vain to *find* history in America—it has been replaced by spectacle, with advertisement as its motor:

> He has learnt fact—he learns greatly in America—to mistrust any pleas for it [history] *directly* made by money, which operates too often as the great puffing motor-car framed for whirling him, in his dismay, quite away from it . . . he sees the same [sources], which are the references by which interest is fed, used again and again,

with a desperate economy; sees the same ones, even as the human heroes, celebrities, extemporized lions or scapegoats, required social and educational figureheads and "values," having to serve in *all* the connections and adorn all the tales. That is one of the liveliest of his American impressions. He has at moments his sense that, in presence of such vast populations and instilled, emulous demands, there is not, outside the economic, enough native history, recorded or current, to go round. (p. 183)

The historical dislocation James was able to chart was the eradication of public history at the behest of avoracious publicity. Mrs. Jarley's waxwork show in *The Old Curiosity Shop* had advertised itself by staging history, putting on an ever-changing show where historical figures made chameleonlike changes according to the needs of the audience. American advertising denatures history like the waxwork show on a grand national scale, indiscriminately using the same troupe of heroes and celebrities to produce history as a spectacular panorama, performed to the dictates of the money behind the scenes. James is jarred by the enormity of history's absence, which forces his own journey to reenact the freeze-frame spectacles of historical magic lantern shows. All that is visible is "the whole American *spectacle*" (italics mine). Advertising sets the conditions for James' own essayistic sections, precedes his vision and frames America for him like Chad and Madame de Vionnet.

James looks for the theater of operations of this spectacle, knowing of course that it has capital behind it. One place he finds an analog to it is in the theater itself, where relations of the audience to the play have been drastically rearranged along the lines that have reordered the body politic. As an index of this rearrangement James describes the consumption of candy in the theater, the addition of a purely *advertised* good to the setting where narcissistic identification once reigned supreme. If James had once found the "very flower of the ideal" in one of Barnum's theater shows, he now envisages America as if it were a vast theater, but one that has lost the secret eros of identification between the actors and the audience. He imagines a Shakespearean theatrical dynamic with a vital, multivalent appeal to all classes, now replaced by an alienating theater whose audience does not know the lines, needing to be placated by candy since they are precluded from understanding the play. The poorer classes who visit the theater have been inoculated into a "cult of candy," and James moves from this symbolic inoculation to the entire range of advertising-induced desires:

> Wages, in the country at large, are largely manners—the only manners, I think it fair to say, one mostly encounters; the market and the home therefore look alike dazzling, at first, in this reflected, many-colored lustre. It speaks somehow, beyond anything else, of the diffused sense of material ease—since the solicitation of sugar couldn't be so hugely and artfully organized if the response were not clearly proportionate. But how is the response itself organized, and what are the other items of that general budget of labor, what in especial are the attenuations of that general state of fatigue, in which so much purchase power can flow to the surprisingly superfluous? The wage-earners, the toilers of old, notably in other climes, were known by the wealth of their songs; and has it, on these lines, been given to the American people to be known by the number of their candies? (p. 197)

James is not overly obsessed with confectionery here; in a meticulous way he has traced the pattern whereby an artificial need has come to be a substitute for indigenous culture, a species of aesthetic class erotics.

Other venues for the selling of spectacle include the store and the hotel. James' famous disquisition on the Waldorf-Astoria, embodying the "hotel-spirit" of America, relates directly to his critique (p. 102–3). The hotel acts as an incoherent temple and labyrinth of money, which turns out also to be a maze of display where an unattached and de-historicized populace gathers. James returns to this image later in the book and darkens it—this time the "hotel" of mass culture becomes a cage:

> I seemed to see again the whole housed populace move as in a mild and consenting suspicion of its captured and governed state, its having to consent to inordinate fusion as the price of what it seemed pleased to regard as inordinate luxury. Beguiled and caged, positively thankful, in its vast vacancy, for the sense and the definite horizon of a cage, were there not yet cases and connections, in which it still dimly made out that its condition was the result of a compromise into the detail of which there might some day be an alarm in entering? (p. 239)

Throughout the text the metaphors of reflection, gilding, mirror, store window, and stage sound the note of a culture whose entrapping fictions are fueled, through the conduit of advertising and publicity, by the "raw wealth and power" of capitalism.

Another note sounded in *The American Scene* makes explicit the sexual side of this image system. James finds that American capitalism has stratified itself, not only across class lines but across sexual ones as well. American women have to bear the entire freight of aestheticizing and embroidering the cultural veils shrouding commercial activity. For James, American men on the whole are ciphers, completely taken over by business, while the women do not enjoy, as Ann Douglas would have it,[17] free cultural reign, but are instead commodified:

She has been, accordingly, about the globe, and . . . infinitely amused the nations. It has been found among them that, for more

An early version of the woman serving as the interest on the money; a home-grown example of the placement of women within the commercial nexus of the commodity form.

Advertising photographs taken by Mrs. G. Bowen at her photographic studio, Waterloo, Iowa, 1890. From the Bella C. Landauer advertising collection.

Courtesy of the New-York Historical Society, New York City

reasons than we can now go into, her manner of embodying and representing her sex has fairly made of her a new human convenience, not unlike fifty of the others, of a slightly different order, the ingenious mechanical appliances, stoves, refrigerators, sewing-machines, type-writers, cash-registers, that have done so much, in the household and the place of business, for the American name. (p. 347)

The commodification cuts both ways in James' analysis; not only is the American woman marketed globally in order to sell the products of capitalism, but she is also marketed *to*. James imagines a young American girl cognizant of this fact and wondering how "I can supply *all* the interest, all the interest that isn't on the money?" (p. 431). American girls literally provide this interest in the denuded cultural scene James observes; but they also provide more and more of the representational scheme of the consumer society. Isabel Archer and others like her become images powerful enough to create desire and to market it. The American girl is encountered in "the great glare of her publicity," a publicity that has produced a monstrous misalliance with the "bagmen" of commerce. James' novels had previously approached the subject of woman as the reflecting icon of culture, and here he points directly toward this process as a mainstream activity of consumer culture.

James' texts parallel the national fascination with the American girl. His heroines are nearly all representative of this type: Isabel Archer, Verena Tarrant, Daisy Miller, Milly Theale, Maggie Verver, and others are all, whatever their differences, counters of "innocence" in tangled commercial dramas. American advertising mirrored this cultural preoccupation by pushing the American girl to the fore of its own staging. The invention of the Gibson girl by Charles Dana Gibson at the turn of the century is one instance of the commodification of the image of the American girl, and American advertisers found that she was as exportable as James' American girls had proven to be.

The cooptation of a certain type of female beauty for wider cultural ends causes James to question whether there can *be* a place for the aesthetic in capitalist culture. In the internal movement of the book he has first addressed the problem of history—how it can become virtually invisible in such a society. Looking for cultural space for the beautiful, James is forced to conclude that it has been usurped by the spectacles of publicity. Returning full circle to the theatrical metaphor that always activates his thought, James ends his text by conjuring America as a vast stage of entertainment, a theatrical spectacle forced on a populace who have no other viable methods of staging themselves. The spectacle hides the actual currents of power in the society, but it also does more—it insists on producing the desire for itself.

> All this constitutes a vast home-grown provision for entertainment, rapidly superseding any that may be borrowed or imported, and that indeed already begins, not invisibly, to press for exportation. As to quality, it looms immense. . . . It is the public these appearances refer us to that becomes thus again the more attaching subject; the public so placidly uncritical that the whitest thread of the deceptive stitch never makes it blink, and sentimental at once with such inveteracy and such simplicity that, finding everything everywhere perfectly splendid, it fairly goes upon its knees to be humbuggingly humbugged. (p. 459)

James' critical vision returns to invoke Barnumization once more, as the conqueror of the American scene, the literature of a fallen romance. I have called *The American Scene* an allegorization of the discursive rivalry between advertisement and literature; each romance *topos* James cites, from the regional landscapes to the romantic topos or space of the American girl, is an allegorized site of the struggle. No mere "witness" to the eviscerating energies of advertisement and publicity, James permits his own writing to become the scene of battle. The romance *topoi* of the scenes of the book are like pitched tents on that battlefield—James allows his own pivotal textual nodes to take the fire of the advertising system. Everywhere James transforms his apparatus of theatrical metaphor to deploy it against the culturally theatrical stagings of advertisement.

The erotics of advertisement was thematized in *The Bostonians*, in Verena Tarrant's hypercharged advertising glamour; in *The Ambassadors* advertisement is a kind of carnal epistemology, a writing so "knowing" it can constitute desire. If we read *The American Scene* as a heightened allegory the erotic text is similarly heightened, not to say galvanic—the public becomes a ravished, insatiable Public, brought "home" again and again by the sexual ministrations of advertising as a scene of writing. To return to the quote above, where the public "becomes thus again the more attaching subject," it takes little over-reading to discern the public on its knees, at the end of this passage, begging for what James might call, following Strether, "well—a practice," the superlative erotic surrender to humbuggery. This is consensual humbuggery, it is clear—the public, too, goes down humbuggingly, with no provocation whatsoever. Humbuggery is an erotic thralldom that relies on the pleasure principle of repetition, where individual advertisements are those repetitions with a difference.

Advertising has gone beyond romance, in James' textual engagements with it—in *The American Scene* it achieves the status of an American sublime. This sublimity will rearrange all the counters on the cultural board, especially the position of literature. James' work testifies to the porosity of modern discourses to the invasion of advertisement, a trick that has been played out in the relatively brief span of years from his own enchanted boyhood thralldom in the kingdom of Barnum. Acknowledging the hegemony of a discourse that draws on the enchantments of theater, the scene of narrative, the thrust of desire, and the mythologization of history, James' text pulls back to see its own place within these nets of desire. What Mrs. Luna had once said about Verena Tarrant, a comment then safely lodged within James' own novel, is now appropriate as an allegorical recognition, as well as judgment, of America itself—America is a walking advertisement.

4 • Advertising & the Scene of Writing in *Ulysses*

> Our language can be seen as an ancient city: a maze of little streets and squares, of old and new houses, and of houses with additions from various periods; and this surrounded by a multitude of new boroughs with straight regular streets and uniform houses.
>
> Ludwig Wittgenstein, *Philosophical Investigations*, 18

HAVING BORROWED ITS TECHNIQUES FROM those of aesthetic representation, most specifically narrative fiction, and having created a system of exchange modeled on that of literary production, advertising by 1920 had established itself as a prerequisite for doing business of any kind. Ads had become a self-referential system, an exotic form of social reading whose meanings far exceeded the original ostensive meaning of early ads: here is announced my product. The configuration of ads told a collective story—a narrative—to its society at a given moment. The sudden profusion of ads and their creation of social narrative in a newly dis-continuous way naturally reshaped the reception of narrativity as a whole.

Advertising succeeded because it pried loose other languages from their referents, and set them in juxtaposition, creating a new represen-tational system. *Ulysses'* own juxtaposition of absolutely disparate styles, its use of language as counter and emblem, can only take place in this context. The book's constant advertising refrains—for Plum-tree's Potted Meats, Epp's Cocoa, Pear's Soap, Hely's men, etc.— reiterate the voices of advertising culture, emanating from invisible sources, yet filling all the interstices of the world. The wrapped lemon soap, Sunday-supplement calendar picture of a nymph, et al. are among the objects Joyce chooses to remythologize, because they have already been mythologized through advertising. *Ulysses* is a narrative in a culture being expressed, furthered, and masked by a new literature with no discernible author and no particular reader—advertising.

This opens a chink in the traditional reading of *Ulysses* as the hallowed text of modernism. Advertising and mass cultural forms become the matrix of its textual practices, set within a parody frame of scholastic and classical reference. The materiality, the pervasiveness, the hieroglyphic and the collectively authored characteristics of advertising become the enabling situation of modernist prose. This chapter will approach advertising as typifying the modern condition of writing: it presages the "death of the humanist subject" of contemporary theory, produces the first intersubjectivity of reading and the formation of the subject in a uniquely historical and imagistic way, and offers a glimpse, however fallen, of the utopian powers of collective consciousness in a mass age.

I have been exploring the collision of literature and advertisement, in each case claiming that a by-product of the investigation has been a critical reappraisal of the novelists in question. In this chapter the focus is on one signal work—*Ulysses*—and the secondary proposal is that the lens of advertisement[1] offers a serious new vantage point on this text.

Two of the most stimulating recent critiques of the book have come from Fredric Jameson and Franco Moretti, whose essays were published when this study was essentially complete.[2] Jameson sets *Ulysses* against the background of the reification of life, and especially city life, in the late capitalist period. The repetitive network of the novel, which demands a back-and-forth reading, like thumbing through an encyclopedia in some ways, can

> be equally understood as a process whereby the text itself is unsettled and undermined, a process whereby the universal tendency of its terms, narrative tokens, representations, to solidify into an achieved and codified symbolic order as well as a massive narrative surface, is perpetually suspended. I will call this process "de-reification," and I first want to describe its operation in terms of the city itself . . . the classical city is defined essentially by the nodal points at which all those pathways and trajectories meet, or which they traverse: points of totalisation, we may call them, which make shared experience possible.[3]

Jameson enlarges his determinative term "de-reification" to serve as an explanation of the linguistic nature of this text as well.

Unsurprisingly that mediation will have to be linguistic, yet it will have to define a kind of speech which is neither uniquely private nor forbiddingly standardized in an impersonal public form, a type of discourse in which the same, in which repetition, is transmitted again and again through a host of eventful variations, each of which has its own value. That discourse is called gossip. Gossip is indeed the very element in which reference—or, if you prefer, the "referent" itself—expands and contracts, ceaselessly transformed from a mere token, a notation, a short-hand object, back into a full-dress narrative.[4]

Franco Moretti will also locate the book at a crisis point in the modern world, the "long good-bye" to the liberal form of bourgeois society and the definitive decline of the self-regulating market, of which World War I was only symptomatic. "As the poet of the crisis of classical capitalism in its classical area of development (overproduction), Joyce offers us a monumental autopsy of an entire social formation."[5] Social relationships in *Ulysses* will appear only through the lens of consumption; for Moretti, Joyce scathingly satirizes Bloom as a petty-bourgeois philistine, Molly as the quintessential consumer, Stephen as an intellectual worker who can put his culture to no use. Moretti emphasizes that, in contrast to T. S. Eliot, Joycean mythology and history are complementary, both presupposing and neutralizing one another. Advertising, as the apotheosis of commodity fetishism, supplies the mythology: "Stream of consciousness and crisis of the ideology of the free individual meet under the ensign of advertising. This is the new 'myth' to which Bloom . . . succumbs with increasing regularity."[6] *Ulysses* utterly refuses to give priority to any literary style or "high art" expression, as "the fundamental intention of his novel [is] the systematic refusal to assume *one* style as the privileged vehicle of expression. What has been said for style is also true of ideology in *Ulysses*. There is nothing *but* ideology in this novel: it is a universe of false consciousness."[7]

Reification, commodity fetishism, capitalist crisis are analyses held in common by Jameson and Moretti, and surely do offer pivotal bases on which to establish a new reading of the book and its modern importance. *Pace* Jameson, however, I will attempt to show in what follows that a de-reifying *Gerede* does not shape the language of *Ulysses*—always and everywhere that *Volksprache* has been replaced by a linguistic form much more truly formative of the linguistic response of Joyce's text—advertising. And *contra* Moretti, whose placement of the book in the context of mass culture is highly convincing and, in my view, a critically important step, it is not the case that all cultural languages are given equal weight in the text: advertising is the premier language of the book, and Joyce's novelistic response to this is neither dour, despairing, nor condemnatory in a Lukácsian sense.[8]

By pursuing advertisement through *Ulysses* several key elements become clear. My primary, and no doubt most disturbing, claim is that advertising language is responsible for the techniques of "high modernism"—to dissect, analyze, valorize these formal achievements purely from within the novelistic tradition, or as a "high art" phenomenon, is to be blind to the exhilarating *realism* of *Ulysses*. Advertising language out in the actual streets turns the tricks that *Ulysses* then imports into its structures—on a strictly formalist level, the innovations flow from the mass cultural paradigm to the novelistic techniques, and not in reverse order. The whole book performs a tango with advertisement, and is set to its music.

This may sound like an abrupt demotion from canonical status: what is still sacred if the great forger of modernism, Joyce as the sublimely rarefied artificer of a notoriously difficult book, is essentially a forgerer, borrowing advertisement's capital to turn to his own uses? In fact, several salutary things happen at once. The radical separation of mass and "high" culture, never tenable in practice but generally a received truth in criticism, becomes impossible. The endless circular mystifications of "how he did it" vanish as well, to be replaced with a more fruitful consideration of languages coming into conjunction. *Ulysses* becomes part of a recognizable and still contemporary modern world, and its form no longer languishes as scripture for critics to pore over— the language of *Ulysses* is a material register of mass, modern culture's inroads in language and thought. This chapter will focus on advertising as a new and crucial literature with the power to transform literary writing.

A second focus, then, attempts to illuminate these mechanisms. What are the features of advertising language built into, re-deployed, eviscerated, or celebrated by *Ulysses?* Advertising is a material thematic in the book, beginning with Bloom's job but not stopping there; advertising reorients the nature of print and reading; it reinfuses the mythological into daily life and language practice; it substitutes for the authoritative desire structures of religion; it redefines the relationship of language to referent, of word to thing; women are refracted in advertising discourse in altered ways; and finally, advertisement allows for the metacommentary on language itself that is the hallmark of *Ulysses*.

Ulysses represents the third phase of the dialectic of literature and advertising. In the early stage, culminating in the example of Dickens' work, advertisement shares conditions that bring the realist novel into being, and it begins to model itself on literature. The second development brings literature and advertisement into open rivalry, with literature on the defensive, as evidenced in the examination of James' work. By the time of the writing of *Ulysses* advertising has begun its *floruit:* so firmly ensconced as the necessary accompaniment to production of all kinds that literature begins to be colonized by it.[9] *Ulysses* records this process, but by no means succumbs passively to advertising's takeover. The novel incorporates the interloper, and puts advertising language to work for its own purposes. One does not diminish the novel by showing how it refashions advertising techniques—*Ulysses* is all the more central as the site of a Pyrrhic victory over advertising.

This victory is Pyrrhic because literature cannot flick away advertising like a bothersome fly, as Nietzsche enjoined the transvaluated man to dismiss those of lesser sensibility. Advertising's presence changes the scene: *Ulysses* absorbs it to get beyond it, leaving Joyce the final option of creating his own language or nothing. Voilá, *Finnegans Wake*. It is important to stress, however, amidst these military metaphors, that Joyce was a devotee of advertisement, relishing its Promethean features. He was addict of *Tit-Bits*-style puzzles and contests, an ad collector, and an avid fan of mass-cultural lore. One also remembers that Joyce ran a film theater for a brief period, writing its advertisements which he even published abroad, that he asked friends to send him ads when on trips, advised Harriet Weaver incessantly about advertising campaigns for his own work, and was shattered when he did not win one of the grand prizes for his solution to a London newspaper puzzle contest. "I make notes on the backs of advertisements," he wrote in 1917. He loved punning on advertising slogans—"His Mastiff's Voice"—and writing "fake" ads, like this one for Italo Svevo's *Zeno:*

—a colored picture . . . representing two young ladies seated at a table on which a book stands upright, with title visible, and underneath the picture three lines of simple dialogue, for example;
Ethel: Does Cyril spend too much on cigarettes?
Doris: Far too much.
Ethel: So did Percy (points)—till I gave him *Zeno.*[10]

And now that the new version of the Ellmann biography has come out, one can breathe new meaning into Bloom's imagined ad for a lover, "To aid gentleman in literary work." Joyce's identical ad brought him an actual love affair.[11]

These biographical shards can at least convince us that Moretti is perhaps too swift to impute disdain, contempt, or hatred for Bloom to Joyce. Bloom may be a "parody of Benjamin Franklin," but we're meant to love him. The extent to which *Ulysses* idealizes Bloom seems rather shameless, but here it is an important corrective to the automatic assumption that Joyce, or *Ulysses*, loathes and reviles the empty mediocrity of advertisement and advertising culture. The unabashed sentimentality of *Ulysses* is rarely acknowledged; nonetheless, critics and readers including myself participate in it in all the endearing analyses they write, and all the day-long Bloomsday festivals they support. One has to be willfully incensed by the moralistic abstraction of commodity fetishism to miss seeing that while *Ulysses* anatomizes modern, reified existence, much of its pleasure stems from the melodramatic grandeur of Bloom, a Chaplin as advertising agent, and the pratfalls he takes, which Joyce himself loved, within mass commodity culture. This "sentimentality" is a core feature of the book, and a core *strength*, as it was for Dickens. *Ulysses* is indisputably allied to mass cultural narrative roots, to Chaplin films, fancy postcards, to *Tit-Bits* itself. The "everyday" is charged with an extraordinary effusion of sentiment and wonder taken from popular culture, mass culture, above all working class culture. Advertising is here a class diction.

ADVERTISING AND EVERYDAY LIFE: BLOOM AS BRICOLEUR

If advertising acts as an organizing principle in *Ulysses*,[12] and also as a necessarily prior condition for the creation of its "literary" techniques, the veritable site of advertisement within the text could be concretized in the figure of Leopold Bloom. Immediately upon his appearance in the "Calypso" chapter the textual bonds that have linked its "Telemachiad" to a previous work, *Portrait of the Artist as a Young Man*, are snipped. Bloom is ensconced in a different textual, as well as historical, world: the waves of his thought blow in from no Aristotelian shores, but rather lap against the real-life flotsam of *Matcham's Masterstroke*, *Tit-Bits*, posters, exercise pamphlets, Plumtree's potted meat, and Hely's sandwichboard men. Language vigorously inserts itself in the world of Dublin, 1904, thinking itself through Bloom even as he begins his everyday activities.

Leopold Bloom is imbricated in the world of advertisement in the literal sense, as well as insofar as he demarcates an alternative textual positioning to those Stephen Dedalus or Molly Bloom make available. He works as an advertising canvasser, and through most of the book practices his job, albeit in a desultory and haphazard manner, one in fact related to the nature of advertisement itself. Bloom's position as an advertising canvasser is somewhat anachronistic by the professional and institutional standards of advertising even in 1904. Advertising canvassers harkened back to a previous stage before agencies had established their sway over advertising activity. In this sense, Bloom replicates the actual historical position of Ireland vis-à-vis England at the time, in that the deluge of professional advertisement that is shown to cover Dublin is virtually all produced outside it, in London, or, in rare instances, in America. The secondary, colonized position of Ireland's general economy holds true for its control over the flow of advertising images and texts. These proceed from an outside source, while the local needs for advertising that are inevitable in a world transformed by it are supplied in old-fashioned and often *personal* ways by those, like Bloom, connected with advertising at its periphery.[13]

The canvasser operated as a free-lance liaison between the newspaper and the company or manufacturer, trying to interest both sides in coming together for an ad. It was incumbent on a canvasser, as an intermediary, to seek out a variety of newspapers, learn their circulation and styles, ingratiate himself with editors, account managers, and even printers, and correspondingly to find shops, firms, or businesses willing to place appropriate ads in those papers. Canvassing was a highly tenuous activity because so much could go wrong at both ends of the transaction—newspapers could be recalcitrant about accepting ads, harsh about demanding payment, and also liable to inflate their rate of circulation to unscrupulously attract advertisers. On the other hand, canvassers had to convince small firms of the very value of advertisement, particularly in urban "villages" like Dublin, either to invent the ads or refashion them, and then to continue pleading with their clients to run the ads regularly, or risk losing an entire account. Translated into the sexual force-field of the novel, Bloom as canvasser is pimp, matchmaker, fertilizer, and midwife simultaneously. His advertising canvassing can be superimposed over the Circean transformations he undergoes in a direct parallel. The system Bloom works in most nearly resembles the conditions obtaining before Mitchell founded the first advertising agency in England in the 1840s, where independent middlemen, often coffee-house owners, set up shop as go-betweens for newspapers and small companies. Bloom is pursuing an outdated and very minor-league aspect of the career of advertising, but one that reflects the imperial status of British advertising firms and their more highly developed connections to capital and to urban markets, both impossible to attain in Ireland. In 1904, advertising agencies in London numbered in the hundreds, whereas newspapers had formed their own account managing departments specifically to sell advertising space. Advertising had become too complex and too integral a part of the economy to be left to the vagaries of the individual canvasser. The "art" and "science" elements of advertising increased the pressure for trained copywriters and for statistically informed salesmen, squeezing out the marginal roles played by Bloom and others like him. Neither competent to write and illustrate "big" ads, nor conversant with the marketing information needed to snare the really big accounts—for example, one of the only export items indigenous to Dublin, Guinness Stout, had its ads prepared by the top London firms—Bloom is permanently on the periphery of advertising, barely making a living in one of the few astronomically growing businesses before World War I. The incredible specificity of Bloom's labor, gleaned in bits throughout *Ulysses*, starkly disputes the traditional complaint that there is no work shown in the book, but additionally makes possible new historical and political readings. Bloom occupies a language colony, performing a variety of services for it, but also standing in a dialectical relation to it. In this sense his work is akin to the textual labor of the book as a whole, written outside Ireland but also in opposition to the British control of the English language. Bloom cannot achieve mastery over the advertising process that forges connections within Dublin, but he is able, in the profusion of his advertising ideas and in his reworking of the advertising slogans running through him, to fashion a mosaic of advertisement that does become independent of and dominant over its source.

Once it is clear that Bloom's job is a carefully chosen and pivotal element in *Ulysses*, it still remains to be seen why Bloom is marginalized in just this way. The range of other petty bourgeois occupations is apparently large enough to make this particular choice a significant one—Bloom could be a bookseller, a small-time promoter of musicales, a minor journalist, a lab assistant, for example, but he is none of these. These putative occupations cannot perform the same textual function that "advertising canvasser" apparently can—Bloom's nominal job is seminal to the novel in ways that have nothing to do with the naturalistic need to find a career for the novel's protagonist. Bloom's job is as accidental as are the erstwhile careers of Bouvard and Pecuchét; "advertising" participates in textual meaning here to the same degree that "copying" locates the textual provenance of Flaubert's book.

First of all, the advertising canvasser not only occupies an intermediary business role by definition, but mediates in the life of the city, especially the modern city, as well. Bloom stands between the economic base of Dublin—its manifold shops, pubs, and private services, and what could be called its superstructure, i.e., the newspaper offices, cultural productions, and social rituals he has contact with. Advertising is the only profession that subtends these two demarcated areas of modern urban society, participating in both the commercial and the aesthetic faces of Dublin. Bloom's constant perambulations are the famous basis for the laying down of the text's structure, but his canvassing traversals are also commodity paths carved through Dublin. The geography of the text not only obeys a diagrammatic parallel to Ulysses' voyages, it also maps itself along the networks of transportation, communication, and monetary exchange available in Dublin. Bloom's path follows the pub connections, it roams from store to store; he himself suggests a new tram line direct to the cemetery, sets up a classified ad network, and follows up on concert tour ideas. His ad background alone makes him a Hermes of Dublin.

Dublin also has a unique relationship to advertisement, one that is analogous to the position of Ireland as a whole. Despite being the capital city, Dublin has no vital economic or cultural function. As mentioned, virtually the only export product is Guinness Stout, and

Ulysses makes much mention of the brewery, the bottles, and the ale itself. As a colonial possession of Great Britain, Ireland remains deliberately undeveloped, and this stasis and sense of redundancy is particularly acute in Dublin as Joyce writes of it. Advertising figures prominently in Dublin's colonial underdevelopment. One index of this is that the litany of advertising tags and slogans so often encountered in the book are nearly without exception exhortations for British or American products. Epps Cocoa, Plumtree's potted meat, Pear's Soap, Crown Derby Porcelain, and Hamilton Long's syringe each have distinctive and ineluctable narratives attached to them, and their "voices" are constant refrains in the novel. However, these are also outside voices, the visible and audible expressions of the very real economic triumph of England over Ireland, taking up most of the language space available. Cultural hegemony is not only a matter of enforcing political and social standards; advertisements too can be a language of colonization. Any citizen of Dublin can theoretically retreat into a bar, speak Gaelic (a practice reserved for obtuse Englishmen in *Ulysses*) and discuss the political vagaries of the Sinn Fein, but it is still impossible to escape the haunting refrain: "Good morning, have you used Pear's Soap today?" Advertisements seep into the unlikeliest places, lodging in new cultural interstices, so that a city like Dublin finds itself linguistically colonized through it as well.

The first two chapters of Bloom's appearance in the novel, "Calypso" and "Lotus Eaters" using the traditional terms, inaugurate the everydayness of the speech of advertising. Bloom's matutinal duties are scrutinized with care, but this is not chiefly a matter of establishing his profoundly "earthly" nature, in contradistinction to Stephen's more rarefied concerns. Bloom is established as a powerful alternating current of language, and also as a transformer station for everyday language. Bloom receives the signals that the culture is sending out, and he makes his own mix of them. Every activity, however humble, underscores Bloom's conduction of this electrical current, not because some facile equation of language and text is being made, but because the new mode of orientation Bloom expresses is indeed language as a *form of life*, language with epistemological, visual, political, and sexual consequences, shaped through a mass lexicon. In this reading, Stephen Dedalus no longer takes precedence as an "artist" or an "intellectual." Bloom is in fact our text's intellectual figure: his energetic consciousness, comprised though it is of the leavings of mass languages, is a kind of window into the general intellectuality that Gramsci made a case for.[14] Is this to exalt *Tit-Bits* and the Sunday Supplement over Stephen's discussions of *Hamlet?* In a sense the text does make available a rereading of those materials and of what their presence entails for culture as a whole, and it is not a univocal one.

As Bloom moves through Dublin advertising is one of his primary ways of reading the inner and outer worlds that surround him. He charts his bearings through his culture's most salient signs. The constantly unfurling "stream of consciousness" that is Bloom's narrative style is largely made up of his "mind" wending its way through the eddies, currents, and shorelines of advertising or advertised goods. Bloom is preternaturally alert to all advertising tokens. Like Adam, who is given the gift of naming all things in the world, Bloom enters an already named world that he nonetheless takes the time to articulate. Beginning his day's agenda, he peeps into his own hat to read its mute sign—"Plasto's high grade ha" with the "t" of resolution sweated off. Bloom starts his itinerary by donning this hat and simultaneously accepting himself as the subject of advertising, and in a larger sense, as a subject formed by advertising. The strong reference here is to *Bouvard et Pecuchét*. The two copyists first discover their affinity for each other by each staring into their worn-off hat-bands, and in fact "introduce" themselves through the arbitration of that remnant of commercial language. For the doughty French copyists, about to embark on a fallen pastoral idyll where the language of the metropolis (of institutions and public discourse) can ostensibly be shed, the hat bands serve as a harbinger of the power names will have to define them, leaving them accepting their final fates as eternal copiers. Bloom has no foil, nor will he accept language and social life as strictly *idées reçues:* you *can* do things with words, however monolithic they may seem to be. Bloom dons his hat, but not in order to become a copyist. There is a private message for him in the special way the words have been sweated off his hat—his own alchemical perspiration has already altered the equation. And Bloom will continue to be an alembic filter of advertisement.

As Bloom steps out into the sunlight on this Adamic day he passes a labeled van carrying Boland's bread. This innocuous moving advertisement prompts a reverie about bread that immediately jolts Bloom into the dark gloaming of an exotic advertisement; in the middle of the sunlit sidewalk a scenario unfurls, the Oriental exotica adumbrated in so many advertisements, particularly those for cigarettes. "High wall: beyond strings twanged. Night sky moon, violet, colour of Molly's new garters" (p. 57). Bloom's inner theatre reprises an advertisement that magically transports him to the stage, although it is a dramatization in which items from his own everyday life figure prominently.[15] The ad acts as a miniature cinematic moment, its desire structure—toward the Orient, voluptuous women, indolent settings—redirected from the product to Bloom's private stock of worries and fantasies about his wife, their sexuality, and possible modes of representing it (violet garters).

Insinuated back into the quotidian, Bloom is brought up short by passing Larry O'Rourke's pub. "No use canvassing him for an ad. Still he knows his own business best." He meditates on the good location and positioning O'Rourke's has, as a pub that can still manage to make money without needing to be called to public attention in an ad. Bloom wistfully contemplates the old-fashioned emanations of the bar, which gives off "whiffs of ginger, teadust, biscuitmush," in an olfactory rush. He evaluates the location of the bar sagely; it lies on a particularly direct vector if one imagines Dublin, as Bloom does, plotted on the radiating spokes of pub locations. City geography is laid down by markets and promotion as much as by traditional landmarks for Bloom, and part of his intimate knowledge of it is in measuring how the lines of communication between establishment and prospective customer will be arranged.

> "Where do they get the money? Coming up redheaded curates from the country Leitrim, rinsing empties and old man in the cellar. Then, lo and behold, they blossom out as Adam Findlaters or Dan Tallons. Then think of the competition. General thirst. Good puzzle would be cross Dublin without passing a pub. Save it they can't. Off the drunks, perhaps. Put down three and carry five. What is that? A bob here and there, dribs and drabs. On the wholesale orders perhaps. Doing a double shuffle with the town travellers. Square it with the boss and we'll split the job, see?" (p. 58)

Pubs do become "establishments" in Dublin through fierce accounting, and reliance on an alcoholic population, but they manage without the ministration of ads—his midwifery would be superfluous.

A nominal purpose of Bloom's early walk is to buy breakfast meat, but even this transaction is saturated with the image and print of advertising. Bloom first muses over the various meats seen through Dlugacz's butchershop window, responding first to the visual display. Much of Dublin seen through Bloom's eyes is refracted off the glossy surface of a store window, just as Dickens and James sent off a variety of urban strollers to stand mesmerized before the enthralling window displays of the city. This window has an even more galvanic attraction for Bloom, the perfect advertising subject, since it has written ads pasted up inside the window frame. Bloom pauses here for a moment of absorbed reading, accepting the window as a natural page for perusal. He takes up one of the advertising circular sheets lying on the counter, and as he reads it, he again unreels an internal cinema—the ad, in Bloom's hand, becomes the occasion for a complete scenario.

> He took up a page from a pile of cut sheets. The model farm at Kinnerath on the lakeshore of Tiberias. Can become the ideal winter sanatorium. Moses Montefiore. I thought he was. Farmhouse, wall round it, blurred cattle cropping. He held the page from him: interesting: read it nearer, the blurred cropping cattle, the page rustling. A young white heifer. Those mornings in the cattle market the beasts lowering in their pens, branded sheep, flop and fall of dung, the breeders in hob-nailed boots trudging through the litter, slapping a palm on a ripe-meated hindquarter, there's a prime one, unpeeled switches in their hands. (p. 59)

Bloom moves here from what is clearly an inner reading verbatim of the promotion for a model farm, to a seamlessly sutured imaging of moving page and print, to a dramatization of a farm complete with pigs and their caretakers. The rather bald message of the ad is nonetheless capable of engendering an interior spectacle, as well as a strange space on the page of *Ulysses* itself, for what arises to be described there is not "read off" from any outside landscape, nor from some personal memory of the "character." A real material artifact from the "outside" world collides with language that seems to be confined within the book itself, and their collision is a hybrid language. Bloom reads and produces text which we then read, but only because we, too, are experienced readers of ads and promotion. "He held the page aslant patiently, bending his senses and his will, his soft subject gaze at rest." The active connotation of bending senses and will is belied by the second half of the sentence, where Bloom's gaze is in thrall to the compunction of his reading. This analysis is not meant to suggest an agonized involuntary seizure on Bloom's part. Instead, Bloom's very patience and his eagerness to read, to embroider a meager advertisement with

a lush and detailed scene, presents us with the advertising consciousness par excellence. Bloom not *only* reads as ads have taught him to
do, he directs his gaze to a new, personal narrative beyond the mere
print on the page, to a mysterious inner reading that only a practiced
advertising subject can produce at will.

Bloom continues to "read" as he makes his way homeward, trans-
lating advertisements into perfervid, exotic scenarios:

> Agendath Netaim: planter's company. To purchase vast sandy tracts
> from Turkish government and plant with eucalyptus trees. Excellent
> for shade, fuel and construction. Orangegroves and immense mel-
> onfields north of Jaffa. You pay eight marks and they plant a dunam
> of land for you with olives, oranges, almonds or citrons. Olives
> cheaper: oranges need artificial irrigation. Every year you get a
> sending of the crop. Your name entered for life in the book of the
> union. Can pay ten down and the balance in yearly installments.
> Bleibtreustrasse 34, Berlin, W. 15. (p. 60)

He is particularly susceptible, as a Jew married to a woman from
Gibraltar, to conjuring, as he proceeds to do, a resplendent Middle
Eastern world, replete with oranges, eros, and satisfaction, from the
more monetary incentives offered in the ad itself. Yet the effulgent
world that had come to mind, prompted by the advertisement, subsides
into a dark, historical vision, a cumulative past, as opposed to the ever-
radiant present and future tenses of advertising narrative. Bloom leaps
from this narrative to an adjacent mental area of narrative, Old Testament history:

> A dead sea in a dead land, grey and old. Old now. It bore the oldest,
> the first race. . . . The oldest people. Wandered far over the earth,
> captivity to captivity, multiplying, dying, being born everywhere.
> It lay there now. Now it could bear no more. Dead: an old woman's:
> the grey sunken cunt of the world. (p. 61)

The two incommensurable readings occupy the same subject.
Bloom, instead of literally traversing the world like his great avatar,
Ulysses, experiences his voyages as advertising hallucinations, brought
up short by his counterknowledge, derived from alternative narratives
that demystify those promised voyages. Bloom doesn't resolve the
contradiction between the heavenly version of Jaffa and the desolate
weight of history, although on the surface level he surely rejects the
zionist project of colonizing Palestine. He decides the deadness of the
latter vision may be brought on by physical weakness as much as by

historical apprehension, and his advertising self prompts him to vow to practice Eugene Sandow's exercise system more faithfully. Sandow, a British Charles Atlas, appears again in the Circe episode; here, Bloom's internal gaze comes to rest on the promises of Sandow's ads as if they were a potential cure for the abuses of history. Advertising narrative is so omnipresent that it is ever ready to occupy the space vacated by consciousness of something outside its confines. Moments of historical clarity are slippages in Bloom's internal text—advertising rushes into the breach to reclaim him as subject. Its subtle power over his gaze extends to the haphazard advertisements clustering on a parlor floor window, to which his eye is drawn as he rounds the corner. "Plasters on a sore eye," he thinks, making ambiguous whether it is the advertising window as eye that is sore, or his own arrested gaze that becomes plastered over with the sight of anonymous bills. The entwinement of ads, reading, and the eye is underscored en passant.

Bloom's early-morning excursus around his neighborhood is marked by all these acts of reading, the myriad exposures to advertising copy opening up new spaces in the mundane geography of that walk. Bloom is both a conduit for the language of advertising and a reshaper of it. It directs his gaze, determines the trajectory of his desire, yet is rewritten or revised in internal colloquy as well. This altered vantage toward language does not stop at the threshhold of Bloom's home, either. Advertising language has set up shop there, too, reordering the terms of domestic life.

Chief among the domestic totems is Bloom's picture of the Bath of the Nymph, hanging over their bed. This picture is an advertising artifact above all else. As an art object, it comes with this announcement: "Given away with the Easter number of *Photo Bits:* splendid masterpiece in art colors" (p. 65). This picture is not marked with ad copy, but it is an advertisement nonetheless, an aesthetic giveaway reproduced in thousands of copies, meant to extend the reach of its parent magazine, *Photo Bits*. The nymph is of course related to the Calypso motif of this chapter—she is an erotic goddess, an erotic ideal, an evocation of Molly's sexuality, and an echo of the force that held Ulysses under a benign spell on the way homeward. Bloom's "Nymph," his private piece of mythology, has been given to him, and to countless others, by *Photo Bits*. This nymph beds down between the covers of celebrity gossip, puzzle contests, crime features, and a host of advertised commodities. Beyond being art in an age of mechanical reproduction with a vengeance, the nymph also underscores the textual matrix of this mass-produced art—it comes carrying a whole set of textual luggage. Where Benjamin had offered the possibility of posters and film as new modes of perception, as access to art from "close-up," sans aura, it has never been within this contingent, advertised context.[16] The promiscuity of art in its mass cultural bed is almost literalized in Joyce's chapter, and the condition of art among the soiled sheets of *Photo Bits* et al. is enacted in the "Circe" chapter. The assemblage recenters the text of *Ulysses* itself: if mythological nymphs can disport themselves between the covers of the prime mass market advertising tabloid, this implies that textual "purity" is an impossibility also. Scraps of Aristotle and Shakespeare coexist with Epps Cocoa, street hoardings, and newspaper captions. If *Ulysses* makes itself out of language, its realism is this fidelity to the modern ecumenical scene of language.

Hanging the nymph picture on the wall does not diminish its advertising context. First it is still embedded in the advertising aura of its publication, which is the language Bloom uses to describe it. And secondly, the picture belongs to the set of other advertised desire objects, not to the "high art" collection its promotional caption boasts of. Bloom uses it as a private shrine, but what he worships there is the commodified, advertised female. This becomes explicit when, in the Circe chapter, the Nymph comes to life and announces herself to Bloom. She speaks neither in hallowed, mythological tones, nor with the gravity of fine art. Instead, the nymph unfolds her universe of erotica, and it is all advertised.

THE NYMPH
Mortal! You found me in evil company, highkickers, coster picnic makers, pugilists, popular generals, immoral panto boys in flesh tights and the nifty shimmy dancers, La Aurora and Karini, musical act, the hit of the century. I was hidden in cheap pink paper that smelt of rock oil. I was surrounded by the stale smut of clubmen, stories to disturb callow youths, ads for transparencies, trueup dice and bustpads, proprietary articles and why wear a truss with testimonial from ruptured gentlemen. Useful hints to the married.

BLOOM
(Lifts a turtle head towards her lap.) We have met before. On another star.

THE NYMPH
(Sadly.) Rubber goods. Neverrip Brand as supplied to the aristocracy. Corsets for men. I cure fits or money refunded. Unsolicited testi-

monials for Professor Waldman's wonderful chest exuber. My bust developed four inches in three weeks, reports Mrs. Gus Rulin with photo.

BLOOM
You mean *Photo Bits?* (p. 545)

Bloom's wistful hope that the two of them have met before on another star, perhaps in the Homeric incarnations as Ulysses and Calypso, is sadly contradicted by the resolute nymph. What the two of them share is the narrative language of advertising, a mythological stream that occasionally permits a goddess within its midst. Bloom's consciousness, as the subject of desire, is inextricably entwined with advertising discourse. The bits of *Photo Bits* language that cling to the nymph are the discourse the two of them have in common.

Advertising still delivers the wondrous promise of mythological narrative. The nymph testifies to this when she relates how Bloom had borne her away, framed her in oak and tinsel, and, with kisses, shaded in her erogenous zones with a pencil. Bloom acknowledges his anachronistic, mythological adoration: "Your classic curves, beautiful immortal. I was glad to look on you, to praise you, a thing of beauty, almost to pray." The dialog between the nymph and Bloom is not meant to mock the fallenness of contemporary culture, but to bear witness to the eruption of pure desire within the nets of advertising language. Amid bust developers and rubber goods, the adoring sensibility of Bloom can still conjure a creature of pure, mythological desire, an ideal figure to watch over his marriage, itself a Penelopean skein of girdles, rubber goods, and *The Sweets of Sin*.

The "Circe" chapter gives us the unique, and unprecedented, opportunity to hear an advertising artifact speak for itself. In the textual universe of *Ulysses* pieces of advertising language have the ability to dramatize themselves, to reformulate the narratives they participate in. Part of this uncanny power is only the reverse of the "normal" modern world of advertising, as *Ulysses* makes quite clear. Advertising, in all its myriad forms, offers up a narrative to be read, engaging even the most desultory stroller in an enforced act of reading. Print, storefront, and hoardings present innumerable miniature dramas, a kind of language on stage that cannot be ignored. The nymph speaks up in the Circe chapter, but she and Bloom have really already had their conversation, which Joyce does us the favor of enacting. The energy of metamorphosis is inherent in advertisement's self-referentiality; even a bar of lemon soap can leap into the sky like a sun, crying "we're a capital couple are Bloom and I; He brightens the earth, I polish the sky" (p. 440). The dynamism of "Circe" represents the magic, Ovidian language of objectification already installed by "normal" advertising.

The materiality of the mass cultural status of language in Bloom's everyday life is underscored in the finale to "Calypso"—Bloom's trip to the outhouse, prize story from *Photo Bits* clutched under his arm. *Matcham's Masterstroke* is modest—"It did not move or touch him but it was something quick and neat. Print anything now."—and "he envied kindly Mr. Beaufoy who had written it and received payment of three pounds thirteen six" (p. 69). Its reading time is perfectly coincident with the span of time Bloom has planned to take moving his bowels, and upon completion, a page of the now-digested story is perfect for toilet paper. Bodily rhythms of digestion, defecation and sex are matched against the duration of reading that is advertising consumption. Bloom's double reading process enters in here, too—he not only finishes Beaufoy's story, he makes a start on one of his own, a domestic story to arise from stray sayings of Molly's while she is dressing.

If "Calypso" sets out the rearrangement of private vision and language that brings *Ulysses* into modernity through Bloom's mass-cultural existence, then "Lotus-Eaters" begins to demarcate how differently groups of people interact under the auspices of mass cultural forms. All the meetings in this presumably intimate, villagelike Dublin are previously conditioned or determined by an advertising context; as Joyce sets things out in this chapter, advertising is the invisible grid of their connection.

Central to Bloom's concerns here is his receipt of a letter from Martha Clifford, his secret pen pal. Their correspondence comes about from an ad Bloom has inserted in several newspapers, anonymity insured by the pen name Henry Flower and by the post office box number. Bloom links his ad—"to aid literary gentleman in his work"—with George Russell and his young female protégée, whom he later sees on the street, but in fact his epistolary partnership with Martha Clifford is entirely a product of its advertised origins. Bloom's eros takes shape as a categorized request accompanied by a box number, and he is aware that other answers to his ad are piling up, unread, in other postal corners. Martha Clifford comes into "being" by answering an ad, not by appearing in person, and her responses could easily be substituted for by the wealth of other letters drawn by the advertising mechanism, which renders them all equivalent. Martha's letter is placed in direct correspondence with the one Bloom receives from his daughter Milly, the "photo girl." Despite being a personal, family missive, Milly's letter also has its place in the advertising catalog, since as a photo girl, Milly works as a living advertisement. The seaside photo girls were nominally photographic assistants, but largely attractive advertisements for the booths they represented, and available to have their picture taken with gentlemen customers. "I am getting on swimming in the photo business now," Milly writes, her job a miniature version of one of the ads Bloom will later imagine for stationery. This job has taken Milly away from Dublin, where there is little employment for her, but it also indicates the rearrangement of domestic and erotic space brought about by mass-cultural forms. Her mother has worked as a professional singer of sorts, a kind of employment that relies on an earlier form of social organization: Molly sings in church choirs, at lecture halls, on concert tours with a publicity circuit connected to the common life of the city and its small talk. The photographic apparatus takes photogenic Milly outside that earlier sphere of entertainment into a space of reproduction, image, and popular song ("Oh, those sea-side girls!"). She is a modernized version of Nell, a photo-girl instead of a waxwork-child, an advertising vessel.

Bloom does enter one demesne in the chapter that seems to have escaped being defined by advertisement when he visits the chemist, whose haunt is almost medieval in its evocation of scents and its old-fashioned nostrums. Even in the apothecary environment Bloom is reminded of the classic advertising line, "Good morning, have you used Pear's soap today?" Pear's soap was perhaps *the* most well-known product in Britain: its slogan appears in innumerable joking ads (the embarrassment of meeting Queen Victoria and involuntarily asking her whether she had washed that day, for instance), and it had the distinction of achieving the first endorsement, when the famous painting "Bubbles," by Sir John Millais F.R.A., was allowed to have "Pear's" inscribed on its surface in reproduction, above the little boy gazing at a bubble he has blown. The bubble bursts yet again in Bloom's mind, transfiguring the ordinary shop.

The chapter is replete with Bloom glancing at the hoardings crowded on every block, standing transfixed before the military recruitment poster, and creating his own suggestion for successful ad:

College sports today I see. He eyed the horseshoe poster over the gate of college park: cyclist doubled up like a cod in a pot. Damn bad ad. Now if they had made it round like a wheel. Then the spokes: sports, sports, sports: and the hub big: college. Something to catch the eye. (p. 86)

The centralizing, arresting movement of the ad Bloom conceives as a replacement is also a synechdochic representation of life transfigured in the face of the textuality of advertisement—all eyes equidistant from the same ads, all auditors equally aware of the same slogans, all the city arrayed along invisible lines of spectatorship, desire, and response; social reading is in progress.

The great leveling provided by advertising is transformed in "Hades" into a secularized response to the problem of death, which Bloom, ever creative, imagines in terms extended beyond the Plumtree's ad. The ad in full has particular resonance throughout *Ulysses*, a motival refrain amply discussed by Joyce's commentators:

> What is home without
> Plumtree's Potted Meat?
> Incomplete.
> With it, an abode of bliss.

Bloom reads this ad, which he has seen innumerable times, when engaged in desultory conversation with the importunate McCoy, who is called a "talking head" years before the advent of television. At that juncture, the ad has a direct connection to Molly's forthcoming assignation with Blazes Boylan, the person who is "getting up" more than Molly's singing tour, in face of Bloom's absent potted meat. By the Hades chapter, the same ad is darkly specific, especially when Bloom, to his disgust as a savvy ad-man, discovers it appearing under the obituary column. The ad runs in counterpoint to the religious rhetoric occasioned by the funeral, in some ways a preferable response that emphasizes the egalitarian materiality of death as potted meat.

Ruminating on corpses, Bloom imagines an ad of his own that connects the garden of desire imagery so associated with his ad reading that morning to the problem of death in a secular world:

Chinese cemeteries with giant poppies growing produce the best opium Nastiansky told me. The Botanic gardens are just over there. It's the blood sinking into the earth gives new life. Same idea those jews they said killed the christian boy. Every man his price. Well preserved fat corpse gentlemen, epicure, invaluable for fruit garden.

A bargain. Buy carcass of William Wilkinson, auditor and accountant, lately deceased, three pounds thirteen and six. With thanks. (p. 108)

Beyond the coincidence that the price for the corpse is exactly the same as the prize money offered for the story contest in *Photo Bits*, the text implies that even a dead body could enter into the scheme of circulation and commodification advertising lends its narrative to.

The circuit of Bloom's everyday life which has been sketched here depends on the flow of advertising experience he becomes aware of. Another name for this flow is "stream of consciousness," which is perhaps the writing technique most identified with *Ulysses*, even when the usual differentiations from Dujardin and Richardson have been made. If advertising is responsible for much of the panoply of style in the novel, then surely it is implicated in its most famous practice. Umberto Eco has described stream of consciousness in *Ulysses* this way: "Remaining within the conscious facts—all recorded with absolute fidelity as so many equivalents—*personal identity itself is questioned*. In the flow of overlapping perceptions during Bloom's walk through Dublin, the boundaries between 'inside' and 'outside,' between how Bloom endures Dublin and how Dublin acts on him, become very indistinct."[17] Perhaps the foregoing tour of Bloom's mental activity has made clear the extent to which "personal identity" is a constructed patchwork. "Bloom" in the text is a collocation of outside languages, the vanishing point of a private language. A primary constructor of this interior flow is, demonstrably, advertising language, its imagery and desire. Ads locate and fix "Bloom," rather than the other way around. Such "construction of the subject" is manifest in language at all periods; an entire wing of modern critical theory has taken this power as its defining characteristic. Advertising language brings a new technique to this "interpellation," however, because its sole purpose *is* to seek out a reader and insist on that reader's absorption of a piece of language. The interpellative force is militant and unabashed. Advertising becomes the first entirely public language directed at *every* person; in so being, the extent to which human subjects are "made" by language becomes manifest to all, even when not theoretically expressed. *Ulysses* contains one passage that seems almost fortuitously to muse on the constitutive power of advertising language, its force on the language scene which renders language a stream that passes through all interlocutors alike.

His eyes sought answer from the river and saw a rowboat rock at
anchor on the treacly swells lazily its plastered board.
Kino's
11/-
Trousers.
Good idea that. Wonder if he pays rent to the corporation. How can
you own water really? It's always flowing in a stream, never the
same, which in the stream of life we trace. Because life is a stream.
All kind of places are good for ads. That quack doctor for the clap
used to be stuck up in all the greenhouses. Never see it now. Strictly
confidential. Dr. Hy Franks. Didn't cost him a red like Maginni the
dancing master self advertisement. Got fellows to stick them up or
stick them up himself for that matter on the q.t. running in to loosen
a button. Fly by night. Just the place too. POST NO BILLS. POST
100 PILLS. Some chap with a dose burning him. (p. 152)

No place is safe from advertisement, neither the water, which would
seem too Heraclitean an element on which to inscribe a message, nor
the outhouse, shut off from public observance but not sequestered
from advertising's gaze. Advertising language can tackle the problem
of mutability and change, even making it an advantage, because in
this case no one "owns" the surface on which the ad is written. No
matter how inaccessible the terrain, advertising only gains additional
power if it can be there first with its message—one knows this feeling
of being inexorably anticipated by advertising if one has ever seen the
Wall Drug ad posted 14,000 feet up a seemingly primitive Rocky
Mountain trail. In the dark privacy of the public toilet, each person is
addressed "confidentially." Advertising can mime the act of whispering
a secret, even as it trumpets itself, obviating secrecy. The Kino's ad
Bloom sees "creates" his subsequent stream of thoughts; it also suggests that advertising language is the only stream to swim in, now.
Other language events will take place *within* its ubiquitous perimeters.

"GIVE US THIS DAY OUR DAILY PRESS"

The intimate history of advertisement and newspaper has been
repeatedly underscored in this study. The newspaper room of "Aeolus"
marks the conjuncture of these "prints" as it replaces the literal map
of Dublin with the textual space of mass communication, while the
"central space" of the city becomes a dematerialized place, an interface

of the commercial and the public as they are textualized in advertisement and news. The textual is presented as material in this chapter, which marks the first departure from the quasinaturalistic style that introduces both Stephen and Bloom, to replace these "personalities" by the stark rivalry of print styles as they perform every rhetorical trick. The newspaper format, with its headlines that come from no locatable narrative "voice," has the power to squeeze authorial narration right off the page, substituting the anonymity, the ubiquity, of the advertising voice. And after this foray into the newspaper, all language is up for grabs—the chapter is followed by the arbitrary voices of "The Wandering Rocks," the dramatics of "Circe," the tour of English prose in "Oxen of the Sun." The setting of "Aeolus" is decisive in this process, however; the power of advertising-cum-newsprint serves to prove that language is material, that it can be "fabricated," like any other commodity, and that advertising covers over and circumscribes the rival forms of political rhetoric, historical legend, and literary style.

Bloom enters this place to do his bit of business—to secure an ad for Alexander Keyes Wine and Spirits that will be accompanied by a puff in the "news" column. "It's the ads and side features sell a weekly not the stale news in the official gazette," he avers, which is indubitably true throughout newspaper history. Unfortunately, the ad Bloom wants to place is rather penny-ante, and the various powers and personalities of the newspaper collude in making it difficult for him. Bloom can imagine as a private print "utopia"the cozy collision of styles a country weekly newspaper offers, seemingly the perfect home for his scrap of ad, but he can also sense the overwhelming autonomy of print and its actual impersonality, better represented by the city daily:

> Nature notes. Cartoons. Phil Blake's weekly Pat and Bull stories. Uncle Toby's page for tiny tots. Country bumpkin's queries. Dear Mr. Editor, what is a good cure for flatulence: I'd like that part. Learn a lot teaching others. . . . The machines clanked in threefour time. Thump, thump, thump. Now if he got paralysed there and no one knew how to stop them they'd clank on and on the same, print it over and over and up and back. Monkeydoodle the whole thing. (p. 119)

The newspaper printing press not only fabricates language wholesale, it can render it as well, chopping it into bits the way the imperturbable Red Murray snips out ads to scissor and paste them, parceling out language to different neighborhoods and villages according to their advertising links, even turning language inside out—the typesetter reading type backwards, "mangiD. KcirtaP.," performs a secular Kabalism parallel to the sacred reading of Hebrew text Bloom's father used to practice. The demystification of language offered by its decimation into letters and even reversed letters is correspondingly, paradoxically, remystifying as well, suggesting a transubstantiating mystery of the part becoming the whole.

Respiration is a perfect metaphor for the cultural activity of the newspaper/advertising process in modern capitalist economies, whatever relevance it may have in linking "Aeolus" to Odysseus' cave of the winds. The centripetal exhalations of the press lay down all the lines of communication that establish civil society in Gramsci's sense; the centrifugal inhalation brings history, language and politics within one encompassing breath. One way of reading "Aeolus" is to track the movement as key historical and political events and legends enter the maw of journalism/advertisement—the latter's linguistic control and preeminence proves ineluctable. It should be carefully noted that the press as language machine cannot be taken to "stand for" some abstract property of language, a given that is only being discovered, not invented, in the deconstructive prose of James Joyce. To reduce this matter to an intrinsic property of language in toto leaves out the dynamic conflict and rivalry between languages, the struggle within the linguistic economy prompted by the rise of advertising as a self-sufficient linguistic force. *Ulysses* surely does not shrink from portraying a cannibalistic process of language feeding on language. A chief leitmotif of the chapter, the Phoenix Park murders, indicates just how engulfing the press has become, as history and legend are almost literally placed within an ad.

Myles Crawford tells the admiring newsroom of the extraordinary career of the journalist Ignatius Gallaher, whose biggest scoop happened to be transmitting the news of the Phoenix Park murders abroad when ordinary transmission was forbidden by censors. By embroidering on Gallaher Crawford already displaces the historic event, with its enduring repercussions for Irish destiny, into the lore of journalistic triumph, a "how I got that story" narrative. But far more decisive is that Gallaher's solution to putting out this important news involved embedding it into an advertisement:

. . . Look at here. What did Ignatius Gallaher do? I'll tell you. Inspiration of genius. Cabled right away. Have you Weekly Freeman of 17 March? Right. Have you got that?

He flung back pages of the files and stuck his finger on a point.

—Take page four, advertisement for Bransome's coffee let us say. Have you got that? Right. . . .

—F to P is the route Skin-the-Goat drove the car for an alibi. Inchicore, Roundtown, Windy Arbour, Palmerston Park, Ranelagh. F.A.B.P. Got that? X is Davy's publichouse in upper Leeson street. . . .

CLEVER, VERY

—Clever, Lenehan said. Very.

—Gave it to them on a hot plate, Myles Crawford said, the whole bloody history.

Nightmare from which you will never awake.

—I saw it, the editor said proudly. I was present, Dick Adams, the besthearted bloody Corkman the Lord ever put the breath of life in, and myself.

Lenehan bowed to a shape of air, announcing:

—Madam, I'm Adam. And Able was I ere I saw Elba.

—History! Myles Crawford cried. The Old Woman of Prince's street was there first. There was weeping and gnashing of teeth over that. Out of an advertisement. (p. 136–37)

Advertising determines the viability of newspapers, coexists on every page with its prose, enters into news reportage itself as if the columns of print were permeable membranes, and now shows an even more mysterious power: the advertisement is a secret code, a discrete sign on which to superimpose a historical diagram that will lose, in being placed inside an ad, whatever independence as historical representation it could have claimed. Ads are banal, if you will, but also mystical. In telling the tale of Gallaher the historical narrative *per se* is absent, invisible; what remains is the cunning abyss of the ad, whose language and even letters can have the multivalence once reserved for literature, the dynamism reserved for historical event.

Ads can now cannibalize historical reference, and the chapter extends their representational covetousness to oral speech, to rhetoric, and to literature. One by one advertisement manages to absorb them; the colloquy among the members of the press is a nostalgic remembrance of these forms before their usurpation. Under the mantle of the press come all the disparate languages, an *omnium gatherum* nullified by the job of getting the paper out.

—All the talents, Myles Crawford said. Law, the classics . . .
—The turf, Lenehan put in.
—Literature, the press.
—If Bloom were here, the professor said. The gentle art of adver-
tisement. (p. 135)

Ripe styles of oratory past and present are compared, the merits of fine
speeches are vaunted. Unwitting of their textual "location" under the
staccato headlines, the group wistfully harkens back to public speech
and words as memory:

His listeners held their cigarettes poised to hear, their smoke as-
cending in frail stalks that flowered with his speech. *And let our
crooked smokes*. Noble words coming. Look out. Could you try your
hand at it yourself?
—"And it seemed to me that I heard the voice of that Egyptian
highpriest raised in a tone of like haughtiness and like pride. I heard
his words and their meaning was revealed to me." (p. 142)

The sacred and the profane magic of spoken word, of political debate
and of the tradition of Irish letters flowers amid a language that inexorably supplants and realigns them. Bloom, who is both Ariel-like and
Chaplinesque in this chapter, on a mission in support of the master-
language of advertisement, but himself still sentimentally tied to an
anachronistic sacred mode of reading, skims past Stephen Dedalus,
who tries to create a literary parable that is also quashed by the superior
force of journalistic language. Delicious as it is, the parable of the
plums makes way on the page for the newspaper headline, expanded
to full narrative length, a complete *translation* of the literary/historical
into advertising prose:

DIMINISHED DIGITS PROVE TOO TITILLATING FOR FRISKY
FRUMPS. ANNE WIMBLES, FLO WANGLES—YET CAN YOU BLAME
THEM? (p. 150)

Advertising language has its own parabolic necessities.
To return to a nominal plot element of "Aeolus" that emblematizes
the change in language: consider the Alexander Keyes ad itself. Un-
remarkable in its own right, a local ad with a homemade touch that
could never produce much revenue for either the wine shop or the
newspaper, its presence generates an allusive network that lasts
throughout the book. Of course, the subject of keys had been broached
before—Stephen had lost his; Bloom, we will later learn, has left his

at home. But the Keyes ad really inaugurates the inplicit ongoing discussion of the sui generis nature of advertising language, building on the crossing of literal housekeys.

—Like that, see. Two crossed keys here. A circle. Then the name Alexander Keyes, tea, wine and spirit merchant. So on. Better not teach him his own business.
—You know yourself, councillor, just what he wants. Then round the top in leaded: the house of keys. You see? Do you think that's a good idea? The foreman moved his scratching hand to his lower ribs and scratched there quietly.
—The idea, Mr. Bloom said, is the house of keys. You know, councillor, the Manx parliament. Innuendo of home rule. Tourists, you know, from the isle of Man. Catches the eye, you see. Can you do that? (p. 120)

Spiritual and temporal power are both allegorized in the advertisement, although not in the way that Ignatius Gallaher was able to turn an ad into an allegorical diagram encrypting an historical event. The more immediate level of allegory, and the one Bloom counts on to catch the eye of the public, is the ad's connection of an unprepossessing wine shop, which a man named Keyes happens to own, with the desire for home rule in Ireland, something that has only been realized in the parliament of the Isle of Man, and that is *there* symbolized in the blazon of two crossed keys. Since the ad is able to invest its pun on the word *key(e)s* with a literal reference to the design of the Manx parliament "sign," and beyond that, to a collective if often nascent public desire to be freed of British rule, it is an extraordinarily dense document with an ontology all its own. The kind of recognition, of reading or "eye-catching" it calls forth is a double one (in fact, it may be too subtle altogether for the foreman). The linguistic pun, bolstered by the picture, has to work, and then the level of what Bloom calls "innuendo" has come into play. The ad ultimately depends on its incorporation of political dissatisfaction with the British imperium, but that unhappiness and anger vanish into the ad as if into a black hole. In allegorizing such a vital, if inchoate, public emotion, a revolutionary desire, the ad has made it disappear into its own design: the "innuendo" about home rule, a fraught political problem, does not survive the social reading process as a galvanizing artifact because the reference cannot stop at the level of analysis or even agitprop. To be read *as an ad*, the House of Keyes motif must be glued to the wine shop itself, like a label. So advertising language can set up shop in the heart of contemporary cultural and political reference, but it subsumes such reference for its own purpose, bracketing the ad's allegorical frame. No one will be mobilized to agitate for British removal after seeing the Keyes ad, although that potential must exist for the ad to "read," because the home rule pun is placed in suspension, eviscerated as the premise, as the rhetoric, of the ad.

One must hasten to add that this allegorization is not being stigmatized as either malevolent or conspiratorial. Bloom's idea is ingenuous and ingenious, and certainly not symptomatic of a villainous plot against public language, revolutionary or otherwise. The intentionalist fallacy can rear its head in studies of advertising language, under the guise of seeing in it a monolithic totalization of capitalist control. Far more appropriate than assigning blame is to consider, as *Ulysses* does, in this example and in others, the actual operations of advertising narratives, which batten on the body politic because that is their only source of narrative energy, turning suppressed discourses into allegories of themselves.

If the body politic plays host for advertising references, and if puns are permissible in such a suspect atmosphere, then one can say advertisement ultimately becomes a host itself: the religious metaphors of the Alexander Keyes episode leave no doubt that *Ulysses* conceives advertisement as the substitute for holy communion. This allegorical level is not, of course, one that can be read by the audience for the ad; it is reserved for us, readers of *Ulysses*, to see that it happens to them like that. Almost too much religious metaphor inheres in the Keyes ad; first, it publicizes a wine shop, placing us referentially in the New Testament, both at the marriage of Canaan, and inside St. Paul's wine bottles. That Keyes is a "spirit merchant" means he sells liquor, ordinarily enough, but ads in general are also involved in a species of spiritual merchandising. The crossed keys offer the keys to the kingdom of heaven, a shortcut to the transformations of paradise that render mere politics moot. Additionally, the crossed keys are the harbinger of the later crossing of Bloom and Stephen, when they finally conquer the "parallax" that has kept them textually apart. Beyond this, the key motif suggests that the multiple reception of advertisements is a simulacrum of religious ceremony.

Advertising does not deliberately mimic religious practices, nor exist as a travestied modern form of religion, something F. R. Leavis was to claim. Rather, the transcendent promises of Catholic theology and ritual, and the promissory form and communal metaphysics of advertising intersect, particularly in a colonized Catholic country where such ideology always has a political subtext. The host is a wafer that can become the actual body of Christ (only during sacralized public observance), a transformation accomplished by words. An ad also has its only genuine *ontos* or being in public space, and when ingested in all the multiple acts of reading it undergoes a transformation—"all very fine to jeer at it now in cold print but it goes down like hot cake that stuff" (p. 158)—into active cultural currency. Each person can read or see the ad in private assimilation, but it belongs to everyone and to no one; it is brought to life by the framing of consensus that agrees, "This is an ad"; it penetrates and even becomes the language of its readers. While "everything speaks in its own way" (p. 121), especially the language of objects that is advertising, simultaneously "no one is anything" (p. 164). Individual identities are fictions, being comprised, as they are, of shared pieces of this host language. The moment of absorption of that host, both a private and a public ceremonial, is transcendently ineffable albeit materially concrete.

In another religious vocabulary the hopes for incarnation and resurrection are manifested in transmigration of souls and "metempsychosis," and advertising's textual and social dynamics are shown to be close relatives of these spiritual epistemologies. "Met-him-pike-hoses" rests on a belief in the unity of all matter, including human souls, and the infinite exchangeability of the relatively insignificant bodies that enclose those souls. A continuity of being along the otherwise impersonal chain of history is presupposed. "The cords that all link back, strandentwining cable of all flesh. That is why mystic monks. Will you be as gods? Gaze in your omphalos. Hello. Kinch here. Put me on to Edenville. Aleph, alpha: nought, nought one" (p. 38).

The "Aeolus" chapter recapitulates this umbilical image, but it inscribes the metempsychotic into the urban setting, where strandentwining cables are tram lines and boat canals, telegraph wires and pulsating switchboards. HELLO THERE, CENTRAL!—the cry goes out. Just as George Rowell had predicted that only advertising lines of force could collocate as a "nerve center" in the complex web of industrializing America, so advertising in *Ulysses* stretches its Ariadne's cord across the labyrinth of modern Dublin, invisibly interconnecting and underlying all its social functions.

The most powerful representation of the *cordon sanitaire* advertising creates in the city, and its "metempsychotic" ability to string the citizens of Dublin along its wire, comes in "The Wandering Rocks," a microcosm of the structure of the novel as a whole. As the cast of characters covers their daily rounds the "voice" of the chapter elides from each one of them, never coming to rest in any singular or more omniscient vantage point. All the manifold traversals of the city the citizens make are coordinated so that only a few minutes of textual time elapse, making the "time" of the chapter a composite time that is the sum of the different characters' narrative moments. Without their knowing it, each person in "Wandering Rocks" achieves an exchangeable identity with every other person "there"; they are all transfixed and held in equivalent "subject" positions by the advertising posters of Marie Kendall, "charming soubrette," and Mr. Eugene Stratton, black vaudevillian, as these spectacular faces gaze from their hoardings. Denis Maginni connects all these disparate citizens by their stares at his "self-advertisement," and the march of the Hely's sandwichboardmen gives them virtually algebraic configurations. One could say that these characters are constellated in and through advertisement.

"From the hoardings Mr. Eugene Stratton grinned with thick niggerlips at Father Conmee" (p. 222), a private smile between the two of them that leads Father Conmee to muse on the wastefulness of God's damning all the "black and brown and yellow souls" who have died unbaptised. Miss Dunne at her typewriter watches the solemn enfilade of H.E.L.Y.'.S. alphabet men parade by, and can see from her window Marie Kendall, always demanding the automatic appellation "charming soubrette," even when the sight of her elicits disapproval. "Mustard hair and dauby cheeks. She's not nicelooking, is she?" (p. 229). Her coy dauby smile presides over Lenehan and McCoy's conversation, and she enters the febrile mind of Patrick Dignam *fils:* "Buttoning it down, his chin lifted, he saw the image of Marie Kendall, charming soubrette, beside the two puckers. One of them mots that do be in the packets of fags Stoer smokes that his old fellow welted hell out of him for one time, he found out" (p. 237).

This unfurling frieze of textual moments becomes a mosaic, where the chips of individual experience are exposed as a design, when the viceregal cavalcade wends its way through the streets. This luncheon group, wielding the power of the British in absentia over Ireland, has the same galvanizing effect the ads do: the passing of their car halts the whole cast of characters, commanding their gaze, creating them as audience. Earl and Lady Dudley and lieutenant-colonel Hesseltine have no particular political agenda on this afternoon; they are merely returning from lunch with a modicum of pomp. But their passage is a media event, ironically described in the chapter in the newspaper tone reserved for the powerful: "The viceroy was most cordially greeted on his way through the metropolis." Presumably the description would remain the same were potatoes to be thrown at the car, which in fact doesn't happen. However, elevated as they convince themselves they are, the viceregal party receives but dubious homage from the advertising figures who provide the "continuity" of the narrative. "A charming *soubrette*, great Marie Kendall, with dauby cheeks and lifted skirts, smiled daubily from her poster upon William Humble, earl of Dudley, and upon lieutenant-colonel H. G. Hesseltine and also upon the honorable Gerald Ward A.D.C." The sandwichboardmen go by, although the aristocratic party loses the full effect of H.E.L.Y.'.S. since H. has halted at the corner. "Mr. Eugene Stratton, his blub lips agrin, bade all comers welcome to Pembroke township." The advertised ones seem to grab the noblesse oblige for themselves; they smile their ecumenical smiles at all and refuse to bestow especial grace on the powerful ones, who, themselves, become part of the pageant passing before the ever more contained power of advertisements. There is certainly nothing counterhegemonic about these ads, but their dauby laughter is subversively unsettling. The chapter has balletically shown the material life of Dublin pivoting about these impersonal advertising greeters, who bid welcome to everyone and to no one at the same time (pp. 253–54). Their impersonality absorbs politics, history, and religion. A *pièce de résistance* remains: an ad that narratively links all these scraps of incident and encounter, yet which remains invisible and un-"read". This is the "Elijah is Coming" throwaway ad, pasted up or passed out to announce an evangelistic revival at a concert hall.

> A skiff, a crumpled throwaway, Elijah is coming, rode lightly down the Liffey, under Loopline bridge, shooting the rapids where water chafed around the bridge piers, sailing eastward past hulls and anchorchains, between the Customhouse old dock and George's quay. (p. 227)

And again:

Elijah, skiff, light crumpled throwaway, sailed eastward by flanks of ships and travelers, amid an archipelago of corks, beyond New Wapping street past Benson's ferry, and by the three-masted schooner *Rosevean* from Bridgwater with bricks. (p. 249)

"Elijah is Coming" has a magical constellation of properties. Almost by definition as a throwaway ad it is ephemeral, inconsequential. This particular piece of paper, no more special than the other copies made and pasted up, has been tossed away—following instructions, one might say—and plies the river, a barque of forgotten advertisement. To revise Berkeley's argument: does an ad exist if it is crumpled and thrown into a river with no one to see it or read it? The magicality invoked here is that "Elijah," albeit unperceived, does create eddies of significance in its wake. As a throwaway, the ad is a piece of pure contingency that contravenes the ostensibly impeccable design of the book—but not really; like all other "accidents" in *Ulysses*, the throwaway is recuperated as and by design. However, the purpose it serves narratively, as a prophetic message of salvation and rescue for Ireland, both contradicts and confirms its nature as an ad. Contradicts it because as an ad it has fallen out of circulation, arrests no gaze, has become singular rather than multiple and no longer points to its own referent, in this case the actual evangelical meeting. Yet the confirming paradox is that "Elijah" may also be read as advertising *an sich*. As a form of writing, it can penetrate consciousness, crystallize desire, and circulate among thousands or millions without ever losing its substance. And this particular "piece" of it retains that potency even when "thrown away," in an almost religious sense.

Ads are compared to institutional religion continually through the book. Bloom himself points out the ways that the Church's rituals, ceremonies, and promises are constructed to prey on fears and desires, to keep people hoping that the church will fulfill them. "Pray for us. And pray for us. Good idea, the repetition. Same thing with ads. Buy from us. And buy from us" (p. 377). The institutions of advertising and the church are so similar in the Irish context that they can meld as bizarre hybrids. "Where was that ad some Birmingham firm the luminous crucifix? Our Saviour. Wake up in the dead of night and see him on the wall, hanging" (p. 151). Their props are well-nigh interchangeable; advertisement and the church both have a product to sell; the promises of one signifying system are not that alien from those of the other. The Elijah throwaway, on the other hand, is no mere thematic parody of organized religion and its methods. Rather, the religious vocabulary of incarnation, grace, and communion, otherwise translatable as communal, collective desire, transcending individual boundaries and de-reifying all the hopes of the body, is mapped onto advertisement in the exemplary "Elijah" throwaway. This is not a sinister, sardonic, or despairing correlation; Joyce, after paring his fingernails, is not wringing his hands backstage in T. S. Eliot fashion. *Ulysses* is a perfectly serious and analytic demonstration of the proximal transcendence that is the promise behind every ad. As in organized religion, there is an aspect of advertisement that is authoritarian, manipulative, enervating and fraudulent. But advertisement also invokes, in language, for *Ulysses* at any rate, a rhetorical fulfillment of a dubious metaphysics, and "Elijah" is its prophet.

> Professor Alexander Rustow . . . characterizes the mentality of the modern capitalist by ascribing to him the implicit attitude: 'To produce and to sell belong to the elect, to buy and to consume, to the damned.' . . . Advertising, on the other hand, seems to scream from all the billboards and posters: 'To the buyer and consumer belongs the paradise!' This eudaemonistic deism with which advertising is informed is the same philosophy underlying the faith of Adam Smith, who believed that, by the 'invisible hand' of Providence, the private egotisms of all human individuals are welded together into the common good.[18]

Rabelais meets the patent-medicine salesmen here on the religious hustings; American fundamentalist promises ring out vulgarly here, but there is also a wild energy and a carnivalesque performance style that yokes merchandising and transcendent hopes. Leo Spitzer points out the connection of advertising style and language with the "preaching style" of American Protestant capitalism, extending Weber's analysis of the links between economics and religious ethos to an entire performative universe.

> Christicle, who's this excrement yellow gospeller on the Merrion hall? Elijah is coming washed in the Blood of the Lamb. Come on you winefizzling ginsizzling booseguzzling existences! Come on, you dog-gone, bullnecked, bettlebrowed, hogjowled, peanutbrained, weaseleyed fourflushers, false alarms and excess baggage! Come on, you triple extract of infamy! Alexander J. Christ Dowie, that's

yanked to glory most half this planet from 'Frisco Beach to Vladivostock. The Diety ain't no nickle dime bumshow. I put it to you that he's on the square and a corking fine business proposition. He's the grandest thing yet and don't you forget it. Shout salvation in King Jesus. You'll need to rise precious early, you sinner there, if you want to diddle the Almighty God. PFLAAAP! Not half. He's got a coughmixture with a punch in it for you, my friend, in his backpocket. Just you try it on. (p. 428)

The fervid peroration which ends "Oxen of the Sun" emanates from no particular speaker, as the climax to a shifting display of the prose styles that have literally made the English language. In a final cacophonous blast, a huckster's dream-style language of universal paradise exhibits the transcendental roots of advertising language, and the transformation of prophetic speech into the coinage of advertising's privatized, commodified world.

POSTCARDS FROM FARAWAY PLACES

While the advertising excesses of "Circe" mobilize all the anthropomorphic potential of ads in a pyrotechnic hallucination, to which I will return, the ostensibly pedestrian "Eumaeus" chapter offers a fiercely political overview of international advertising that extends advertising's inroads even further. The general critical reaction to Eumaeus involves noting its tediousness; in efforts to recuperate its banal prose, especially after the fireworks of "Circe," critics like Fredric Jameson have presciently suggested that Joyce is bringing off a somewhat bungled parody of Henry James, or H. G. Wells, or Arnold Bennett, or delivering an exercise in boredom for its own sake.[19] But if advertising is the critical focus of attention, "Eumaeus" doesn't need subtle apologetics: the wacky cabman's shelter is the perfect textual waystation for a meditation on tourism as it replaces travel, on the narrativization of history and politics by advertising styles, on the "eternal return" of mass culture, and on literary labor as advertising's amanuensis, ads themselves gilding with a commercial charge even the "pure" friendship of Stephen and Bloom.

The doughty red-bearded sailor figures large here, answering the need in the text to consummate the Odyssean parallels with a pseudo-Odysseus as red herring. W. B. Murphy of Carrigaloo fits the bill; he has been gone for years to exotic venues, he has left behind a long-suffering wife, he is rife with highly suspect stories, and, ultimately revealed as a "bit of a literary cove in his own small way," he can don sea-green spectacles and be apotheosized as an author-surrogate. Before this final sea-change, Murphy's presence illuminates both the disappearance of "travel," and the lability of political images, traceable to the world of advertising as the supplanting narrative fabric.

Murphy reveals himself to Stephen and Bloom as the result of a strange coincidence; when he acts out a shooting exhibition he has once seen, and then ascribes the talent to the sharp-shooter Simon Dedalus, they are stunned by this "false sighting." He draws the story from the sailor's boundless fund of lore, and can jadedly chalk up the coincidence in names to the "small world" of the world traveler. Odysseus, of course, had made free with this perquisite of exotic voyaging—his stories of disguise all turn upon chance meetings at sea. Murphy's dissimulations, however, take place in a world mediated by publicity and showmanship. He recites a snatch of a Buffalo Bill publicity song—"Buffalo Bill shoots to kill, Never missed and he never will" (p. 624)—apropos of having seen this Simon Dedalus ten years ago in Stockholm on a tour with Hengler's Royal Circus. The sailor's private knowledge of ports of call, his closer relationship to "seeing" the world in its untrammeled and unvisited state, have vanished. Odysseus' own voyages had only his words to vouch for them, but the possibility of travel and individual testimony to the previously unknown was clearly there. *Murphy's* privileged information rests on having been a public spectator at a public spectacle. Advertised entertainment on a Barnumized scale has preceded him, and every other "traveler," as he rounds the globe. Flaubert remarked on the mediated nature of modern travel as he described climbing a pyramid in Egypt: "Imbeciles have written their names everywhere: 'Buffard, 79 Rue Saint-Martin, wallpaper manufacturer,' in black letters; some Englishman has written 'Jenny Lind'; almost all the names are modern."[20] The red-bearded sailor intersects with the tourism industry, the advertising gloss on exotic places, so that his narrative is not just at the deceptive one remove Odysseus deliberately essayed—his narrative agenda is set up for him by advertising.[21]

A case in point: the sailor's most stirring tale, pathetically hyperbolic as well as Swiftian, concerns cannibalistic natives he has known in Peru. The tale no longer suffices on its own in the modern world: only the souvenir, a kind of reified advertisement, will confirm the eruption of the exotic into the everyday.

—Khan! Like that. And I seen maneaters in Peru that eats corpses and the livers of corpses. Look here. Here they are. A friend of mine sent me.
He fumbled out a picture postcard from his inside pocket, which seemed to be in its way a species of repository, and pushed it along the table. The printed matter on it stated: *Choza da Indios. Beni, Bolivia.*
All focused their attention on the scene exhibited, at a group of savage women in striped loincloths, squatted, blinking, suckling, frowning, sleeping, amid a swarm of infants (there must have been quite a score of them) outside some primitive shanties of osier.
—Chews coca all day long, the communicative tarpaulin added. Stomachs like breadgraters. Cuts off their diddies when they can't bear no more children. Seen them there stark ballock-naked eating a dead horse's liver raw. (p. 625–6)

The talismanic postcard not only identifies a scene in Bolivia, absent any sign of raw horse liver, but Bloom surreptitiously discovers it is addressed to an A. Boudin in Santiago, Chile, and it bears no message. The universal currency of postcard reproductions, the ambivalence of their "view" of faraway places and the peculiar fictional gap left by their message spaces—a *mise-en-abyme* when left blank—serves to do more than burlesque the tales of the sailor-figure. When Bloom goes on to imagine his own dreamed-of trip, a typical English seaside tour, his language for the sights and pleasures is adopted from postcard captions, and it segues into dreams of a successful traveling Tweedy-Flower grand opera company, "providing puffs in the local papers could be managed by some fellow with a bit of bounce who could pull the indispensable wires and thus combine business with pleasure. But who? That was the rub" (p. 627).

Travel, heroic, epic, or otherwise, is emptied out in *Ulysses*, but not only because the scene resolutely remains set in Dublin. The ubiquity of advertising has penetrated even geography—a more bona-fide sailor than Mr. Murphy would still have his travel experiences filtered through the screen of advertising's tourist images. A brisk, commercial tone attends Bloom's ruminations on these proto-adventures; a seedy, petty-bourgeois pamphleteer's prose appraises the benefits of travel for young men: "Because of course uptodate tourist traveling was yet merely in its infancy, so to speak, and the accommodation left much to be desired. Interesting to fathom, it seemed to him, from a motive of curiosity pure and simple, was whether it was the traffic that created the route or vice-versa or the two sides in fact" (p. 628). Bloom has heretofore been extremely knowledgeable about the invisible paths of commerce that advertising carves through Dublin, and his reflection on the superimposition of tourism on travel is similarly canny. As he ponders the sailor's experiences, his thoughts make a loop back to the kind of shows and exhibitions about travel so common in Britain in the nineteenth century, the stark forerunners of modern travel advertisement:

> —Mind you, I'm not saying that it's all a pure invention, he resumed. Analogous scenes are occasionally, if not often, met with. Giants, though, that is rather a far cry once in a way. Marcella, the midget queen. In those waxworks in Henry street I myself saw some Aztecs, as they are called, sitting bowlegged. . . . However, reverting to friend Sinbad and his horrifying adventures (who reminded him a bit of Ludwig, *alias* Ledwige, when he occupied the boards of the Gaiety when Michael Gunn was identified with the management in the *Flying Dutchman*, a stupendous success, and his host of admirers came in large numbers, everyone simply flocking to hear him through ships of any short, phantom or the reverse, on the stage usually fall a bit flat as also did trains) . . . (p. 636)

Just as Dickens' work shows the transformation of carnival, circus, and street show into advertising systems, so the vestigial remnants of exotic sideshow acts and music hall stagings peek appealingly out from the twentieth-century tourist world of advertisement. The excitement of melodrama and the collective memory of spectacle still informs its allure; the theatrical practices have become encapsulated in the act of reading ads.

Collective social memory exists not only for departed music-hall stars and faded singers, but for historical heroes as well. The sailor who has been set into a travel frame aestheticized by advertisement, not fiction, also blurs into a resurrected Parnell, whose death cannot be accepted by Ireland at large. The chance that Parnell could come back, even disguised as a sailor, is bruited about by the interlocutors. Of course the joke is that Mr. Murphy, in his chameleonlike way, could just possibly be Parnell himself. On a subsidiary note, if there must be a parallel to Odysseus in the novel, Parnell's ghost haunts the text more thoroughly than that of any other candidate. Dead for the requisite twenty years, the constant subject of rumors, the focus of political hopes, and a father figure par excellence, it is nonetheless interesting that Parnell *redivivus* can only be conceived by all concerned in the chapter in mass-cultural terms. Unlike Odysseus' stealthy reconnoiter upon landing back in Ithaca, Parnell's reappearance would be heralded by the tabloid press, in the style of those National Enquirer articles that ask, "Did Marilyn Monroe Really Die, or Has She Been in a Mental Asylum for Twenty Years?" (artist's reconstruction accompanying). "One morning you would open the paper, the cabman affirmed, and read *Return of Parnell*" (p. 648). All the counters of Parnell's narrative are sutured into mass cultural expression; even the picture of his lover has had mass distribution in barber-shop windows. For political and historical hopes to have aggregated around the narrative styles of mass cultural forms ensures that Parnell and the revolutionary history he suggests have slipped beyond social grasp. Parnell is now "incarnated" as a tabloid press commodity, as a wraith of photograph and newsprint, his allure spread out upon Dublin in these communion wafers. Thus "Eumaeus" underscores even more pungently than such pyrotechnic chapters as "Circe" the vanishing horizon of political possibility. The sacrosanct Parnell must become a part of the pantheon of publicity.

Literary production is cast upon the slag heap of advertisement in this chapter, although not because Joyce recoils at the "debasement" of high literature; the text acknowledges that literary discourse, too, makes its way along the same tracks of publicity and showmanship that invest political authority. Bloom starts to hope he will be able to front for Stephen Dedalus, who after all has a B.A., "a huge ad in its way," although most commentators seem appalled or bemused at this transaction. Yet the "pure" literature Stephen had hoped to make had already vanished in the wavelets of his own urine, as he drowned his book with a vengeance along the strand. Bloom may not have a B.A., but he knows that nothing can happen anymore without an "opening" being cleared; advertising is the key in the lock.

All kinds of Utopian plans were flashing through his [Bloom's] brain. Education (the genuine article), literature, journalism, prize tidbits, up to date billing, hydros and concert tours in English watering resorts packed with theatres, turning money away, duets in Italian with the accent perfectly true to nature and a quantity of other things, no necessity of course to tell the world and his wife from the housetops about it and a slice of luck. An opening was all was wanted. (p. 658)

Multiple erotics invest this position vis-à-vis the literary: Bloom would be midwife, pimp, procreator, mother. That the joint enterprise is doomed, to say nothing of being shabby and ill-conceived, doesn't vitiate the cultural picture drawn here, where disparate languages and activities coexist and compete, with advertising as both the leveling element and the catalyzing agent they depend upon. Travel, history, and literature can be "worked up" to the effacement and yet interpenetration of all three.

NEBRAKADA FEMINUM

Still to be assessed is the novel's highly particular placement of a feminine position within advertising language, a question which involves engaging the sexual politics of *Ulysses* as a whole. *Ulysses* is a structurally, rather than thematically, misogynist book, and the importance (i.e., the specificity) of this misogyny cannot really be elicited by studies that revise and reverse the immense negativity of Molly Bloom, proving, for example, that she is not a lazy slut but a household drudge, not a promiscuous adulteress but a neglected, still-young wife at her sexual peak, not a foolish Wife of Bath but a sage and pithy exponent of eternal female wisdom and cynicism. Regardless what spotlight one fixes on Molly Bloom by reversing the terms of her portrait, the far more interesting sexual politics of the quintessential modernist narrative will remain obscure. Redeeming Molly Bloom, even from the likes of Hugh Kenner et al., is a side issue. The paradox of gender, both erotically and politically, is determinative of *Ulysses* as a whole. How does this mesh with all the foregoing arguments, which have placed advertising as a central technical problematic in the text? The answer to this lies in what advertising has become in the early twentieth century, having wended its way out from between book covers and taken over print wholesale. By the time of the publication of *Ulysses*, both advertisement and realist narrative are caught in the toils of sexual encoding. For *Ulysses*, this will occasion a nonpareil textual construction. For advertisement, this sexualization will mark the final step beyond "simple" public announcement.

Those who want to valorize the avant-garde techniques of *Ulysses* as politically progressive exercises in literary language, rather than as a product of the cross-fertilization of the novel with mass-cultural and specifically advertising modalities, have had special problems recuperating it along sexual lines. Colin MacCabe, for example, devotes a chapter of his excellent *James Joyce and the Revolution of the Word* to an analysis of "Penelope" that gives Molly Bloom's speech the revolutionary power to obliterate male patriarchal pretensions, especially as they inhere in language.[22] Ending the text with a female monologue has decisively positive implications in and of itself, he claims, as MacCabe is not troubled by the ventriloquial nature of that speech. The Lacanian and Kristevan approach he adopts has the real virtue of emphasizing and foregrounding language itself, rather than character or psychology or authorial "sexism." But the desire to give Molly's supposedly affirmative and rebellious speech the last word avoids the compromised, composite, nature of the text's language as a whole. At least in my reading it has borrowed its decenteredness, its stream-of-consciousness, its conjunction of styles and its circularity from advertising's forms, *not* a purely "revolutionary" source. In addition, the sexual conundrum of *Ulysses*, that seemingly breaks down masculine/feminine polarities only to reinstate them in more absolute terms, is the paradox of consumption in advertising as well.

It would take an exhaustive study to document the consistency of sexual structuring throughout the novel, but shorthand versions of such a review can be made. The "feminine" is everywhere correlated with acts of consumption; either the woman figures in an advertising scenario, or she is implicated in *wanting* to buy something. Somehow, Bloom is tapped as meta-commentator on advertising and women's place within it, while Stephen unnaturally escapes advertisement altogether, excepting the auto-advertisements of street walkers, his vision of women fixed on their infinite and eternal capacity for betrayal. Women have fallen into the abyss of advertisement, since they can neither control it nor remain above it. The radical instability of the masculine/feminine that gives way in "Circe" to a rondelay of sexual metamorphosis is also replicated in advertising's use of the female as desire object, concomitant with addressing most advertisement *to* women.

"Best place for an ad to catch a woman's eye on a mirror" (p. 372), Bloom says, in one line consolidating a vast literary and social tradition that places women raptly before their mirrors. The metaphysics of the formula is complex and clearly this is not a throwaway line: so much of *Ulysses* is oriented around just this moment of halted, reflected vision. Women presumably would notice ads without fail on their mirrors because they are narcissistically drawn to mirrors in any case. But ads are always already structured like mirrors—they position themselves on transparent shop windows, over "open" space, on blank walls, only to open up a site of reflection there. They arrest the eye, where once it might have roamed freely, to poise it before a scene that then becomes *reflected*, in two senses of that word. First, there is a reflection of a social scenario, presumptively taking place somewhere: a college cyclist crosses a campus, an entertainer stands against footlights, etc. A simulacrum of what exists somewhere in social space or social possibility is being represented. The second sense of reflection involved is the placement of subjects within these ads. When one reads off an ad, one also becomes part of it by having an imaginary space for oneself created within it. The ad reflects where "you" (in advertising's uncanny you-personally/you-all mode of address) could or should be within it. A spectral mirroring takes place on both these levels: a sort of through-the-looking-glass glimpse of another social scene, and a glimpse of oneself as read *by* the ad, which somehow already knows "you." This doubly charged mirroring grounds all ads as representations; positioning a woman in front of an ad on a literal mirror infinitely complicates matters.

The construction of women within discourse already operates as a form of mirroring, since only relatively rarely have women figured as the instigators of their place within language. Consequently, this woman before a mirror is already the shadowy reflection of language, imported into a text to "stand for" women in general. Looking into a mirror is also the classical act of self-recognition and self-knowledge, but these categories cannot obtain for the "woman" who is by definition blind to any self-reflexivity, since she is "found" outside herself. Add to this, finally, that ads themselves install women within their scenes as a means of arresting the eyes of men, and an infinite regress of mirrors is set up. At what point along this chain of mirrored representations can women's desire to buy, which is a desire to be placed within the scene, be located? *Ulysses* can only resolve this by making women the mythologized creatures of advertisement, like the Nymph, or the debased coiners of their own images, as when Molly, so erotic to Bloom for being like the Turkish sultana on a package of cigarettes, is fixated on a pair of violet garters she "needs."

Advertising as a system was similarly beset by worry over an irresolvable tension at that historical moment. A changeover to ads encouraging general consumption was being effected during the first two decades of the century, and while advertising agencies in their in-house documents were not hesitant to explain the business reasons for this—the shift to an economy of consumption due to excess productive capacity, in the wake of monopolization—an interesting apologetics is at work in the professional literature of the period. A fiction of the "reasonableness" of ads, at least during the recent present, was created and cultivated. Advertisement, so the self-explanations went, was devoted to rational exposition of the merits of various articles, in a well-regulated and scientific system of writing. However, market research had discovered that women did the majority of the purchasing and this fact was used to legitimate the "irrational" rhetoric surrounding the literature of advertising. Evolutionarily speaking, one copywriter claimed, men had risen above art and narrative, but primitive peoples and women were still entranced by such shiny toys, and women, as consumers of unrivalled power, would have to be satisfied. *Because* women were irrational, weak, attracted by stories and pictures, ads accommodated them, through sheer necessity. Nonetheless, advertisement deplored this "propensity", while relying on it; "The woman who will not read advertisements is not a woman," declared George Fowler.[23] Ads became thought of as a sort of minor literature specifically for women, although the fiction persisted that they were easy to entice and that a far "superior" literature could exist if only men would pay attention. The peculiar logic of this advertising teleology blamed women for its low estate, but prided advertisement on its irresistable representational power. The most striking fallacy in all the collective demurrals of modern advertisers is that advertisement could ever have been a "rational" discourse; when not excoriating women for their childlike credulity, advertising managers frankly admitted there was not a scintilla of difference between, say, Woodbury and Lux soaps—called "parity products" in the ad business. Establishing them as products required that they be given fictional incarnations, since only narrative techniques could distinguish them. The abstracted, rationalist calculus of capitalist production had to be accompanied by a narrativized, fictional, and "feminized" representational system. The powerful impetus toward measured, scientific market studies and "scientific" psychological research operated in tandem with a driving hyperaestheticization, even if it could not be openly acknowledged other than by being blamed on a female audience as a temporary deviance. A female "reading" begins to displace social reading at large, which I will return to in the final section.

REPETITION AND THE SCENE OF WRITING

"—Because you see, says Bloom, for an advertisement you must have repetition. That's the whole secret" (p. 323). No small secret, this, however apparent it may seem in retrospect. In his formula Bloom provides a skeleton key to the confounding of the literary and advertising apparatuses, and above all, to advertising's spur to "modernism." Advertising has two modes of repetition available to it, and this is one more resource than the realist novel has been able to command.[24] Ads are literally repeated in their very mode of production: an ad is always a reproductive copy, always suggests its shadow siblings whenever and wherever it is seen. In doing so, to recapitulate Benjamin's famous argument, it destroys or at least vitiates the aura surrounding the singular artifact, the work that can only be produced once and for all, and never copied legitimately. Fiction has always had an interstitial position with regard to this aspect of repetition—it is clear that Benjamin's argument works much better for the plastic arts, where artifacts of sculpture, painting, architecture can possess the lonely grandeur of booty. In the textual world, only a document like the Book of Kells or the Gutenberg Bible can take on such retrospective and rarefied glory. Postmedieval literature *counts on* mechanical reproduction and its aesthetic is similarly open to the repetition at the heart of its fabrication. However much literary production may have wanted to distinguish itself from "cheap" printed productions, newspapers, broadsides, etc., this was impossible on the grounds of their common physical existence. Literature in the modern world, then, has always fought for acknowledgment on a contested terrain, sometimes using its limbic similarity to other printed material as disguise, subject, covering cherub, what have you. A certain tatty egalitarian quality has obtained for printed productions, so the shocks of the "age of mechanical reproduction" should not, for literature, necessarily have been shock waves.

And yet they were. Advertising has a second, distinctive process of repetition, which will make clear why it could not be ignored by modern literature. Any individual ad, as argued above, is in itself always a copy and presupposes other ads just like itself. But imagine, for example, that I go down the street and see a Marlboro cigarette billboard. That individual billboard can only get its meaning, both semantic and social, from repetition. In other words, the single ad is not sufficient to establish any process of signification. For the meaning of the Marlboro billboard "Come to Marlboro Country" to emerge (and that meaning is a very active exhortative one, crudely translated as "Smoke Marlboro cigarettes"), a whole network of similar ads must surround me, past, present, and future. I must see other copies of the ad, on other billboards, in magazines and in stores, and I must see other versions of it over time. No one definitive reading event can ever be said to take place: advertising has to make a repeated world for its productions to inhabit, the campaign. "One" ad makes no sense—not because of commercial considerations, although these are affected, but because of the ontology of the advertising text, which can only be made up of repeated instances, instances that have no meaning attached to them until the whole parade of repetitions has been grasped. It is true I might happen to see a certain ad only once in my life, but the one time I see it, I read it as an ad because I know there are other copies of it—I read it as multiply disseminated and as meant for other people's readings, not just my own. For some ads, a single form endlessly repeated over time will do; "Chew Mail Pouch Tobacco" painted in blue and orange on America's barns could use a single image in infinite multiples, the one image continuing to accrue repetitive textual power as the meanings and circumstances of America's rural areas changed over time. The Marlboro ads are Protean repetitions of the rugged western scenario, sometimes zooming close to the weathered men who smoke crouched in snow by the calving pens, sometimes letting us infer them on the skyline of a Montana ranch. Nonetheless, no one ad for Marlboro can ever "mean" independent of any other: a repetitive network that does not exhaust or extinguish itself is made available in advertising language.

When Bloom speaks of the secret of repetition he does not delineate these circuits of repetition as an exegesis of the secret, but if we stand back from the text, we see that *Ulysses* as a whole is an exposition of them. For repetition, in the first and the second senses given above, is the secret of *Ulysses*, of what is called its modernism, although the fire is borrowed from advertisement and Joyce acknowledges this.[25] The text of *Ulysses* is not a text of history—i.e., a written exposition of what has happened or is happening (excusing momentarily this simplification of novelistic narrative)—rather, it is a text in the process of being made, and it makes itself *with* repetitions. All the vast efforts expended on documenting the repetitive allusions of *Ulysses* are ultimately uninteresting unless the structural necessity for their existence is assayed. And that impetus comes from mapping the repetitive structure opened by the nature of advertising language onto the field of the novel. *Ulysses* writes itself *as being written*, as a reproducing process whose fabricating medium is language. The interior architecture of repetitions is not a static design within which critics and readers can flag recurring bits—the man in the mackintosh, the green bowl of the sea, *Sweets of Sin*. Advertising, whatever its limitations and however fierce the efforts to defend against it, is the exemplary language system for modernism, and particularly for Joyce's *Ulysses*. Advertising's second form of repetition is the model of a semantic system composed of repetitions which can only be read in dynamic process, in other words in relation to both spatial and temporal repetitions along the plenum of its textual world. The epiphanic moments of memory and repetition literature could be envisaged as supplying are effaced or surpassed by advertising's easy ability to engender epiphanic repetition as a feature of everyday language and everyday life.

Were all these epiphanic repetitions to coalesce into one monadic advertisement capable of making all the individual acts of reading simultaneous and of perfectly representing the quintessence of advertisement, a sort of mystic rose of the modern text would be produced. Such a dream is broached in "Ithaca," within its catechistical language, and it has all the luminous fixity of the paradisial rose in Dante's heaven.

> What were habitually his final meditations?
> Of some one sole unique advertisement to cause passers to stop in wonder, a poster novelty, with all the extraneous accretions excluded, reduced to its simplest and most efficient terms not exceeding the span of casual vision and congruous with the velocity of modern life. (p. 720)

This would be a moment such as modern literature could never dream of, a kind of ultimate unity and unanimity before one sacral text, so utterly self-sufficient that the "product" it would nominally be advertising drops out of consideration altogether. This is advertisement as pure form, as a literature unto itself. Hoping for a unique ad that would stop repetition in its tracks is otherwise seen as magical thinking; more often the text focuses on the proliferation of advertising possibilities, on the Protean nature of advertising as a literature. Its printed powers are defined and categorized:

> What also stimulated him in his cogitations? . . . the infinite possibilities hitherto unexploited of the modern art of advertisement if condensed in trilateral monoideal symbols, vertically of maximum visibility (divined), horizontally of maximum legibility (deciphered), and of magnetizing efficacy to arrest involuntary attention, to interest, to convince, to decide.
>
> Such as?
>
> K. 11. Kino's 11/-Trousers
> House of Keys. Alexander J. Keyes. (p. 683)

The trinitarian aspect of ads as symbols is clear here—they have the divine visibility of God, the force of Christ as *logos*, and the magnetizing efficacy of the Holy Ghost. Aesthetic response is coextensive with active will; in arresting attention, they also prompt decision. Even the terse little line about Kino's trousers becomes, as an ad, much more than those humble words on the page. Bloom is a fervent believer in this kind of writing, and "there's a touch of the artist about old Bloom." The somewhat horrible prospectus for the Wonderworker, an aid for flatulence, is nonetheless a literature; it interests, convinces, and decides. "What a pity the government did not supply our men with wonderworkers during the South African campaign! What a relief it would have been!" (p. 722). If the wonderworker is rather ironically described as a thaumaturgic remedy, the modern art of advertisement is also a thaumaturgic language, a wonderworker in appropriating the symbology once reserved for literature.

The extraordinary conjunction of literature and advertisement *Ulysses* represents has a *locus classicus* in the text—it is a long passage, but important to analyze in its entirety.

> A procession of whitesmocked men marched slowly towards him along the gutter, scarlet sashed across their boards. Bargains. Like

that priest they are this morning: we have sinned: we have suffered/ He read the scarlet letters on their five tall white hats: H. E. L. Y. S Wisdom Hely's. Y lagging behind drew a chunk of bread from under his foreboard, crammed it into his mouth and munched as he walked. Our staple food. Three bob a day, walking along the gutters, street after street. Just keep skin and bone together, bread and skilly. They are not Boyl: no: M'Glade's men. Doesn't bring in any business either. I suggested to him about a transparent show cart with two small girls sitting inside writing letters, copybooks, envelopes, blotting paper. I bet that would have caught on. Smart girls writing something catch the eye at once. Everyone is dying to know what she's writing. Get twenty of them round you if you stare at nothing. Have a finger in the pie. Women too. Curiosity. Pillar of salt. Wouldn't have it of course because he didn't think of it himself first. Or the ink bottle I suggested with a false stain of black celluloid. His ideas for ads like Plumtree's under the obituaries, cold meat department. You can't lick 'em. What? Our envelopes. Hello! Jones, where are you going? Can't stop, Robinson, I am hastening to purchase the only reliable inkeraser *Kansell*, sold by Hely's Ltd, 85 Dame Street. (p. 154)

This specimen paragraph begins with the way advertising has brought print into the street, as a literal human alphabet, the humans subsumed into their letters and suffering in the body in an echo of Christ dragging his cross to Calvary. The second way station is the transparent show cart, Bloom's idea for a better stationery ad that also is the book's most vivid image of the transfigured modern scene of writing. The clear glass show cart conflates two of the central advertising histories this study has been discussing. On the one hand, the performative, country-fair, folk carnival aspects of early advertising nexes are brought out— the show cart can't help but call to mind the traveling show cart of Little Nell, early advertising avatar. On the other hand, the transparency of the cart modernizes the scene, because it borrows from the spectacular vocabulary of advertising, most especially from the shop window scenario, where the clear pane of glass is the new proscenium of advertising's social stage. There is both active performance and voyeuristic reading occurring in this image of writing, which needless to say is transpiring out in the street. The practicioners of the writing will not be sagacious professors, lettered reverends, or busy salesmen and budding authors like Bloom. Significantly, two chic young girls will display themselves as writers: the iconic status of women within advertisement adds its lure here, and furthermore, the secret writing they will produce has been eroticized, too. The "two smart girls" would not, one imagines, be envisioned as writing feminist tracts, letters to Parliament, Gaelic League defenses. Presumably a billet-doux would cover the crisp Hely's stationery. Part of the surprise here is that women, who are generally representationally *excluded* from the realm of writing, can be italicized as writers here because their writing is pure display. There is an interesting syntactical slippage in the first sentence of this section that suggests the paradox of advertising on display and advertising as produced writing: the two smart girls are sitting inside the cart writing letters (and they could perhaps be writing copybooks too), but by the time one arrives at reading "envelopes" and "blotting paper" the words have become an inventory, not a description of what the girls would be writing. The advertisement scheme sets them up in the street but hesitates over whether they actually produce any writing. The semblance of writing, and the erotic charge of writing as a hieroglyph of woman's secret, are key here. Advertising becomes a collective literature of desire whose *enactment* substitutes for its written content. Advertising can *stage* literary production and make it a galvanizing, eroticizing, and utopian scene.

Advertising also mimes other features of writing in this paradigmatic paragraph. One of Bloom's ideas is for an ink bottle with a false celluloid stain. It is not putting too much pressure on this image to see in it a candid textual reflection of the unlimited false ink of advertisement, an infinite flow whose relation to authorial production, witnessed here by the ink bottle, is extremely moot. Bloom's consciousness is then invaded by the colloquy of Jones and Robinson, whether this represents an actual advertising tag, like "Good morning, have you used Pear's soap today?" or whether Bloom is inventing this, too. The process of writing has reached its limit point here—the endlessly flowing inkwell that advertising is free to dip into is reversed by an inkeraser that can also cancel out writing, that "can sell" it as commodity or obliterate it at will. The movement in the paragraph sets up an alphabetic calvary where the letters themselves do the bidding of advertisement; a charged scene of writing is then staged, where *what* is written becomes an eroticized secret—advertising using the power of writing to focus attention on itself. The ink bottle stain abstractly reveals advertising's now cavalier relation to print: it can use writing, manufacture it, and when it comes to the *Kansell* metaphor, put it under erasure, to adapt a current theoretical metaphor to a highly politicized struggle between discourses.

Put under erasure—*Ulysses* dramatizes the realignment of the field of literary language necessitated by the powerful success of advertisement, a motile literature that now encompasses literature, rather than modeling itself upon it. Is this dramatization wholly mournful, and *Ulysses* then a species of swan song? I would answer by reinscribing the text in its dialectic with advertisement, as has been the practice of the foregoing chapters. The modernist techniques so celebrated about the book derive, in many ways, from the exposure of the novel to the energies of advertising language: stream-of-consciousness, the free play of print, the emphasis on interconnectedness, the ability to frame styles of language and to deny any a hierarchical primacy, all are advertisement's gifts.[26] The unabashed sentimentality of the book, which one could call its mass-cultural aspect, and the creation of Bloom are also the fruits of an intercourse with advertisement. And given over in dialectical exchange is the myth of "pure" literature, the vitality of historical and political discourse, the vision of an exchange that is not one of consumption, but of genuine transcendence. Finally, one can sense a rueful resignation, not on Joyce's part (he was sanguine enough to hope mass advertising would sell *Ulysses* like hotcakes), but on our own behalf at the closure of such a massive artifact of literature. If, as I have claimed, *Ulysses* is a text in process, part of that process is to admit that advertising may have made it too late an hour to read such a book, at all. Walter Benjamin balances the epigram from Wittgenstein that began the chapter:

> Printing, having found in the book a refuge in which to lead an autonomous existence, is pitilessly dragged out into the street by advertisements and subjected to the brutal heteronomies of economic chaos. This is the hard schooling of its new form. If centuries ago it began to lie down, passing from the upright inscription to the manuscript resting on sloping desks before finally taking to be in the printed book, it now begins just as slowly to rise again from the ground. The newspaper is read more in the vertical than in the horizontal plane, while film and advertisement force the printed word into the dictatorial perpendicular. And before a child of our time finds his way clear to opening a book, his eyes have been

exposed to such a blizzard of changing, colorful, conflicting letters that his chances of penetrating the archaic stillness of the book are slight. Locust swarms of print, which already eclipse the sun of what is taken for intellect for city dwellers, will grow thicker with each succeeding year.[27]

With both conviction and ironic humor, *Ulysses* gives notice from its archaic stillness, that *Après moi, le déluge.*

• Epilogue: Advertising
Terminable and Interminable

N ADVERTISEMENT FOR BEECHAM'S PILLS, appearing in *The Illustrated London News* in 1889, encapsulates—as it were—the interpenetration of advertising with the other social discourses, above all the literary, that surround it. We see the backs of nine men wearing sandwich-board placards as they proceed down an abstract street; each man is strongly coded as a particular discursive type, although we see them only from rear view, so that we easily recognize the poet by his flowing locks, pipe, and battered hat, while the Shakespearean actor carries sword and buckler and the scholar is mortar-boarded and doffing his spectacles. Each placard reiterates an advertising claim about Beecham's that appears in isolation in their other ads: "Beecham's Pills Arouse and Revive Depressed Spirits," or "Beecham's Pills, Affirmed to be Worth a Guinea a Box." In this case, however, we encounter a virtual *mise-en-abyme* of advertisement. Not only are all these placards arrayed out in a line before us, but each is tailored to its individual "bearer," and beneath the picture there is running copy that devotes a message to each one of the nine men, as if they were "speaking" their advertisement in a mutual colloquy. For example, the Shakespearean actor figure is quoted as remarking, below the "line," "Is that a 'Pill' I see before me? Marry! I do remember an apothecary." The eccentric professorial figure puns: "If I and Beecham's can't from sadness win you, I'm Don(e)—there's not a laugh left in you!" An apparent stand-in for a newspaper editor, whose placard reads "What is Truth? Beecham's Pills are a Wonderful Medicine," opines in his statement that "We both make Pills;—'tis Beecham's to combine his with consummate skill. I print all mine!" And bringing up the rear of the sandwich-board line is the aforementioned poet, inscribed with a message that wonderfully enmeshes Beechamism within the nets of poetry:

> What are the wild waves saying
> To invalids all day long?
> Why suffer ills?
> When Beecham's Pills
> Will make you well & strong

In a switch from the punning or elaborate professional allusions of the other captions in the dialogue of the nine members, the final couplet simply underscores the presence of this Tennysonian figure amidst the throng proclaiming Beecham's: "Where statesmen lead the van, it is most clear/ a laurelled poet may bring up the rear!"

What the Beecham's ad can "do" is to make the ad consist in the usurpation of the tags and symbols of these differing social offices and roles, creating a kind of forced march of these parodied discourses, hauled into service as sandwich-board men for the dissemination of the name of Beecham. At the same time, the ad itself is built out of layers of print—extremely complex intra- and interreferentialities multiply in the spaces between the placard messages, the ostensible quotes, and the outer world of other Beecham's ads cited and reproduced—to say nothing of the place of the ad itself within the newspaper columns it mimes.

The advertisement puts all the major, modern—model—discourses on parade, with literature infiltrating throughout, all in the service of advertisement, which is wittily produced as the subject of the advertisement itself. What I have described in the preceding chapters has been the progression of the advertising institution in its rivalry with the most publicly word-centered discourse, literature. This Beecham's piece helps to literalize that analysis, in that advertisement here blithely frames and deracinates the discourses it "borrows," deploying both poetic and narrative strategies to insist on the primacy of advertising rhetoric in the public sphere. Another crucial demonstration the advertisement makes, in its sheer complexity, its "blizzard of print," to cite Benjamin afresh, is the preponderance of print and references to print media in advertisements up until the 1920s. The ad requires an almost fetishistic devotion to styles of social reading to decode it, with the emphasis on reading. An obeisance to the multifarious realm of reading is the necessary prelude to reading this advertisement—there is still a powerful link to the procedures of "the laurelled poet," still a narrative poetics that exults in its propinquity to and its distance from the literary.

I have brought my narration of the dialectic between literature and advertisement to a slightly artificial climax with Joyce's *Ulysses*, although that text does help to define a genuine terminus, or at least a parting of the dialectical ways. The year 1922 is by no means a completely arbitrary one for ringing the curtain down on a certain relationship between advertising and fiction, nor is *Ulysses* an arbitrary textual space within which to chart the separation.

The 1920s mark the international consolidation of advertising interests, as well as important national mergers that produce the mega-agencies—the advertising corporations—we now recognize as the social and economic form of advertisement. Most commentators give 1920 as an approximate date for the coalescence of techniques, technologies, business styles, and economic change that translate into the modern advertising apparatus, which is perceived to have undergone only minimal organizational shifts since that period. Let me briefly rehearse these transformations: by the twenties, diversification of large companies, rather than their vertical integration, had become the major vehicle of business growth, as corporations became decentralized, multidivisional organizations. Marketing segmentation became the primary imperative and the guide for focusing advertising dollars, while a shift to service industries rather than product manufacture in the older sense transformed the condition of "products" to be advertised. This internal corporate elaboration wrought lasting changes in the advertising institution as well, beginning to crystallize in the two decades after World War I; advertising agencies developed ancillary marketing services and subsidiaries themselves, with research and development branches, public relations sectors, links to film, photography, and art concerns, and growing ties to media beyond the newspaper. The technological developments that allowed for but also were demanded by new cultural media, like movies and radio and high-speed color lithography, orchestrated a new ensemble for advertising production, and consequently gave a volatility to its relation to "print," once its primary abode, its ancestral "home" within cultural discourse.

The dialectic I have been tracing out, the discursive rivalry and mutual interdependence of advertising and literature, wanes during these watershed years, but not because of instrumentalist changes within either discourse. Above all, I would resist the explanations of criticism on both the left and the right that advertising pulls out of the dialectic because it "wins," traducing the sacral space of literary production and reception for once and for all. Another way of regarding the cultural and ideological realignment of these discourses—and this is also germane to the political implications one can draw—is to stress that advertisement reaches a point of cultural primacy where its universe of discourse comes from the culture of advertisement itself. Advertising no longer derives its cultural momentum from its shocking, coquettish, or ironic replications of the paradigm of literature.

The emphasis within advertisement from the mid-1800s on had to be placed on the question of reading, on creating a readership, which was in no way an easy, "manipulative," or conspiratorial gesture. I have tried to show the intricacy of this process, as social reading proceeded out of a close imitation and modulation of the "reading" required by literature. The danger here lies in excoriating advertisement as a fallen literature, a perverse and successful realization of the fictionality of fiction. It is politically a bit hysterical to look on this scene as if a vampirish reified Advertisement were caught turning away in bloody glee from the ebbing body of innocent Literature—an allegory that wends its way into the most unlikely of critiques. Nor is it politically satisfactory to merely establish advertisement as a cultural symbology, unproblematically signifying within a larger ideological framework.

In short, the question of what advertisement has become in modern capitalist social conditions since the end of World War I is a material question about a discourse that uses aesthetic means as a powerful social and economic agency. Michael Schudson's recent *Advertising, the Uneasy Persuasion*, advances the notion that advertising is "capitalist realism," analogous to socialist realism in that it tries "to picture reality as it should be—life and lives worth emulating."[1] Advertising, he claims, is neither a false mode of belief on the order of religion, nor a denigrating and manipulative secular propaganda, but a way of experiencing which is, essentially, "Capitalism's way of saying 'I love you' to itself."[2] Schudson is oblivious to the contemporary discussion of ideology as lived relations which emerges from Althusser and others and is crucial to cultural critique, nor is he concerned to place advertising in relation to other cultural forms of address. The emphasis on the self-referential and even excessive character of the discourse is important, nonetheless. Coming from another direction politically and hermeneutically, thinkers like Jean Baudrillard have also departed from the Frankfurt School model of the culture industry and have theorized advertising as an extraordinary imagistic level within exchange, becoming, for Baudrillard, so simulacral that advertising now approaches the conditions of architecture—it is the imagistic stuff that constructs the simulated edifices of social exchange.[3]

It hasn't been my task to produce a full-blown theory of advertising at our current historical moment, but rather to point to the intimate ties of advertising and literature during the approximate hundred years of the installation of the advertising institution, in order to resituate the contemporary debate on advertising by suggesting an alternative genealogy. That genealogy has resonant political and critical implications in that it deflects obloquy against advertisement and casts it back on the social conditions that call for the practice of advertisement, and it also forestalls the tendency to romanticization of many postmodern critics who locate advertising as the despoiler of the gift economy.

Ulysses was a text rife with advertisement, but a text set in the immediate past, a text already nostalgic for the turn-of-the-century *mise en scène* of advertising. The hurly-burly of its place amidst the discourses, its invigorating tutelage of modernism and its winking exchanges with literature are all lamented by the book, in that the abstractness of the modern advertising scene was already being felt by the time of the publication of *Ulysses*. Advertising as social reading was giving way to the advertising sublime, the need to advertise advertising.

Advertising arises out of the economic imperatives of capitalism, in the last instance, but not merely the economic necessity to sell products or even to create and maintain a consumer class, however much this may appear to be the case. The advertising sublime gives witness to another determination of advertising as capitalist art form: advertising speaks about itself in order to narrativize all the relations of and contradictions in the surplus value of capitalist production. Advertising, seen as one vast textual system (*not* as a "language," in semiotic terms), textual despite the many forms it is able to take, still calls on social reading, a reading now of all the multiple possibilities within this excess that lies beyond product or consumer, beyond both of them. Advertising relates, or tells, or displays, the ongoing surplus, the extra that must be deployed in aesthetic form to reveal itself within the social world as a surplus. That extra is of course not superfluous at all, is the product of someone's work, if we translate the notion of surplus value back into the economic register. But all the social discourses, of law, medicine, education, literature, and politics are refigured in the surplus zone of advertisement. Advertising can now proffer them in the cultural narratives it stages, certain of the widest possible social reading.

Advertising performs enormous cultural work, then, on the order of a social literature with its genres, traditions, self-references, and material transformations. It is unlike literature in that it gains this power only across the range of its artifacts, only in its constellation as a floating cultural corpus—the individual instances of advertisement are too embedded in the discursive matrix of advertising for them to be anything other than slight when taken in isolation. Literature's power is discrete and accretive; advertising's power is aggregate, cumulative—almost, one might say, immanent. The institution of advertising doesn't need literature as it once did; advertising was the genie literature let out of its bottle (under social and economic pressure), another tongue within its many languages that ultimately took social precedence. Advertising *is* interminable, at least in the foreseeable future, because there will be a plethora of stories to tell, an infinity of social permutations to represent. Advertising once announced fictions—that was its job, to accompany them into the world of discourse as a mediating shield and a triumphal herald. Advertisement was the hieroglyph of fiction, until its own fictions became the book of the modern world.

• Notes

INTRODUCTION: ADVERTISING AND CRITICISM

1. Ludwig Wittgenstein, *Philosophical Investigations*, p. 52.

2. This study will focus on advertising in the nineteenth century, when it first became an institution. However, even its prehistory has illuminating links to literary production.

3. Elizabeth Eisenstein's magisterial *The Printing Press as an Agent of Change* provides the best source for this early history; Lucien and Martin Febvre's *The Coming of the Book* is another key text for this section.

4. Eisenstein, p. 392.

5. Eisenstein, pp. 228–229. It is important to note that literature and advertisement bifurcate here, but that advertising will reenter its relation to printed literature in the nineteenth century.

6. Michel Foucault, "What is an Author?" gives a supplementary etiology for this, which is much more in the political spirit of my investigation.

7. Eisenstein, p. 156.

8. Eisenstein, p. 158.

9. My subject will be just this modern transformation of the advertising system.

10. See especially Theodor Adorno and Max Horkheimer, "The Culture Industry: Enlightenment as Mass Deception." Other works are fully listed in the bibliography. Stuart Ewen's deservedly influential study, *Captains of Consciousness*, borrows the "conspiracy theory" latent in the former essay, making his text somewhat reductive if historically deeply informative. John Fekete's *Critical Twilight* contains an important if one-sided critique of McLuhan. Basic to cultural investigation of this kind is Georg Lukacs' essay "Reification." Williams' essay is found in his *Problems in Materialism and Culture*, an extraordinary contribution.

11. Important correctives to this history exist in Ian Watt, *The Rise of the Novel*, and George *Altick, The English Common Reader: A Social History of the Mass Reading Public* 1800–1900.

12. Francis Mulherne, *The Moment of 'Scrutiny'*.

13. F. R. Leavis and Denys Thompson, *Culture and Environment: The Training of Critical Awareness*, p. 81.

14. Leavis, p. 80 and passim.

15. Elizabeth Eisenstein credits publicity for having saved the oratorical tradition, p. 242.

16. Deconstruction and Derrida may seem out of place in advertising company, but see John Fekete on the Derrida/McLuhan confluence, in "Reconsidering McLuhan." McLuhan's key texts for advertising topics include *The Mechanical Bride*, "The Age of Advertising," and *Understanding Media*.

17. Leavis, p. 46.

18. John Berger, *Ways of Seeing*.

19. Roland Barthes, "The Rhetoric of the Image."

20. Although Barthes does reformulate his thinking on this in "Change the Object Itself, Mythology Today."

21. Walter Benjamin, "The Work of Art in the Age of Mechanical Reproduction."

22. See Michael Chanin, *The Dream That Kicks*. Chapter 2.

23. Walter Benjamin, *One-Way Street*.

24. Richard Simon, "Advertising as Literature."

25. M. M. Bakhtin, *The Dialogic Imagination*, p. 262.

26. Ibid., p. 262. ·

27. Ibid., p. 418.

28. Many histories of advertising have been consulted in writing this book, and they appear in the bibliography. A valuable overview is Daniel Pope's *The Making of Modern Advertising*, despite its resolute business orientation.

1. THE DICKENS ADVERTISER

1. George Orwell, "Charles Dickens," p. 136.

2. This "newness" refers to advertising as an industry, not to the techniques of advertising originating with the printing press, as discussed in the introduction.

3. See especially Steven Marcus, *From Pickwick to Dombey;* Humphry House, *The Dickens World;* and Phillip Collins, *Dickens and Education* and *Dickens and Crime*.

4. John Gloag, *Advertising in Modern Life*, p. 167.

5. Gloag, pp. 137–144.

6. Raymond Williams, "The Magic System," in *Problems in Materialism and Culture*, pp. 231–232.

7. Elizabeth Eisenstein, *The Printing Press as an Agent of Change*, vol. 1, p. 345. See Lennard J. Davis, *Factual Fictions* (New York: Columbia University Press, 1983) for a rich account of newspapers and fiction.

8. F. S. Siebert, *Freedom of the Press in England*, p. 114.

9. Lawrence Lewis, *The Advertisements of the Spectator*.

10. In the *Spectator*, 1750, as collected in Lewis.

11. Anthony Smith, *Goodbye Gutenberg*, pp. 11–12.

12. G. Allen Foster, *Advertising: Ancient Market Place to Television*, p. 47.

13. Lucien Fevbre, *Coming of the Book*, p. 34.

14. John Forster, *Life of Charles Dickens*, p. 128.

15. Forster, p. 130.

16. F. S. Schwarzbach, *Dickens and the City*, p. 26.

17. Schwarzbach, p. 40.

18. Norah Richardson, "Early Advertising in England," *Discovery*, vol. 17, pp. 383–387.

19. Charles Dickens, *Sketches by Boz* (New York: Simon and Schuster, 1961). Hereafter all references in text to this book will be to this edition.

20. Charles Dickens, *The Pickwick Papers* (London: Penguin Press, 1974). Hereafter all references in text to this book will be to this edition.

21. As reported in Georgina Hindley, *Advertising in Victorian England: A Victorian View*, p. 78.

22. Sir Ambrose Heal, *The Signboards of Old London Shops*, p. 65.

23. *The Book of Fairs of 1750 to 1780*, in *A History of Commerce: Historical Reprints*.

24. Percy Fitzgerald, *A History of Pickwick*.

25. Ellen Trent, "Illustrations in Dickens' Work," in *The Dickens Society*, vol. 23, pp. 43–44.

26. Volney B. Palmer, *Mechanical Inventions and their Ads in England*.

27. Bernard Darwin, *The Dickens Advertiser*, p. 46.

28. Ibid., p. 87.

29. Ibid., p. 142.

30. Ibid., p. 60.

31. Charles Dickens, *The Old Curiosity Shop*, 1841 (London: Penguin Books, 1972). Hereafter all references in the text to this book will be to this edition.

32. Alexandra Artley, ed. *The Golden Age of Shop Design*, p. 2.

33. Charles Dickens, *Martin Chuzzlewit*, 1843–44 (London: Penguin Press, 1974). Hereafter all references in the text to this book will be to this edition.

34. Charles Dickens, *Nicholas Nickleby*, 1839 (London: Penguin Press, 1978). Hereafter all references in the text to this book will be to this edition.

35. Charles Dickens, *Letters and Writings, 1844 to 1855*, p. 217.

36. Charles Dickens, *Bleak House*, 1853 (London: Penguin Press, 1971). Hereafter all references in the text to this book will be to this edition.

37. Charles Dickens, *Our Mutual Friend*, 1864 (London: Penguin Press, 1970). Hereafter all references in the text to this book will be to this edition.

38. Walter Benjamin, *One-Way Street*.

39. Charles Dickens, *Collected Issues of Household Words*.

40. Terrence Malley, *The Growth of Advertising as a Profession*, p. 75.

41. Henry Sampson, *A History of Advertising from the Earliest Times*.

42. Ibid., p. 634.

43. Steven Marcus in *From Pickwick to Dombey* presents telling readings of Dickens' involvement in his own texts, in particular ch. 5.

44. Charles Dickens, "A Collection of the Advertisements and Readings from Charles Dickens' Reading Tours," passim.

45. Bernard Darwin, *The Dickens Advertiser*, passim.

2. SPECTACULAR AUTHORSHIP: AMERICAN ADVERTISING AUTHORS

1. Frank Presbrey, *The History and Development of Advertising*, p. 211.

2. Richard Herskowitz, "P. T. Barnum's Double Bind," *Social Text* 4, pp. 133–141.

3. Neil Harris, *Humbug*.

4. Michel Foucault, "What is an Author?"

5. Ibid., p. 121.

6. Ibid., p. 132.

7. Ibid., p. 137.

8. P. T. Barnum, *Struggles and Triumphs*.

9. George Foster, *Advertising: Ancient Marketplace to Television*, p. 12.

10. Russell Lynd, *The Art-Makers*, chapter 2.

11. Harris, p. 43.

12. Harris, p. 252. Special thanks are owed to Jackson Lears here and throughout the chapter for his perceptive comments and broad historical knowledge.

13. Bella C. Landauer Collection of the New York Historical Society.

14. Ibid.

15. Carl Bode, Introduction to *Struggles and Triumphs*, pp. 23–4.

16. As quoted in Constance Rourke, *Trumpets of Jubilee*, p. 324.

17. Harris, p. 58.

18. Guy Debord, *Society of the Spectacle*, paragraph 43.

19. George Rowell, *Men Who Advertise: An Account of Successful Advertisers Together with Hints on their Methods* (New York: Morrow, 1870). Hereafter all references in the text to this book will be to this edition.

20. Bella Landauer, *Literary Allusions in American Advertising*.

21. Bella Landauer Collection.

22. Landauer, p. 4.

3. "THE AGE OF ADVERTISING: HENRY JAMES AND THE ADVERTISING SCENE

1. Raymond Williams, *The English Novel From Dickens to Lawrence*, passim.

2. F. R. Leavis, *The Great Tradition*.

3. Raymond Williams, *Politics and Letters*.

4. Fredric Jameson, *The Political Unconscious*.

5. Marcia Jacobson, *Henry James and the Mass Market*. Jacobson's book has a particularly interesting reading of *The Bostonians*. See pp. 130–31, Mark

Seltzer's *Henry James & the Art of Power* is particularly stimulating; he gives a reading of *The American Scene* under the chapter title "Advertising America," although advertising enters directly only at the endpoint of his argument. Jean-Christophe Agnew's essay appears in *The Culture of Consumption*, Fox and Lears, eds.; his comments are taken from page 87. The entire essay is a masterful reading of Jamesian style and material politics.

6. Henry James, *The Bostonians* (New York: Macmillan, 1886). Hereafter all quotations will be taken from this edition and indicated in the text.

7. Constance Rourke, *Trumpets of Jubilee*, p. 397.

8. As cited in Rourke, p. 401.

9. George Foster, *Advertising: Ancient Marketplace to Television*, ch. 2.

10. The Bella C. Landauer Advertising Collection of the New York Historical Society.

11. Foster, *Advertising*, ch. 2.

12. Richard Atwater, *A History of American Advertising*, p. 76.

13. Henry James, *The Ambassadors* (New York: Riverside Editions, 1960). Hereafter all references in text to this book will be to this edition.

14. Major interpretations include Quentin Anderson, *The Imperial Self*, F. O. Matthiessen, *Henry James: The Major Phase;* and R. P. Blackmur, *Studies in Henry James*. Let me make clear that advertising is not the "key" to interpretation of the novel, but that it permits an important enlargement of its material basis in literary production.

15. Stuart Ewen, *Captains of Consciousness: Advertising and the Social Roots of the Consumer Culture*, passim. Virtually all economic and business historians point to a crisis in overproduction that led to the increased need for advertisement, whether or not this is viewed as deleterious. See Alfred Dupont Chandler, *Strategy and Structure*.

16. Henry James, *The American Scene* (Bloomington: Indiana University Press, 1968). Hereafter all references in text to this book will be to this edition.

17. Ann Douglas, *The Feminization of American Culture*. final chapter.

4. ADVERTISING AND THE SCENE OF WRITING IN *ULYSSES*

1. It should be obvious that advertising is not what *Ulysses* is "about." My reading is not meant to displace all the work on allusion, encyclopedia, and so forth, but to consider the language of the book in conjunction with the mass language of advertising.

2. See especially the collection *James Joyce and Modern Literature*, W. J. McCormack and Alistair Stead, eds., and Fredric Jameson's essay in it, *"Ulysses in History"*; and the chapter on Joyce, "The Long Goodbye: *Ulysses* and the End of Liberal Capitalism," in Franco Moretti's *Signs Taken for Wonders*.

3. Jameson, p. 132.

4. Ibid., p. 132.

5. Moretti, p. 183.

6. Ibid., p. 183.

7. Ibid., p. 198.

8. Both essays are superb, but do cast advertising as stultifying and uncreative, which *Ulysses* itself seems to dispute. While the politics motivating that stance approximate my own, the conflation of advertising with reification, pure and simple, has reductive consequences.

9. Various histories of modern advertising are drawn on here; Daniel Pope, *The Making of Modern Advertising*, is paramount.

10. Alfred Berger, "James Joyce, Adman," A marvelous inventory of Joycean advertisement, this article is extremely useful.

11. See both Richard Ellmann, *James Joyce*, and the revised version of 1982.

12. James Joyce, *Ulysses* (New York: Vintage Books, 1961). All further references to the text will be to this edition, and page numbers will be given in the body of the text.

13. See particularly Jeremy Tunstall, *The Advertising Man in London Advertising Agencies*, and Geoffrey Leech, *English in Advertising*.

14. Antonio Gramsci, *Selections from the Prison Notebooks*, p. 186.

15. The larger importance of this phenomenon is presented in Edward W. Said, *Orientalism*.

16. Walter Benjamin, "The Work of Art in an Age of Mechanical Reproduction."

17. Umberto Eco, *The Poetics of Joyce* (New York: 1968), p. 78.

18. Leo Spitzer, "American Advertising Explained as Popular Art," p. 129.

19. Jameson, *"Ulysses* in History," p. 138.

20. Cited in Francis Steegmuller, *Flaubert and Madame Bovary*, p. 183.

21. For the repercussions of foreign "travel" see Said, *Orientalism*.

22. Colin MacCabe, *James Joyce and the Revolution of the Word*, final chapter.

23. Daniel Pope, p. 248.

24. Important investigations of repetition with special reference to the novel are found in Edward W. Said, "On Repetition," in *The World, the Text, and the Critic*, and in J. Hillis Miller, *Fiction and Repetition*.

25. The repetitions of the novel, with all the echoes of other texts and forms, are not being reduced to advertising. Rather, advertising gives a contemporary cultural correlate, a principle, of stylistic repetition. This is independent of content, of course.

26. This is not at all to *equate* modernism with advertisement, but to set it into play with its mass cultural surroundings.

27. Walter Benjamin, *One-Way Street*, p. 77.

EPILOGUE: ADVERTISING TERMINABLE
AND INTERMINABLE

1. Michael Schudson, *Advertising, the Uneasy Persuasion*, p. 85.

2. Ibid., p. 232. Schudson's idiosyncratic and interesting analysis of "capitalist realism" is located in chapter 7.

3. Much of Jean Baudrillard's work touches on theoretical issues crucial to advertisement. For an extended treatment of material relevant to advertising see *Simulations*.

• Works Consulted

Adorno, Theodore, and Max Horkheimer. "The Culture Industry: Enlightenment as Mass Deception." In *Dialectic of Enlightenment*. New York: Praeger, 1973.

Altick, George. *The English Common Reader: A Social History of the Mass Reading Public, 1800–1900*. Chicago: University of Chicago Press, 1957.

——*The Shows of London*. Cambridge: Harvard University Press, 1982.

Anderson, Quentin. *The Imperial Self*. New York: Random House, 1971.

Artley, Alexandra, ed. *The Golden Age of Shop Design*. London: BFI, 1975.

Atwater, Richard. *A History of American Advertising*. New York: Harcourt, Brace, 1968.

Bakhtin, M. M. *The Dialogic Imagination*. Austin: University of Texas Press, 1981.

Barnum, P. T. *Struggles and Triumphs*. Buffalo: Courier Company, 1879.

Barthes, Roland. "The Rhetoric of the Image." In *Image, Music, Text*. New York: Hill and Wang, 1977.

——*Mythologies*. New York: Hill and Wang, 1972.

——*The System of Fashion*. Richard Howard, trans. New York: Hill and Wang, 1983.

Baudrillard, Jean. *For a Critique of the Political Economy of the Sign*. St. Louis: Telos Press, 1981.

——*Simulations*. New York: Semiotext(e), 1983.

——*La societe de consommation: ses mythes, ses structures*. Paris: S.P.P.P., 1970.

Benjamin, Walter. "The Work of Art in an Age of Mechanical Reproduction" In *Illuminations*. New York: Harcourt, Brace, Jovanovich, 1968.

——*One-Way Street*. New York: Harcourt, Brace, Jovanovich, 1978.

Berger, Alfred. "James Joyce, Adman." In *MLN*, Spring 1964.

Berger, John. *Ways of Seeing*. London: Penguin, 1971.

Bersani, Leo. *A Future for Astyanax*. Boston: Little, Brown, 1976.

Blackmur, R. P. *Studies in Henry James*. New York: New Directions, 1983.

Bode, Carl, editor. *Struggles and Triumphs: The Autobiography of P. T. Barnum*. Penguin edition, 1981.

Book of Fairs of 1750 to 1780, The. In *A History of Commerce: Historical Reprints*. New York: Chadbourn, 1935.

Boyce, George, James Curran, and Pauline Wingate, eds. *Newspaper History: From the 17th Century to the Present Day*. London: Constable, 1978.

Brooks, Peter. *The Melodramatic Imagination: Balzac, Henry James, Melodrama, and the Mode of Excess*. New Haven: Yale University Press, 1976.

Chandler, Alfred Dupont. *Strategy and Structure: chapters in the history of the industrial enterprise*. Cambridge: M. I. T. Press, 1962.

Chanin, Michael. *The Dream That Kicks*. London: Routledge & Kegan Paul, 1981.

Collins, Philip. *Dickens and Crime*. New York: St. Martin's, 1962.

——*Dickens and Education*. New York: St. Martin's, 1963.

Darwin, Bernard. *The Dickens Advertiser*. New York: Macmillan, 1930.

Debord, Guy. *Society of the Spectacle*. Detroit: Black and Red, 1977.

Debray, Regis. *Teachers, Writers, Celebrities: The Intellectuals of Modern France*. London: New Left Books, 1981.

Dickens, Charles. *Bleak House, 1853*. London: Penguin Press, 1971.

——*Collected Issues of Household Words*. New Haven: Yale University Press, Reprints.

——*"A Collection of the Advertisements and Readings from Charles Dickens' Reading Tours."* In the Berg Collection, Monograph Series, 1964.

——*Letters and Writings, 1844 to 1855*. Princeton: Princeton University Press, 1972.

——*Martin Chuzzlewit, 1843–44*. London: Penguin, 1974.

——*Nicholas Nickleby, 1939*. London: Penguin, 1978.

——*The Old Curiosity Shop, 1841*. London: Penguin, 1972.

——*Our Mutual Friend, 1864*. London: Penguin Press, 1970.

——*The Pickwick Papers*. London: Penguin Press, 1974.

——*Sketches by Boz*. New York: Simon and Schuster, 1961.

Douglas, Ann. *The Feminization of American Culture*. Cambridge: Harvard University Press, 1975.

Eco, Umberto. *Le poetiche di Joyce dalla "Summa" al "Finnegans wake."* Bompiani, 1966.

——*The Role of the Reader: Exploration in the Semiotics of Texts*. Bloomington: Indiana University Press, 1979.

Eisenstein, Elizabeth. *The Printing Press as an Agent of Change*. Cambridge: Cambridge University Press, 1979.

Ellman, Richard. *James Joyce*. New York: Oxford University Press, 1959 and 1982.

Ewen, Stuart. *Captains of Consciousness: Advertising and the Social Roots of the Consumer Culture*. New York: McGraw Hill, 1976.

Febvre, Lucien and Martin. *The Coming of the Book*. London: NLB, 1976.

Fekete, John. "Reconsidering McLuhan." *Canadian Journal of Politics and History, vol. 7*.

——*Critical Twilight*. London: Routledge & Kegan Paul, 1977.

Fitzgerald, Percy. *A History of Pickwick*. London: Chatto and Windus, 1924.

Forster, John. *Life of Charles Dickens*. London: 1875.

Foster, G. Allen. *Advertising: Ancient Market Place to Television*. New York: Criterion Books, 1967.

Foucault, Michel. *The Archaeology of Knowledge*. New York: Pantheon Books, 1972.

——"What is an Author?" In *Language, Counter-Memory, Practice*. Ithaca: Cornell University Press, 1977.

Fox, Richard Wightman and T. J. Jackson Lears, eds. *The Culture of Consumption*. New York: Pantheon Books, 1983.

Gloag, John. *Advertising in Modern Life*. London: Heinemann, 1959.

Gramsci, Antonio. *Selections from the Prison Notebooks*. Quintin Hoare and Geoffrey Nowell Smith, eds. New York: International Publishers, 1971.

Harris, Neal. *Humbug*. Boston: Little, Brown, 1973.

Heal, Sir Ambrose. *The Signboards of Old London Shops*. London: B. T. Batsford, 1937.

Herskowitz, Richard. "P. T. Barnum's Double Bind." *Social Text*, 4, 1982.

Hindley, Georgina. *Advertising in Victorian England: A Victorian View*. London: Methuen, 1969.

House, Humphry. *The Dickens World*. London: Oxford University Press, 1941.

Jacobson, Marcia. *Henry James and the Mass Market*. Alabama: The University of Alabama Press, 1983.

James, Henry. *The Ambassadors*. New York: Riverside Editions, 1960.

——*The American Scene*. Bloomington: Indiana University Press, 1968.

——*The Bostonians*. New York: Macmillan, 1886.

Jameson, Fredric. "*Ulysses* in History." In *James Joyce and Modern Literature*. London: Routledge & Kegan Paul, 1982.

——*The Political Unconscious*. Ithica: Cornell University Press, 1981.

Joyce, James. *Ulysses*. New York: Vintage, 1961.

Landauer, Bella C., Collection of the New York Historical Society.

Landauer, Bella. *Literary Allusions in American Advertising*. New York: Monograph, 1947.

Leavis, F. R. *The Great Tradition*. New York: New York University Press, 1969.

Leavis, F. R. and Denys Thompson. *Culture and Environment: The Training of Critical Awareness*. London: Chatto & Windus, 1934.

Leavis, Queenie D. *Fiction and the Reading Public*. London: Chatto & Windus, 1932.

Leech, Geoffrey. *English in Advertising*. London: Longmans, 1966.

Lewis, Lawrence. *The Advertisements of the Spectator*. New York: Morrow, 1973.

Lukacs, Georg. "Reification." In *History and Class Consciousness*. Cambridge: MIT Press, 1971.

Lynd, Russell. *The Art-Makers*. New York: Dover, 1970.

MacCabe, Colin. *James Joyce and the Revolution of the Word*. London: Macmillan, 1978.

McCormack, W. J., and Alistair Stead, eds. *James Joyce and Modern Literature*. London: Routledge & Kegan Paul, 1982.

McLuhan, Marshall. "The Age of Advertising." In *The Commonweal*, 58 (September 1953).

——*The Mechanical Bride*. New York: McGraw Hill, 1951.

——*Understanding Media*. New York: McGraw Hill, 1964.

Malley, Terrence. *The Growth of Advertising as a Profession*. London: Matthews and Brandon, 1974.

Marcus, Steven. *From Pickwick to Dombey*. New York: Basic Books, 1965.

Matthiessen, F. O. *Henry James: The Major Phase*. New York: Oxford University Press, 1963.

Miller, J. Hillis. *Fiction and Repetition*. Cambridge: Harvard University Press, 1982.

Moretti, Franco. *Signs Taken For Wonders*. London: Verso, 1983.

Mulherne, Francis. *The Moment of 'Scrutiny.'* London: NLB, 1979.

Orwell, George. "Charles Dickens." In *Inside the Whale*. London: Routledge & Kegan Paul, 1940.

Palmer, Volney D. *Mechanical Inventions and their Ads in England*. Bella C. Landauer Collection, New York Historical Society.

Pope, Daniel. *The making of Modern Advertising*. New York: Basic Books, 1983.

Presbrey, Frank. *The History and Development of Advertising*. New York: Doran, 1929.

Richardson, Nora. "Early Advertising in England." *Discovery*, vol. 17. London, 1936.

Rourke, Constance. *Trumpets of Jubilee*. New York: Harcourt, Brace, 1927.

Rowell, George. *Men Who Advertise: An Account of Successful Advertisers Together with Hints on their Methods*. New York: Morrow, 1870.

Said, Edward. *Beginnings*. New York: Basic Books, 1975.

——*Orientalism*. New York: Pantheon, 1978.

——*The World, The Text, and The Critic*. Cambridge: Harvard University Press, 1983.

Sampson, Henry. *A History of Advertising from the Earliest Times*. London: Chatto and Windus, 1874.

Schwarzbach, F. S. *Dickens and the City*. London: University of London Press, 1979.

Schudson, Michael. *Advertising, the Uneasy Persuasion*. New York: Basic Books, 1984.

Seltzer, Mark. *Henry James & the Art of Power*. Ithaca: Cornell University Press, 1984.

Siebert, F. S. *Freedom of the Press in England*. Urbana: University of Illinois Press, 1965.

Simon, Richard. "Advertising as Literature." *Texas Studies in Language and Literature* (Spring 1978).

Smith, Anthony. *Goodbye Gutenberg*. New York: Oxford University Press, 1980.

Spitzer, Leo. "American Advertising Explained as Popular Art." In *Interpreting Literature*. Northampton, Massachusetts: Smith College, 1949.

Steegmuller, Francis. *Flaubert and Madame Bovary*. Chicago: University of Chicago Press, 1939.

Trent, Ellen. "Illustrations in Dickens' Work." In *The Dickens Society*, vol. 23 (1976).

Tunstall, Jeremy. *The Advertising Man in London Advertising Agencies*. London: Chapman & Hall, 1964.

Watt, Ian. *The Rise of the Novel*. Berkeley: University of California Press, 1957.

Williams, Raymond. *The English Novel from Dickens to Lawrence*. London: Routledge & Kegan Paul, 1971.

——"The Magic System." In *Problems in Materialism and Culture*. London: Verso, 1980.

——*Politics and Letters*. London: New Left Books, 1979.

Wittgenstein, Ludwig. *Philosophical Investigations*. New York: Macmillan, 1953.

• Index